Taxation and Democracy

DISCARDED

TAXATION AND DEMOCRACY

Swedish, British and American Approaches to
Financing the Modern State

Sven Steinmo

Yale University Press

New Haven and London

Published with assistance from the Mary Cady Tew Memorial Fund.
Copyright © 1993 by Yale University.
All rights reserved.
This book may not be reproduced, in whole or
in part, including illustrations, in any form (beyond that
copying permitted by Sections 107 and 108 of the U.S.
Copyright Law and except by reviewers for the public press),
without written permission from the publishers.

Designed by Sonia L. Scanlon
Set in Times Roman type by Tseng Information
Systems, Durham, North Carolina
Printed in the United States of America by Edwards
Brothers, Ann Arbor, Michigan.

Library of Congress Cataloging-in-Publication Data
Steinmo, Sven.
Taxation and democracy : Swedish, British, and
American approaches to financing the modern state /
Sven Steinmo.
p.   cm.
Includes bibliographical references and index.
ISBN 0-300-05409-2 (cloth: alk. paper)
0-300-06721-6 (pbk.: alk. paper)
1. Taxation—Sweden.   2. Taxation—Great
Britain.   3. Taxation—United States.   I. Title.
HJ2305.S85   1993
336.2—dc20   93-10364
CIP

A catalogue record for this book is available
from the British Library.
The paper in this book meets the guidelines
for permanence and durability of the Committee
on Production Guidelines for Book Longevity
of the Council on Library Resources.

10 9 8 7 6 5 4 3 2

For my love,
Rita

Contents

Figures

Tables

Preface

Taxation is a rather unusual subject for the student of comparative politics. I must admit that it did not immediately grip my attention and fill me with a passion to know more about it. I came to this subject rather through chance when, in the spring of 1982, one of my graduate school professors, Aaron Wildavsky, asked me if I would be interested in earning a little money—a question that no starving graduate student could ever answer in the negative.

Professor Wildavsky was about to embark with Carolyn Weber on a collaborative project that examines the history of taxation and spending from early Mesopotamian times to today. Wildavsky asked me and a few of my fellow graduate students to look at particular historical epochs for background research for his book. I was chosen to write about the politics of taxation in modern democracies since World War II. My mandate was simply, "Tell me something interesting."

At the time, I was deeply engaged in constructing a Ph.D. dissertation prospectus on comparative health care policy. I had recently received my M.P.H. in health policy and planning from the Berkeley School of Public Health and had been interested in this policy arena since writing my senior college thesis at the University of California, Santa Cruz under Grant McConnell and Richard Gunther in 1976. I could not imagine how I would ever find anything interesting to report about a subject as obviously boring as taxation. But the lure of lucre encouraged me to give it a chance.

Having been weaned, like many in my generation of young political scientists, on the antipluralist critiques of American politics written by such scholars as Theodore Lowi, McConnell, and Frances Piven and Richard Cloward, I expected the American tax system to be substantially worse—by which I meant unfair or regressive—than that of other nations. I knew, as most of us "know," that rich people and corporations in America get away with paying virtually no taxes by taking advantage of huge loopholes, while the poor (like myself) and the middle classes have to pay too much. Surely more democratic countries would have fairer and more equitable tax systems. By *democratic* I meant countries (1) in which the kind of hyperpluralism so obvious in America did not run rampant, (2) in which parties are stronger and interest groups weaker, and (3) in which ultimately the balance of power between bourgeois and working-class interests was more close to equal.

I was about to discover my first "interesting" finding. I studied stacks of tables compiled by the Organization for Economic Cooperation and Development (OECD) and, to my amazement, found that the United States received more tax revenue from corporate taxes, both as a percentage of total taxation and as a percentage of Gross National Product (GNP), than virtually any other OECD democracy. (My figures were from the late 1970s; in 1981, as we shall see later in the book, the United States had reduced corporate taxes substantially.) Even more surprising was that Sweden received *less* tax revenue from corporate taxes than any other country in the OECD.

Next I noticed that the United States, together with Sweden and the United Kingdom, was near the top in terms of personal income taxes as a percentage of total taxes. This, though, was only mildly interesting because surely the Swedish—and British for that matter—personal income tax structures were much more progressive than the American.

As I dug further into these nations' tax structures and histories, I came to major surprise number two: marginal income tax rates on the very rich have historically been much higher in the United States than in Sweden and about the same as in Britain and Germany except during the 1970s in Britain; and marginal income tax rates on the poor or relatively poor have been much lower in the United States than in any other country I looked at except France. Sweden and Britain, I discovered to my amazement, had very broad income tax systems, with starting tax rates of more than 30 percent.

Something was amiss. The United States *must* have one of the most regressive tax systems in the democratic world. But I could not find any evidence to support this supposition. In fact, the more specific and detailed my examination became, the less sure I became. I soon discovered, for example, that the United States relies heavily on property taxes and inheritance taxes—both progressive in my view—and slightly on regressive consumption taxes. All other countries I examined, in contrast, had relatively small revenues from property taxes (except Britain) and instead used more or less heavy value added taxes (VATs), a form of sales or consumption tax, to finance their welfare states. When I finally uncovered the fact that Sweden had the heaviest *and most regressive* VAT in the world, 23+ percent with no exemptions for food, clothing, or other basic necessities, I realized that studying taxes could be interesting after all.

I recognized that the interesting data I had collected for Wildavsky presented a theoretically challenging intellectual puzzle. I also figured, quite correctly it turned out, that by changing my substantive focus from health policy to taxation policy, I would be more likely to generate funding for my dissertation research. This decision reached, I began to write a dissertation, and now a book, about taxation.

It has been almost ten years since my baptism in public finance and tax policy. During this time, I have incurred many intellectual and personal debts. Aaron

Wildavsky started me down this empirical path, but my debt to him goes far beyond that. He not only gave me the intellectual space and emotional support to pursue what turned out to be a very ambitious dissertation project, but also brought me back to the real world when my discussions became too obtuse or when I started to wander off into insignificant detail. In short, he allowed me to pick my own intellectual path and then helped me stay on it—often by disagreeing with me and forcing me to defend my positions.

My graduate student days brought me to know a second individual with whom I almost never agree—and who has had an equally important role in shaping both this book and my understanding of politics generally. Over the years, I have sparred, argued, and have drunk with Jonas Pontusson more times than I can remember. I am the better for each of these occasions.

In researching and writing this book I have had the support, help, and advice of a large number of people, far too many to list here—but a few are outstanding. For their willingness to share substantive expertise and knowledge about how to understand tax policy, I thank George Break, Axel Hadenius, John Hills, Mervin King, Carl Olof Klingberg, Nils Mattson, the late Joseph Pechman, Cedric Sandford, Gunnar Sträng, and John Witte. For reading parts of this manuscript—sometimes in its early and embarrassingly crude stages— I am indebted to Kirsten Amundsen, Holly Arrow, Richard Coughlin, Larry Dodd, Anthony King, Nelson Polsby, Colins Ross, Jack Saffel, and Harold Wilensky. I owe a special debt to my mother, Professor Amundsen, who has forced me to think more clearly by attacking any and all "fuzzy-headed" thinking. She also suggested the title of this book.

Most important, I want to acknowledge my gratitude to my family for bearing with me throughout this process: To Siri and Ian, thank you for helping me to remember what really matters in this world. Finally, I dedicate this book to my wife, Rita, without whose support and love it could never have been finished. I hope it is worth it.

Abbreviations

CBI Confederation of British Industries

CBO Congressional Budget Office

CTT Capital Transfer Tax

EC European Community

EPD Excess Profits Duty

ERTA Economic Recovery Tax Act of 1981

GDP Gross Domestic Product

IR Inland Revenue (British IRS)

IRS Internal Revenue Service

OECD Organization for Economic Cooperation and Development

LO Swedish trade union confederation

PDI Personal Disposable Income

PR Proportional Representation

SAF Swedish employers' federation

SAP Swedish Social Democratic Party

SET Selective Employment Tax

SKr Swedish Kronor

SOU Swedish official government publications

TCO Tjänstemännens Centralorganisation

TEFRA Tax Equity and Fiscal Responsibility Act of 1982

TUC Trades Union Congress

VAT Value Added Tax

Taxation and Democracy

1

Introduction

And it came to pass in those days, that there went out a decree
from Caesar Augustus, that all the world should be taxed.
—Luke 2:1

Governments need money. Modern governments need lots of money. How
they get this money and whom they take it from are two of the most difficult
political issues faced in any modern political economy. These are issues that
are settled quite differently in different societies. Yet students of politics have
largely ignored tax policy over the decades. Given the hundreds of studies that
examine the political struggles behind such welfare state programs as health
care insurance, family policy, education, social welfare, and pensions, the
paucity of studies that focus on how welfare states finance these programs is
striking.[1] This gap in the literature is even more surprising when one considers
that taxation is both at the core of the redistributive efforts of the modern welfare state and has been the central instrument of state economic policy since
World War II. Indeed, no other public policy issue has been used so widely for
so many purposes or been so consistently at the center of ideological conflict
over the proper role, size, and functions of the modern state. As modern-day
tax reformers are wont to tell us, virtually everything government attempts
to do with direct expenditure programs they also attempt (for better or for
worse) to do with taxation policy. Today, tax and spending issues cannot be
neatly separated into the categories of "who gets what" and "who pays for
it." A modern tax system is a complex mix of both payments and benefits.

In short, the politics of taxation is one of the most important policy concerns in the modern industrial state; yet we know very little about it.

Indeed, not only do we know little about tax policy, but what we think
we know is often wrong. It is commonly assumed, for example, that social
democratic countries, which have achieved remarkable income and wealth
equalization, will have very progressive tax systems. The corollary is that we
assume that countries like the United States, in which capitalists are politically
powerful and individualism is culturally dominant, will have comparatively
regressive tax systems. These assumptions, however, are false. This book
will demonstrate, for example, that for most of the twentieth century both
the United States and Britain have had more progressive tax systems than

Figure 1.1   Effective Tax Burdens as a Percentage of Income

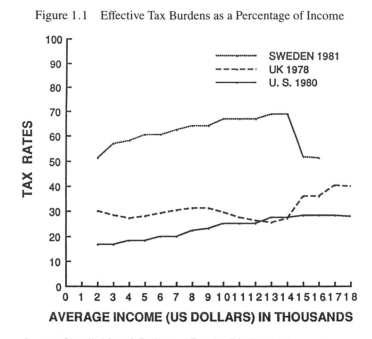

AVERAGE INCOME (US DOLLARS) IN THOUSANDS

Sources: Compiled from J. Pechman, "Taxation," in *Britain's Economic Performance,* ed. R. Caves and L. Krause (Washington, D.C.: Brookings Institution, 1980); Riksrevisionverket, *Statistika Meddelanden,* various years; OECD, *The Impact of Consumption Taxes at Different Levels of Income* (Paris: OECD, 1981).

has "socialist" Sweden. Not only have the United States and Britain relied more heavily on such progressive taxes as income and profits taxes than has Sweden, but also the tax rates in Britain and the United States imposed upon the very rich have been much higher, while the rates paid by the less well-off have been lower. The figure above shows the distribution of effective tax burdens for all taxes by income class in the late 1970s and early 1980s in these three countries.[2]

Contrary to what most people would expect, Sweden does not have a particularly progressive tax system. In fact, by some measures it is regressive. More important than the slope at the end of the tax distribution curve (there are few people in these income brackets anyway) is the very heavy tax burden borne by all income groups in Sweden. The key here is that Sweden, like all social democratic countries, has been able to build a tax system that generates huge revenues to the state. These revenues translate into public spending on housing, education, health, and welfare, and the effects of this spending are substantially more redistributive than steeply progressive taxes.

Table 1.1

"Redistributive" Taxes as a Percentage of Total
Revenue, 1970–89 (Income, Corporate Profit, Property,
and Wealth Taxes as a Percentage of Total Tax Revenue)

	1970	1980	1987	1989
Sweden	55.5	44.3	47.0	46.7
United Kingdom	52.8	49.9	50.4	52.4 (38.9)*
United States	61.8	57.1	54.5	54.5

Sources: "Long-Term Trends in Tax Revenues of OECD Member Countries 1955–1980," *OECD Studies in Taxation* (Paris: OECD, 1981,) table 6,
p. 16, table 7, p. 17; *Revenue Statistics of OECD Member Countries 1965–
1988* (Paris: OECD, 1989), table 7, p. 85, table 11, p. 87; *Revenue Statistics:
1965–1990* (Paris: OECD, 1990), tables 13, 23.
* Figure after elimination of local property tax (rates) revenues (1990).

In the United States and the United Kingdom policymakers have relied
more heavily on explicitly progressive (if not redistributive) taxes than they
have in Sweden. The American and British tax systems are not highly progressive, but the distribution of real tax burdens in these countries is surprising
when compared to the Swedish. In this book I shall explain how and why
these three countries have developed the tax systems that they now use. I shall
in fact make sense of the pictures shown above.

Explaining National Variation

Thus we have a puzzle to solve: Why do these tax systems vary in these ways?
This puzzle is especially intriguing because actual tax outcomes diverge so
sharply from what we expect. Part of the reason we are puzzled is that our
expectations about taxes are overly simplistic. If taxes were simply a means to
generate revenue or instruments of redistributive policy or both, then it would
be reasonable to expect the Swedes to have a more progressive tax system
than Americans. Tax policy, however, involves much more than redistributing
wealth and generating revenues. Any tax system embraces a complex mix
of competing goals, ambitions, and considerations. Raising revenue, redistributing income, encouraging savings, stimulating growth, penalizing consumption, directing investment, and rewarding certain values while penalizing others are just some of the hundreds of goals that any modern government
tries to promote with its tax system. Indeed, taxation is a major instrument, if
not *the* major instrument, through which governments try to affect the private
sector. Particular outcomes, like the distribution of effective tax burdens or
the reliance on one type of tax versus another, are never the result of a single

choice abstracted from the maze of decisions and goals that affect any modern tax system. We must first understand that tax policies are multifaceted instruments that are at the vortex of political and economic relations. Only in this context can we begin to answer the question, Why do these tax systems vary in the ways that they do?

Interests, Values, and the State

While we know a lot about decision-making processes in individual countries, we do not know nearly enough about why the governments of different countries make different decisions and pursue different public policies. The countries of North America and Western Europe are often described as welfare states, the implication being that their governments, all of them, behave in broadly similar ways. We shall see, however, that these broad similarities conceal important wide divergences. These divergences deserve to be explained.—A. King, "Ideas, Institutions and Policies of Governments"

Most analysts who attempt to explain why public policies vary among advanced democracies have posited one of three distinct explanations. These explanations emphasize the importance of either political interests, values, or the state. Each of these explanatory variables has its merits, but I believe that they are inadequate for explaining the "wide divergences" noted by King. The interests explanation argues that policy outcomes vary because the distribution of power among political interests differs from one polity to another. Groups use their power to further their short-term interests. Since the relative distribution of powers between groups differs in advanced democracies, policy outcomes also will differ.[3] Interest theorists assume that groups will always pursue their short-term self-interest and will always displace the tax burden away from themselves if they have the political power to do so. James Alt (1984), for example, has written, "The distribution of taxes is the result of the pursuit of narrowly perceived interests by special interest groups." Louis Eisenstein (1961), similarly, has said, "Tax legislation commonly derives from private pressures exerted for selfish ends." Given this logic, it is perfectly reasonable to assume that the Socialists who have dominated Sweden for so long will tax their own constituencies lightly and the capitalists heavily. But, as I noted above, this is not the case. On the contrary, the most common and obvious explanation of why public policies should vary between countries (the rational pursuit of short-term self-interest) does not appear to explain taxation policy.

The central weakness of the interest explanation in understanding tax policy outcomes is its tendency to treat self-interest as a given. Scholars too readily assume that groups will define their interests in similar ways in different countries. This assumption, however, as numerous cross-national examinations of the politics of particular policy arenas have demonstrated, is empirically false. Instead, groups tend to define their interests in different ways in different national contexts (Immergut 1992; D. King 1992; Hall 1992).

The second common explanation for public policy variations is the values explanation. Proponents of this theory suggest that policies vary because people in different democracies have different policy preferences. The most famous of these arguments is, of course, Louis Hartz's explanation of American exceptionalism. Hartz argues that citizens have different expectations about the proper role of government in society and that this general value frames political debate within a polity. Ultimately, different value premises set nations along different policy paths.[4] This explanation argues, in short, that different publics want different public policies.

A strength of the values explanation is that it does not assume that groups will define their interests or policy preferences similarly in different countries. Rather, it assumes that they will not. Problems remain, however, for the values theorists who would bring their explanations down to the world of real policy making. Because political values and ideas are broad, vague, and sometimes self-canceling, they do not easily translate into specific policy alternatives. Indeed, virtually any policy can be justified by a wide set of political values. Moreover, comparative policy research has often demonstrated that actual policy outcomes do not necessarily match the values that supposedly dominate a nation's political culture. If, for example, individualism and freedom of opportunity and reward are values in the American political culture, how can one explain the fact that the United States has imposed income tax rates of over 90 percent on its most successful capitalists, while Sweden, a socialist political culture, has never imposed tax rates over 80 percent?

Another major problem for the values explanation is the paucity of empirical evidence proving that citizens in different democracies actually have different preferences in key areas of public policy. Almond and Verba showed long ago that Americans do indeed express greater hostility to the government than Europeans. But as other studies have demonstrated, these symbolic statements do not translate easily into robust differences in attitudes toward specific policy choices (Coughlin 1980; Lewis 1982). Very few citizens understand complex policy issues. Moreover, real policy decisions involve choices between competing preferences. Finally, there is more than a little doubt that government elites will do exactly what their citizens want even when they know the majority's preferences (Heclo 1974).

In sum, the values explanation fails to link general ideas to specific policies. In a world that is as profoundly complex as ours, the choice between specific means to achieve general ends is open to broad interpretation. Values, like self-interest, must be interpreted and defined in terms of specific policy choices. Thus simply knowing that Americans are more individualistic than Swedes does not help us understand how their policy structures will vary.

Another weakness of both values and interests explanations is that they ignore the role of the state. Few analysts today would argue that the state is a neutral umpire that simply transmits the preferences of interest groups and parties, yet neither of the above explanations considers the ways in which state structures help define who has power, what kinds of groups have access to power, and who therefore shapes public policy outcomes. Nor do these explanations consider the state's role in shaping and mobilizing political ideas. The Swedish political scientist Nils Elvander correctly expressed frustration with attempts to export American-centric, pluralist models when he wrote that these models "allow little scope for anticipation of wants and eliciting of demands—a fact which plays an important role in modern 'service democracy' of, for instance, Sweden's type" (Elvander 1972, 65).

More recently a new school of comparativists has attempted to correct for this weakness and has proposed the state-centered approach.[5] These analyses focus on the role that state actors play in shaping political outcomes. Specifically, they suggest that state actors can be relatively autonomous from both interest group and mass pressures and that the state's preferences can and sometimes do determine public policy. This insight is substantial. The implicit critique it offers of exclusively society-centered approaches is well taken. Still, this approach leaves much unexplained. First, virtually nothing is said of the motives and preferences of state actors themselves. As in the interests explanation, these issues are left virtually unexplored. There is little in this approach to help us understand *why* state actors have certain preferences and why these preferences can vary. Even a casual look at the politics of any significant policy arena amply demonstrates that various actors within what must be called the state have *different* perspectives and preferences. Obviously these perspectives and preferences matter, but we need to know a great deal more about which state actors' views matter the most and why they make the choices that they make.

In sum, values, interests, and state-centered theories fail to explain how preferences and interests are, on the one hand, shaped and, on the other hand, translated into specific policy choices. This book proposes an approach that can help bridge this gap. In the following pages I shall outline the basic structure of what I call the Historical Institutionalist approach. This analysis builds on the work of other recent institutionalist scholars such as Peter Katzenstein, Peter Hall, and John Ikenberry but attempts to situate the logic of this New Institutionalist school into a broader historical understanding of the ways in which political institutions interact with the historical and economic context in which they operate.[6]

The Institutionalization of Bias

Political institutions are not neutral. They bias policy making toward some types of interests and away from others because they channel participation in particular directions. This understanding draws on one of the insights of E. E. Schattschneider, who, in his penetrating analysis and critique of American pluralism *The Semi-Sovereign People*, suggested that "organization is the mobilization of bias." By this, he meant that the fragmented structure of the American political process stacks the deck against diffuse interests and lends itself to manipulation by highly organized and specific interest groups. Similarly, he argued that a more centralized political system—like British party government—stacks the cards differently, puts political power in the hands of the larger constituencies, and prevents the manipulation of public policy by highly specific and non-national interest groups.

My analysis takes Schattschneider's insight one step further. I argue that institutions do more than alter the relative distribution of power among participants in the policy-making process. It is my contention that the structure of a polity's decision-making institutions also profoundly affects how interest groups, politicians, and bureaucrats develop their policy preferences. Peter Hall (1983, 370) has written in the same vein: "Organization does more than transmit preferences of particular groups, it combines and ultimately alters them." Institutions, in effect, provide the context in which individuals interpret their self-interest and thereby define their policy preferences.

This book will argue that rationality itself is embedded in context. One cannot even define what a rational act is without examining the context of that behavior. It may be perfectly rational for an individual or group to act a specific way in one context, but positively life threatening to act in this way in a different context. In politics, political institutions provide the basic context in which groups make their strategic choices. And any rational political actor will behave differently in different institutional contexts.

This analysis explicitly rejects an economistic or substantive notion of self-interest. Instead, it takes the individual or group's definition of self-interest as problematical. At the same time, this analysis proposes that neither specific policy preferences nor general political values appear out of thin air. Values and preferences are derived within particular contexts. For those who begin with the understanding of human rationality as fundamentally bounded, this argument will be uncontroversial. This approach, then, simply focuses on the environmental context of policy choices over time and demonstrates how specific policy outcomes are derived within different economic and political/structural contexts. As such, this analysis marks a beginning of a better understanding of the linkage between individual preference formation and broader issues of macropolitical behavior and policy outcomes.

The argument of this book is substantially more specific than the argument that institutional structure matters. In addition to demonstrating how and why specific institutional decision-making structures matter, I will suggest that the institutional foundations upon which the U.S., British, and Swedish democracies are built critically affect the character of the decision-making structures themselves. Electoral structures constitute the most basic institutional bias found in any democracy.

The United States, Britain, and Sweden are representative democracies. All three have developed political institutions that attempt in some way to link the wishes, desires, or preferences of the public with the actual policy decisions of the political elite. A central dilemma for these systems, however, is that governing elites must have some degree of autonomy from the public that they represent. They must be able to act when public preferences are confused or split, when citizens are apathetic or ignorant, and even when the public is outright opposed to what the government must do. Taxation is just such a case.

The ways in which democratic states have addressed this basic democratic dilemma of balancing responsiveness and autonomy is a critical variable that helps us understand why these nations have developed such different tax systems during the twentieth century. This book will show that as political rights extended to ever-wider portions of the public in these three democratic nations, they developed different institutional mechanisms to accommodate this change. In the United States, constitution makers, fearing *both* an autonomous and an overly responsive elite, constructed a system of multiple checks and balances and intentionally fragmented political authority. The peculiar character of the American tax system—its complexity, its inefficiency, and its low revenue yield—is a product of this institutional structure.

In Sweden, the conservative bureaucratic oligarchy that dominated the political system at the turn of the century introduced proportional representation for the Lower Chamber on the one hand, and retained a complicated and conservative electoral system for the Upper Chamber on the other hand, as their guarantee against a government that would be too responsive to the will of the masses. In their attempts to construct an effective form of government on this constitutional base in the mid–twentieth century, Swedish elites developed corporatist institutions that ultimately tipped the scales in favor of a government that could dominate, but not predominate, the political agenda. The character of the Swedish tax system—its stability, efficiency, high revenue yield, and surprisingly generous treatment of capital compared to the heavy burden borne by the working class—is a product of this institutional structure.

The United Kingdom never had a constitutional convention. The British electoral and constitutional system instead evolved from a centralized monarchy to a representative democracy. But in this process the British did not institutionalize the kinds of checks on the autonomy of the government that the Americans and Swedes did. The objective of new groups entering politics in Britain around the turn of the century was to seize the reins of government, not hamstring it. The strong parties they mobilized rather naturally became strong governments. Strong British party governments do not have to make the kinds of partisan compromises and build the kinds of long-term coalitions simply to pass legislation that both the Swedish and American governments do. The British tax system—its instability, its inefficiencies, and its ever-changing distribution of tax burdens—is a product of these party government institutions.

In sum, constitutional differences set the stage for dramatically different politics—even when what is being fought over is remarkably similar. British governments have absolute control over policy making because of the unique British electoral process, not because citizens have given majority support to one ideological perspective over another. Conversely, America has no government in the European sense because of its unique electoral process, not because no party can win electoral majorities. It is a twist of irony that it is Americans who vote most consistently for the party of the left, when compared to their counterparts in Sweden and Britain.[7] Yet America is the country which has moved the least far to the left in terms of its social welfare spending priorities. If one objects, "But the strong Democratic vote for members of Congress doesn't imply the same thing as a strong Labour party vote in Britain," one fundamentally understands the point of this book. A vote, like any other strategic choice, can indicate entirely different things depending on the context in which it is cast.

Committee, Party, and Corporatist Governments

A nation's basic constitutional structure does not, however, define either its specific decision-making structure or the structure of its tax policy, although it does help shape the form of both. Constitutions are vague and, in some cases, even unwritten. As a result, every country has had to adapt its political foundations to the realities of governing and, in the twentieth century in particular, to the increasing complexities of modern government. I shall demonstrate how the United States, Sweden, and Britain have adapted their tax decision-making institutions to this growing complexity and argue that the different decision-making systems found in each of these countries are rational adaptations of their basic constitutional foundations to this complexity.

Readers of this book are most likely familiar with the concepts of corporatist government, committee government, and party government and will probably accept the characterization of Sweden as corporatist, the United States as committee government, and Britain as a party government system. These models have long been tried and tested in the comparative politics literature. I will not elaborate on these models here but will reveal how these decision-making systems have evolved in each of these countries during the twentieth century. The reader will see how these different decision-making systems have profoundly shaped the formulation of tax policy in each of these three countries over time. I will also demonstrate how these different decision-making systems have affected both who dominates the tax policy-making process and the strategic choices and ultimately the policy preferences of these same actors.

Fundamentally, the various actors in the tax policy process in these three countries want similar things: politicians want to be reelected, bureaucrats want to manage a stable and efficient tax policy, and interest groups want to promote the well-being of their constituents. But how these general desires get translated into specific policy preferences and specific political strategies depends on the rules of the game; and the rules of the game are written by the institutions through which the game is played.

In British party government, the trading back and forth between ruling parties in government establishes a vicious cycle over time. Politicians in each new government are in a hurry to push through their mandates because they know that their electoral clock is ticking and that what they have not fully ensconced in the tax system will be rejected by the next government. Bureaucrats attempt to turn back or at least slow reform because they are still trying to adapt to and institutionalize the reforms of the last government. Moreover, they feel that big changes should be carefully evaluated. Politicians therefore discount bureaucratic nay-saying because they assume it is simply reactionary. Interest groups sit on the sidelines and, being uninvolved in the detailed formulation of new policies, are confused and often scared. Actual outcomes only rarely meet their expectations. Whether the policies go too far or not far enough, support for the government quickly wanes and opposition intensifies. The electoral clock ticks louder.[8]

Neither Swedish politicians, bureaucrats, nor interest groups are in a hurry. For most of the last fifty years at least, interest groups and opposition parties alike have known that the Social Democrats will be in power or near to power for a long time to come. They have also known that the Social Democrats are forced to make deals on the one hand, but that they have enough power to make deals stick on the other. In this context it is perfectly reasonable to exchange tax concessions for long-term nonrevenue policy commitments. Moreover, the long association of a single government with the permanent elite bureaucracy, combined with the government's dependence on technical support, has built a deep mutual trust and respect between the Social Democratic leadership and their chief civil servants. Thus in Sweden these major players are not antagonistic, as they often are in the United Kingdom. Instead their perspectives and preferences have become so intermixed that it is sometimes difficult to distinguish who is directing whom. Indeed, members of the recently elected Conservative government in Sweden often complain privately that they are unable to get the Social Democratic bureaucracy to accommodate the new Conservative thinking.[9]

The openness and fragmentation of the American policy-making system similarly frame the perspectives of the many participants in tax policymaking. Because no one is in control, no one can guarantee a deal. Therefore, it is in the interest groups' self-interest to fight for tax reductions, even when they want spending increases. With some luck, they can get both. Because authority and responsibility for taxing and spending decisions are separate, the incentive structure facing congressmen on revenue committees encourages them to offer particularistic tax reductions that they can claim credit for and fiercely oppose tax increases that they can be blamed for. In the United States, the full-time bureaucracy is relatively shunted to the sidelines of tax policymaking. Though they push tax policy in the same direction as Swedish and British officials, that is, toward efficiency, simplicity, and rate moderation, they must dress up their reform proposals as tax cuts.

Dynamic Institutions in Historical Context

The argument that institutions can bias policy outcomes is hardly new.[10] Currently there are a number of superb analyses which emphasize the role of institutions in shaping policy outcomes. But these analyses suffer from two weaknesses. First, they do not specify which institutions are relevant. The following definition of institutions from Peter Hall (1986, 19) is illustrative: "The concept of institutions is used here to refer to the formal rules, compliance procedures, and standard operating practices that structure the relationship between individuals in various units of the polity and economy." Similarly, Ikenberry (1988, 227) defines institutional structure to include "normative order defining relations between state and society." The problem with these definitions of institutions is that they are so vague that they leave nothing out. Stretching the concept to this extent dilutes it and undermines its analytic utility. Or, to put it somewhat more bluntly, if institutions are everything, then they are nothing. As Theda Skocpol suggests, "We should not shy away from the idea that institutions do not explain everything." [11]

A second problem with most recent institutionalist analyses is that they treat institutions as static variables. The focus on how institutional structure shapes politics has yielded compelling accounts of policy continuities within countries over time and differences in policy outcomes across countries, but the explanations that come out of institutional analysis can appear uncomfortably static. Such explanations flow naturally from an approach like the new institutionalism, which explicitly emphasizes constraints. Ikenberry is quite right when he concludes that institutional approaches have been better at explaining what is not possible in a given institutional context than what is (Ikenberry 1988, 242). Comparative institutional analysis, by extension, tends toward the study of "comparative statics," focusing on how country x and country y produce different policy outcomes because of their respective (stable) institutional configurations. This argument, however, invites a kind of institutional determinism. What often comes out of such analyses is a fairly mechanical explanation that essentially deduces outcomes from institutional constraints.

The following analysis attempts to avoid this through a historical account of the development of both tax policy outcomes and the political institutions that write tax law. In addition, the analysis focuses on both institutional change and on the changing political, economic, and international context in which these institutions operate. Institutions are not everything in politics. Indeed, a central argument presented in the following pages is that *domestic political institutions operate within—and must be understood in the context of—the broader social, economic, and political setting in which they are embedded.* Understanding the ways in which domestic political institutions shape policy choices goes a long way toward helping us understand why, given certain choices, one country takes one path and another country takes another. But looking at these political institutions rarely tells us why these choices were available or necessary in the country in the first place.

In the following chapters we shall see that all three countries have followed broadly similar policy paths over the course of the twentieth century. I identify four major phases in the development of taxation common to all three countries. I shall show how the particular domestic political institutions in the United States, Sweden, and Britain shaped each nation's tax policies in the context of these differing historical phases or agendas. But I do not argue that these institutions are responsible for or explain why these phases came about in the first place. To offer such an explanation would be to imply a much larger theory of politics than is offered in this book. The question of why certain countries democratized, for example, is of perennial interest to students of comparative politics, but it is a question on which I offer no particular insights. This book is instead concerned with the question of how the particular form of democracy that developed in particular countries shapes public policy choices.

Because there is little written about taxes and tax policy that is intelligible to the average social scientist, I begin with a general discussion of taxation policy in industrial democracies. If I were analyzing health or housing policy I could more easily rely on what the reader already knows. With taxation I do not have this luxury. Chapter 2 of the book, then, offers an overview of tax policy in industrial democracies. I present a series of tables and graphs in order to give the reader a sense of the various systems found in modern democracies. The American, Swedish, and British tax systems are then described in greater depth with the objective of giving the reader a sense of the variation in these systems. I shall not attempt to describe each tax system in detail, for this would take several thousand pages, but shall instead characterize the systems and highlight the basic, most consistent differences between them.

In the four chapters that follow, I demonstrate how and why the political institutions in these countries have shaped the policy outcomes described in chapter 2. The aim will be to show how both political institutions and tax policy outcomes have evolved over the past century. I do not give a blow-by-blow account of each major revenue source but will instead highlight some of the major features of the systems as they have developed. The final chapter will draw out the major implications of the evidence and arguments presented for our understanding of the relationship between democratic political institutions, taxes and the welfare state.

2

Common Paths—Divergent Patterns

> There is no part of the administration of government that
> requires extensive information and a thorough knowledge of
> principles of political economy so much as the business of
> taxation.—Alexander Hamilton

Most people think taxes are confusing and unpleasant. That may explain why they have been so little studied by political scientists. Most people cannot figure out their own taxes, let alone understand an entire system. Even seasoned scholars who have spent much of their adult lives researching, analyzing, and writing about how governments spend money usually know little about how governments raise money. This chapter is intended to fill some of the gaps in our knowledge about tax policy and tax policy development generally. It is, one might well be surprised, an interesting story.

In many ways two stories can be told about the politics and development of taxation in modern democracies. The first is about how much modern tax systems have in common. In the late twentieth century, every OECD democracy relies on a small number of taxes with which to generate the vast bulk of government revenues. Just five taxes (personal income, corporate profits, general consumption, property, and social security charges) today contribute an average of 79.5 percent of total government revenues in OECD nations (fig. 2.1). Most of these taxes did not exist a hundred years ago. Modern democracies not only rely on broadly similar types of taxes, but have also tended to change, adapt, and reform their tax systems at almost exactly the same times and in roughly similar ways throughout the twentieth century.

But having said that these tax systems are broadly similar, I can tell another story about how much they differ. Although these countries may depend on the same types of taxes, the degree to which they rely on one type of tax versus another, for example, can vary dramatically (fig. 2.2). Second, the structure and incidence of any particular tax in one country can be quite different from the structure and incidence of the same type of tax in another country. Two countries, then, could collect approximately the same amount of revenue from a tax (for example, the income tax), yet the actual incidence of that tax could be wildly different. I will not delve into the potential diversities among the various taxes here—such a discussion would take us too far afield. The point is that just knowing that a country uses a particular type of tax or

Figure 2.1 New vs Traditional Taxes as a Percentage
of Total Revenue, OECD Nations, 1989*

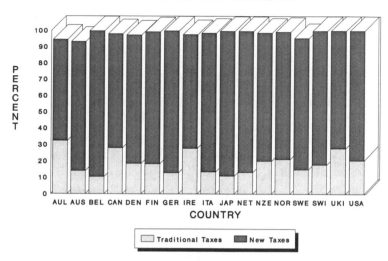

Source: OECD, *Revenue Statistics 1965–1990* (Paris: OECD, 1991).
* New taxes are taxes on personal income, corporate profits, general consumption, and social security. Traditional taxes are taxes on property, customs and tariffs, and excises on particular goods or services.

Figure 2.2 Tax Types as a Percentage of
Revenue, Selected OECD Nations, 1989

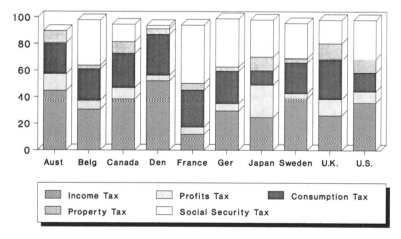

Source: OECD, *Revenue Statistics 1965–1990* (Paris: OECD, 1991).

knowing how much revenue the tax generates will not tell us much about who pays the tax and who, in fact, is able to avoid (or evade) the tax.

Common Paths

In the world nothing is certain, except death and taxes.
—Benjamin Franklin, 1789

If you could magically transport a finance minister from, say, Sweden in 1890 to Sweden in 1990 and introduce him to the tax system found in his country today, he would be lost. The major taxes he knew and understood have either been totally abolished or are insignificant parts of the modern tax system. New taxes that the centenarian finance minister could not have imagined when he was the head of the national budget—including progressive income taxes, social security taxes, corporate profits taxes, and VATs—now make up approximately 80 percent of total government revenue. Government revenue would also far exceed our finance minister's wildest imaginings. In 1900, total government revenue constituted only 10 percent of a much smaller GNP in Sweden; today it is over 50 percent of GNP.

If we could next transport a U.S. treasury secretary and a British chancellor of the exchequer from the late 1800s to the late 1900s and introduce them to their countries' current tax systems, they would be equally lost. In short, over the past one hundred years, the ways governments raise money for public spending have been radically transformed. Indeed, as varying as modern tax systems are, they have more in common with each other in the 1990s than with the tax systems from which they each evolved.

There are profound differences among modern industrial democracies; this book is in large measure about some of them. But it is also important to recognize the similarities, or else the analysis can end up explaining too much. Clearly there have been forces at work *in all capitalist democracies* that have fundamentally shaped tax policy development in the twentieth century. Common political ideas, social forces, economic imperatives, and technological advances have each pushed and pulled modern tax systems along the path on which we find them today. This path is a broad one, and it has had many twists and turns. Yet the very fact that we find the revenue systems of all advanced capitalist nations somewhere along this path tells us something about the common forces that shaped each system.

What accounts for the commonalities among modern industrial states? The best explanation is that tax policymakers in such democracies are faced with two common dilemmas. The first is aptly summarized in the following quote from John Maynard Keynes's *General Theory*:

Since the end of the nineteenth century significant progress towards
the removal of very great disparities of wealth and income has been
achieved through the instrument of direct taxation. . . . Many people
would wish to see this process carried much further, but they are deterred by two considerations; partly for fear of making skillful eva-
sions too much worth while and also of diminishing unduly the motive
towards risk taking, but mainly, I think, by the belief that the growth
of capital depends upon the strength of the motive towards individual
saving and that for the large proportion of this growth we are dependent
upon the rich out of their superfluity. (Keynes 1936, 372)

In short, taxation has been a major weapon for income and wealth redistribution but a dangerous weapon, both for the politicians who wield it
and for the economy in which its use is threatened. Democratic capitalism
is caught between the desire for greater social and economic equity and the
apparent need for a degree of economic inequality. In democratic and capitalist societies the history of modern taxation can be seen as the tug and pull
between these political realities.

The second dilemma is simply that citizens have a virtually insatiable desire
for increased public spending, yet they hate to pay taxes. I disagree with
those public choice theorists who conclude from the evidence that citizens
hate taxes, that the modern welfare state is the product of some kind of elite
conspiracy and also unwanted by citizens (see Brennan and Buchanan 1980;
Buchanan 1987; Peacock and Wiseman 1961).[1] The fact is that citizens want
higher public spending *and* lower taxes. This puts public officials in a difficult
political position; to accommodate citizen preferences on one side of the budget, they must go against what citizens want on the other side of the budget
(Downs 1960). Public officials in all advanced democracies are thus under
immense pressure to devise taxes that generate huge and growing amounts of
revenue but that can be made acceptable to (or hidden from) the constituents
who pay those taxes. The most common fiscal policy trend in all modern
democracies has therefore been a move toward broad-based taxes and taxes
whose revenues grow "automatically"—in other words, taxes that virtually
everyone pays and that grow as the economy does. The more automatically
their revenues grow, the more state officials tend to like them.

At the same time, citizens prefer taxes that someone else pays: and, in a
world in which the great majority are middle-class or poor, the rich and the
corporations are the natural targets for tax hikes. The rub is that taxes focused
on the rich and on corporations have real drawbacks. First, despite whatever
our populist gut impulses tell us, there really are not enough rich people and
corporations (or perhaps they are just not rich enough) to pay for the public

programs our taxes currently support. Let us assume, for example, that the U.S. government imposed a new 100 percent income tax surcharge on all incomes over $1 million a year. Even with the unrealistic assumption that incomes remained the same, this new tax would raise only $72.1 billion dollars (or 8.4 percent of total government receipts in 1989).[2] If it imposed a new 100 percent profits tax on all corporations, and corporations did not change their behavior, this tax would raise only $328.6 billion (36.1 percent of total government receipts). The economic consequences of such a policy are too obvious to elaborate on here.

Tax policymakers have thus for good reasons concluded that taxes that everyone pays are fiscally superior to narrow or focused taxes on certain defined goods or social groups. Broad-based taxes can generate huge revenues at low rates. The more focused a tax, that is, the narrower its base, the higher the rates have to be to generate sufficient revenues to justify the administrative expense, not to speak of the political controversy, of having the tax in the first place. In addition, if tax rates are very high, there are strong incentives for taxpayers to limit the kind of activity or behavior that evokes the tax. In eighteenth-century England, for example, a tax on windows was seen as a reasonable and efficient way to generate revenues: people with many windows in their homes had more money to tax than those with few or no windows. It was also easy for the taxman to count windows and assess the tax due. But as the rates of this tax grew, so did the propensity of homeowners to fill the window openings with bricks. Even today in England one can see many large, dark manor houses with bricks where there once were windows.

From a purely administrative or technical point of view the best and broadest-based tax would be a simple head tax. If the U.S. government taxed all men, women, and children living in the United States $5,000 each a year, for example, it could almost abolish all other taxes. Such a head tax, if it could be collected, would generate about $1.25 trillion dollars a year, which is still slightly less than total government tax revenues in 1990. Any such tax is unthinkable, of course, because virtually everyone would consider such a tax to be grossly unfair. Indeed, as we shall see in chapter 6, Margaret Thatcher's attempt to introduce a head tax evoked a massive revolt that substantially contributed to her eventual ouster. Our finance minister of a hundred years ago might have found this head tax reasonable, but finance ministers of today live under quite different constraints and are forced to find taxes with somewhat narrower bases.[3]

Tax Avoiders vs. Revenue Maximizers, or Citizens vs. the State

The Art of Taxation consists of so plucking the goose as to obtain the largest amount of feathers with the least amount of hissing.—Jean-Baptiste Colbert, finance minister to Louis XIV

Given the conflict between the demand for revenue, the desire not to impede economic growth within a capitalist system, and broad public resistance to taxes in general, what have tax policymakers done? There has been an unmistakable trend, especially in the late twentieth century, for tax policymakers to rely on taxes that can either be hidden or that grow on their own (table 2.1).

The major reason that personal income taxes are the largest single source of revenues in the OECD today is that as income increases, income tax revenue does so even faster.[4] This phenomenon is called bracket creep. Bracket creep ensures that once income tax rates are set, revenues to the state will expand dramatically faster than the GNP even if policymakers simply sit back and wait. In fact, state officials are able to cut marginal tax rates (or multiply tax loopholes) and still count on massively expanding revenues from the income tax "cash cow."[5]

Social security taxes have been almost as popular as income taxes because, even though they do not benefit from bracket creep, they are at least partially hidden from taxpayers.[6] In virtually all countries social security taxes are paid in part or in whole for the employee by their employer. Very few taxpayers even know that their employers are paying part of their wages directly to the government.

I do not want to oversimplify the issues involved here; an additional explanation for the growth of personal income taxes is that they are considered more fair than most other taxes. Similarly, social security taxes are often presented as insurance payments, and taxpayers often believe, wrongly, that their contributions are put into an insurance fund from which they will draw benefits later in life. As with income taxes, citizens tend to view social Security taxes as more fair than other kinds of taxes.

A variety of considerations go into the making of tax policy—equity is certainly one of the most crucial of these. The example of the head tax cited above should remind us of this point. But against this general popular constraint, tax policymakers face powerful incentives to raise revenues from taxes that grow automatically. Property taxes, for example, tend to decline as a percentage of revenues in large measure because raising property taxes requires direct intervention by the authorities; not many politicians are willing to take this risk.

Table 2.1

The Direction of Change in Types of Tax
as a Percentage of Total Revenue,
OECD Nations, 1955–85

	Number of Countries	
Type of Tax	Up	Down
Social Security	15	2
Income	14	3
Corporation	5	12
Consumption	0	17
Property	0	17

Sources: "Long-Term Trends in Tax Revenues of OECD Member Countries, 1955–1980," *OECD Studies in Taxation* (Paris: OECD, 1981), 11–20; *Revenue Statistics of OECD Member Countries, 1965–1986* (Paris: OECD, 1987), table 3, p. 83.

Figure 2.3 Trends in Consumption Tax Revenue, Tax as a Percentage of Total Revenues, OECD Average, 1965–89

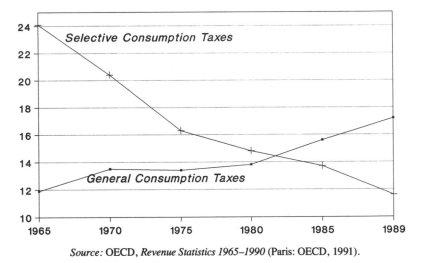

Source: OECD, *Revenue Statistics 1965–1990* (Paris: OECD, 1991).

The mixed revenue performance of consumption taxes provides some insights here. All consumption taxes taken together have gone down in all seventeen OECD countries since 1965. Tax policymakers do not like this form of regressive taxation even if it is an indirect tax. If, however, we differentiate between general consumption taxes such as VATs, which grow with the economy and are hidden from the consumer, and taxes on specific goods and services, which tend to be visible to particular groups of producers and consumers, we see a different picture (fig. 2.3).

In sum, the desire for increased revenue constrained by public resistance to taxes, the demand for more fair taxes, and the need for economic growth are pressures faced by taxing authorities everywhere. As a result of these common forces, income, general consumption, and social security taxes have tended to go up since World War II both as a percentage of tax revenue and as a percentage of Gross Domestic Product (GDP), while property, corporation, excise, and a host of other smaller taxes have tended to decrease. More generally, we see powerful pressures for what Richard Rose identifies in the title of his study "Maximizing Revenues and Minimizing Political Costs" (Rose, n.d.).

Common Trends: A Short History of Modern Taxation

> Who ever hopes the perfect tax to see
> Hopes what ne'er was, nor is, nor e'er shall be.
> —McCulloch's adaptation of Pope

There have been at least four major historical stages of modern tax politics in industrial democracies. Each of these stages can be linked to major developments in the social, political, and economic contexts in which tax policy has developed. The first phase, marked by the introduction of progressive taxation at the turn of the century, was a response by political elites to the changing political reality that surrounded them—chiefly, democratization and the demand for greater social and economic equity. The second stage witnessed a massive expansion of taxation on all classes in society. This change was the result of an uneasy compromise between the Left and the Right over the role of the modern state in the society and economy and over the basic framework for financing that state. The third stage is a product of the huge revenue explosion made possible by both the economic growth of the 1950s and 1960s and the continuance of wartime taxes that produced seemingly limitless sources of revenue at relatively limited political costs. We are currently in the midst of the latest stage of tax policy development in the twentieth century. In this case, the excesses and abuses of taxation policy, on the one hand, and the growing internationalization of the world economy, on the other, are imposing a new set of constraints on tax policymakers. These changes are forcing a reconsideration of the very principles upon which modern tax systems stand. An outline of the major tax policy developments for each of these stages follows. I shall look more closely at the historical and political context in which these developments occurred in chapters 3–6.

Democracy and Tax Policy, 1900–20

The turn of the century marks the turn toward modern taxation in almost every industrializing nation. The modern idea that taxation should be based upon the ability to pay was hotly contested before the end of the nineteenth century. Most countries relied on a dizzying array of duties, fees, excises, charges, and taxes for national revenue. In general this meant that the burden of taxation was borne most heavily by the poorer classes in society.[7] It also meant that the total tax burden in these societies was relatively small; the poor, after all, did not have large amounts of extra resources to tax.

Before the development of modern direct taxation, then, ministers of finance were caught in the trilemma of (a) the need for greater revenue, especially for defense, (b) the political reality that those with political power did not want to pay taxes, and (c) the fact that those with no political power had almost nothing to tax. The twin forces of industrialization and democratization would drastically alter this situation. Industrialization brought with it both a general monetarization of the economy and huge accumulations of wealth. At the same time, the trend toward including more and more citizens in the political system meant that the rising demands for the rich to bear a fair share of taxes became hard to ignore. In many countries the unfair distribution of the tax burden became a major rallying cry for activists mobilizing for popular suffrage.

Throughout the modernizing world the politics of taxation looked as if it would become a major battlefront in an emerging class war. The ensuing battles, however, did not spill as much blood as some had hoped and others had feared. The principal reason for this outcome was a convergence of interests between state policymakers and the political Left: political and administrative elites were under pressure to expand public spending for infrastructure, defense, and nascent social insurance programs at the same time that the demand for fairer taxes was gaining currency. As a consequence, income taxes on the wealthy and on corporations were introduced in virtually every industrializing nation. Though these taxes were minor by today's standards, their introduction established a radically new set of principles upon which tax policy would develop. Just as the Right predicted, only a short time passed before these taxes were increased, and in effect the overall distribution of the tax burden was shifted from the lower to the upper classes. Figure 2.4 shows the top marginal personal income tax rates in Britain, Sweden, and the United States between 1910 and 1921. These taxes were imposed on only the very richest individuals in society. Not until the 1940s did the income tax become a mass tax.

Figure 2.4 Top Tax Rates—Sweden,
Britain, and the United States

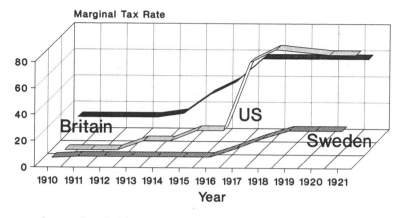

Sources: Compiled from E. Rodriguez, *Offentlig Inkomstexpansion* (Uppsala: Gleerup, 1980); "Report of the Commission of Her Majesty's Inland Revenue" (London: Her Majesty's Stationery Office, various years); J. Pechman, *Federal Taxation Policy* (Washington, D.C.: Brookings Institution, 1987); data supplied by Swedish Riksskatteverket.

World War I explains the jump shown in these data. There is little evidence to suggest that tax rates on the wealthy would have ascended to these levels in the absence of war. But without the expansion of suffrage in the years before the war, there would be little reason to believe that it would have been financed through progressive taxation.[8] This was scarcely the first time that the lower classes had been asked to defend the interests of their nation: it was the first time, however, that they had the political power to demand that the rich pay for it.

The "Historic Compromise," 1920–45

In the years immediately following the Great War the political interests of the Right appeared to be ascendant. Bourgeois parties dominated politically in all three countries under study here. In each case, marginal tax rates on both the wealthy and corporations were reduced while consumption taxes and custom duties were increased (irrespective of the ideological predispositions of the Right in favor of free markets). But the heyday of the Right was short-lived. The Great Depression evoked mass discontent with both capitalism and the politicians who defended it.

The electoral response to the economic crisis was clear and decisive. The Social Democrats in Sweden, the Labour party in Britain, and the New Deal Democrats in the United States swept into office and promised a fairer deal for those that elected them. Somewhat surprising, however, is the fact that in none of these cases was there an immediate turnabout in tax policy. There were two reasons for the Left's apparent timidity. First, although the Left now held the reins of government, in no case were they firmly in control: in Sweden the Social Democratic party (SAP) was forced to form a coalition with the Farmers party; in Britain the Labour party held only 288 of Parliament's 615 seats; and in the United States, though the Democratic party dominated both houses of Congress, President Franklin Roosevelt could not control the Democratic party. Second, irrespective of their political commitment to the principle of progressive taxation, elites in these new governments found that the realities of governing sometimes dictated policies that varied from those promised on the campaign trail.

Though the Left was not able to dictate its tax policy preferences in the 1930s, they were not defeated. The key to understanding tax policy development during the war and afterward, then, is to appreciate that the representatives of capital and labor were each strong enough to protect their interests in their respective legislatures. Each consequently lacked the power to push their agenda through. In Sweden, where labor markets were highly concentrated and class relations were the most acrimonious, the government was able to force a compromise between capital and labor in the famous Saltsjöbaden agreement. In Britain a national coalition government was formed. In the United States, the decentralization of both the economy and the electoral system disabled those seeking either a tripartite or a coalitional solution, but a de facto compromise between the Congress and the executive did evolve. In all three cases, at any rate, the military crisis of World War II forced the feuding parties to pull together; the fiscal crisis required that they compromise over specific policies on the revenue side of the budget. U.S. Treasury Secretary Henry Morgenthau summarized the mood in his nation and in others when he wrote, "The new taxes will be severe, but it's a million times cheaper to win the war than to lose it."[9]

In all three countries, the Right conceded to the imposition of very high rates of personal income tax on the rich (table 2.2). Corporate profits taxes were also boosted radically. But equally vital were the major concessions made by the Left. Consumption taxes, the bane of the political Left, rose in all countries; more important, the income tax was transformed from being a tax on the wealthy to a mass tax. Whereas in the mid-1930s less than 5 percent of the population paid income taxes, by the end of the war the vast majority of income earners paid this tax—and at very high rates.

Table 2.2
Top Marginal Tax Rates, United States, United Kingdom, Sweden, 1930–50

Year	U.S. ($ thousand)		U.K. (£)		SWEDEN (Skr)	
	(a)*	(b)**	(a)	(b)	(a)	(b)
1929–1930			57.50	50,001	30.24	1,000,000
1930–1931	25.00	100	63.75	50,001	30.10	1,000,000
1931–1932	n.a.	66.25	50,001	30.48		1,000,000
1932–1933	25.00	100	66.25	50,001	34.92	1,000,000
1933–1934	63.00	1,000	66.25	50,001	36.46	1,000,000
1934–1935	63.00	1,000	63.75	50,001	35.97	1,000,000
1935–1936		n.a.	63.75	50,001	35.39	1,000,000
1936–1937	79.00	5,000	65.00	50,001	35.04	1,000,000
1937–1938	79.00	5,000	66.25	50,001	36.58	1,000,000
1938–1939	79.00	5,000	75.00	50,001	44.08	200,000
1939–1940	81.10	5,000	90.00	50,001	47.17	200,000
1940–1941	81.00	5,000	90.00	50,001	47.08	200,000
1941–1942	n.a.	97.50	50,001	45.63		200,000
1942–1943	88.00	200	97.50	50,001	46.49	200,000
1944–1945	94.00	200	n.a.	45.63		200,000
1946–1947	86.45	200	97.50	20,001	44.97	200,000
1947–1948	n.a.	97.50	20,001	80.06		200,000
1948–1949	82.12	200	97.50	20,001	80.15	200,000
1949–1950	n.a.	n.a.	80.01			200,000

Sources: U.S.—J. Pechman, *Federal Tax Policy* (Washington, D.C.: Brookings Institution, 1987), tables A-1–A-7, pp. 313–20; U.K.—*Inland Revenue Reports,* various (London: Her Majesty's Stationery Office, 1959); Sweden—Budget Propositions, various years.
* Highest marginal tax rate.
** On incomes over this amount.

In addition to hiking tax rates and expanding the income tax base, each of these governments introduced new systems for collecting income taxes. Instead of having citizens compute their own taxes and then send a payment to the government for the entire amount at year's end, the pay as you earn (PAYE) system was introduced. Now income taxes could be collected with each paycheck, thereby maximizing the immediate yield of this tax and *minimizing the political costs.* Having a percentage of your income deducted from each paycheck is less onerous than having to write a check for hundreds or thousands of dollars, pounds, or kronor once a year. Taken together, these measures—expansion of the tax base, increases in tax rates, and new systems of tax collection—forever changed the revenue picture for modern

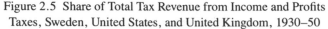

Figure 2.5 Share of Total Tax Revenue from Income and Profits
Taxes, Sweden, United States, and United Kingdom, 1930–50

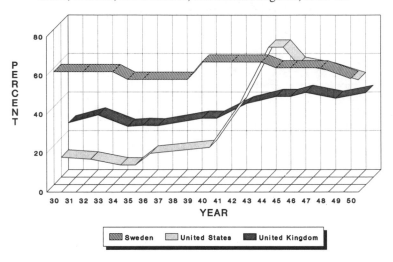

Sources: Compiled from Central Statistics Office, *Statistical Abstract for the
United Kingdom* (Liechtenstein: Kraus Reprint LTD, 1966), various tables;
Central Statistics Office, *Annual Abstract of Statistics* (Liechtenstein: Kraus
Reprint LTD, 1970), various tables; U.S. Bureau of the Census, *Historical
Statistics of the United States from Colonial Times to the Present* (Washing-
ton, D.C.: Government Printing Office, 1975), various series and tables;
E. Rodriguez, *Offentlig Inkomstexpansion* (Uppsala: Gleerup, 1980).

democratic states. Figures 2.5 and 2.6 show the share of the total tax burden
contributed by income and profits taxes during this period and the level of
total government revenue that resulted.

Postwar Tax Policy—Revenue Gain, Less Political Pain, 1945–75

Many expected taxes to be scaled back after the war. They were disappointed.
In the short run, governments felt compelled to maintain high taxes in order
to help retire the national debt. In the long run, however, the compromise
between Left and Right entailed a de facto consensus that both progressive
taxation and welfare state programs were to be permanent features in democratic capitalist states. Immediately after the war, parties of the Left controlled
the government in all three nations, but even after they had been removed
from office in Britain and the United States the postwar compromise held.
Neither the Republicans in the United States nor the Tories in the United
Kingdom embarked on a frontal attack against progressive taxation.

The necessity of wartime planning combined with the acceptance of Key-

Figure 2.6 Total Tax Revenue as a Percentage of
GDP, Sweden and United Kingdom, and as a
Percentage of GNP, United States, 1930–50

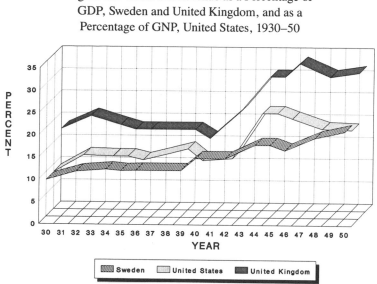

Sources: Compiled from Central Statistics Office, *Statistical Abstract for the
United Kingdom* (Liechtenstein: Kraus Reprint LTD, 1966), various tables;
Central Statistics Office, *Annual Abstract of Statistics* (Liechtenstein: Kraus
Reprint LTD, 1970), various tables; U.S. Bureau of the Census, *Historical
Statistics of the United States from Colonial Times to the Present* (Washing-
ton, D.C.: Government Printing Office, 1975), various series and tables;
E. Rodriguez, *Offentlig Inkomstexpansion* (Uppsala: Gleerup, 1980).

nesian macroeconomic management introduced these governments to new
responsibilities for the health and welfare of the national economy. Political scientists are familiar with the fact that all of these countries, including
Great Britain, which at first eschewed Keynesianism, eventually came to accept the government's responsibility for stabilizing the economy via fiscal
policy (Hall 1989). Less well appreciated, however, is the extent to which
these governments were concomitantly taking on greater responsibilities for
micromanagement of the economy via tax policy.

During the war, given the exceedingly high marginal tax rates on capital
income, governments felt it necessary to offer certain exemptions or deductions or both for certain types of investment and for investments in certain
industries. Although the governments wanted to tax so-called excess profits,
it was in no one's interest to tax away the capital necessary to build a strong
defense. The particular mechanisms varied, but all three countries offered
substantial tax expenditures for key industries. It was generally assumed that
the end of the war would bring an end to high rates of tax *and* an end to many

Figure 2.7 Income Tax as a Percentage of GDP,
Sweden, Britain, and United States, 1930–89

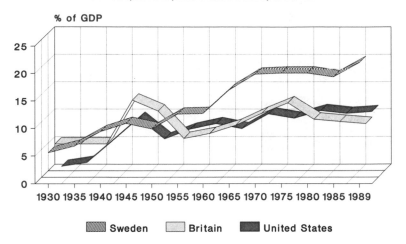

Sources: Compiled from Central Statistics Office, *Statistical Abstract for the United Kingdom* (Liechtenstein: Kraus Reprint LTD, 1966), various tables; Central Statistics Office, *Annual Abstract of Statistics* (Liechtenstein: Kraus Reprint LTD, 1970), various tables; U.S. Bureau of the Census, *Historical Statistics of the United States from Colonial Times to the Present* (Washington, D.C.: Government Printing Office, 1975), various series and tables; E. Rodriguez, *Offentlig Inkomstexpansion* (Uppsala: Gleerup, 1980); C. H. Feinstein, *National Income, Expenditure and Output of the United Kingdom, 1855–1965* (Cambridge: Cambridge University Press, 1972), pp. T10–11; OECD, *Studies in Taxation: Long-Term Revenue Trends 1955–1980* (Paris: OECD, 1991; OECD, *Revenue Statistics 1965–1990* (Paris: OECD, 1991.

if not all of these tax expenditures. Neither expectation was borne out. Tax rates remained high as more and more tax expenditures were introduced.

Postwar tax policy is thus best understood in the context of the convergence of these three forces: first, governments were either unwilling or politically unable to radically reduce formal tax rates on corporations and the rich; second, the political and administrative elites were both developing new tools and seizing responsibility for macro and micro manipulation of the economy; third, the revenue systems established during the war offered huge and automatic revenue surges with relatively limited political consequences. Despite the relative stability of formal tax rates in the postwar years, income tax revenues expanded greatly (fig. 2.7).[10]

How each of these nations dealt with this common set of forces varied considerably. I shall explore this variation in subsequent chapters. In general, however, there were powerful incentives for governments to reduce tax burdens selectively via tax expenditures (or in many cases simply loopholes) and to drive up dramatically public spending.

The Decade of Tax Reform: The 1980s

Since the mid-1970s the world economy has undergone massive changes. The expansion of world trade has been well documented (OECD 1990). Perhaps less well understood is the striking extent to which capital has become more international, more mobile, and more integrated. Such changes have substantively altered the context in which domestic tax policies are made. The result has been a crumbling of the postwar consensus over taxation policy. Whereas it was once widely accepted that tax burdens should be progressive and that the state had a right, if not a duty, to use taxation as an instrument of social and economic policy, today this consensus is under heavy attack.

As mentioned earlier, Keynes suggested that the redistributive potential of direct taxation has been checked by two considerations: the fear of making tax avoidance too worthwhile and the belief that capitalism is dependent upon the rich for economic growth. By the 1980s the internationalization of capital had given these considerations added weight. The common propensity of national government to offer tax incentives, deductions, exemptions, credits, and so on has made tax evasion easier in all countries and has thus undermined the principle of progressivity, even while countries have maintained high tax rates. Moreover, changes in both technology and policy have made "exit" a reasonable, viable, and easy option for capital. "International trade is 15 times what it was 25 years ago, and foreign direct investment is more that eight times what it was in 1980," observed Joel Slemrod, director of the Office of Tax Policy Research at the University of Michigan. Though tax policy "has traditionally been thought of as an entirely domestic matter," Slemrod concludes, "in an increasingly global world economy, nations can no longer afford to design their tax systems without accounting for the effects on international trade and investment" (Hoerner 1990, 516). The result has been the decade of tax reform (Pechman 1987; Boskin and McLure 1990). Table 2.3 shows the changes in top personal and corporate income tax rates in some of the countries that have legislated these reforms.

In addition to the lowering of tax rates, many tax expenditures and incentives have been scaled back or removed, and there has been a general attempt to make tax systems more neutral toward different types of income and investment. But, once again, the manner in which this has been accomplished, the extent to which different countries have embraced these goals, and the means

Table 2.3

Top Individual and Corporate Tax Rates Before
and After Tax Reforms, Selected Countries

Country	Individual Rate (Old/New)	Corporate Rate (Old/New)
Australia	65/49	46/39
Canada (federal)	47/29	36/28
Colombia	49/30	40/30
France	65/53	na
Indonesia	50/35	45/35
Ireland	72/56	na
Israel	60/48	53/48
Italy	72/50	na
Japan	93/50	42/37.5
Mexico	55/40	42/36
Netherlands	71/60	na
New Zealand	57/33	na
Sweden	82/50	56/30
United Kingdom	98/40	52/35
United States	70/33	46/34

Sources: J. Andrew Hoerner, "Tax Reform Around the World," *Tax Notes* 47, no. 5 (April 30, 1990): 516; Joseph Pechman, *World Tax Reform: A Progress Report* (Washington, D.C.: Brookings Institution, 1988), 4–5; Gnossen and Messere, 1989.

by which they have attempted to achieve them have varied widely. Following chapters will show that the differing paths taken in Britain, Sweden, and the United States, at least, are best explained as products of the institutional context through which tax reforms must pass. But the point here is to recognize that the institutions themselves operate within a broader historical context. To understand both the general trends and paths of public policy taken by individual nations, we must appreciate both contexts.

Divergent Patterns

National tax systems of OECD nations are heterogeneous rather than
similar; the average OECD nation is 42 percent distant from the Standard
Tax System.—Richard Rose, *Maximizing Revenue and
Minimizing Political Costs*

I suggested earlier in this chapter that in addition to the story of the common tax policy paths taken by modern democracies, an equally interesting

Figure 2.8 Various Taxes as a Percentage of
GDP, OECD Countries, 1985

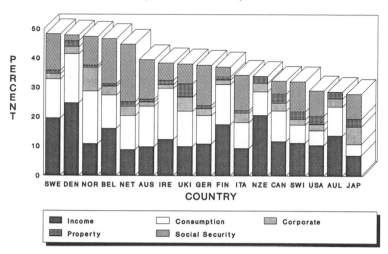

Source: OECD, *Revenue Statistics 1965–1990* (Paris: OECD, 1991).

story is that about the different policy choices they have made along the way. Indeed, when one first compares tax structures in different countries the picture can become quite confusing. For example, when looking at tax policy development over the past thirty years or so one immediately sees that while some taxes go up in some countries, they go down in others and remain quite stable in still others. Furthermore, even countries that have enlarged the total tax burden of society have reduced some taxes that have been quite popular in other countries. In the words of Richard Rose (n.d., 19–20), "In fact, there is no common national pattern of change in taxation. . . . For every example of a tax increasing in importance within a nation, a counter-example can be cited of a tax declining in importance. In 14 of 20 OECD nations more taxes decrease their percentage contribution to the national tax system than increase it. . . . There is thus no homogeneity within nations, notwithstanding the fact that within a nation all taxes are subject to many common political, administrative and economic influences."

Figure 2.8 shows the variation in the gross categories in national tax structures. Even if we look only at the major categories of taxation, we see that the distribution between various taxes can differ enormously (fig. 2.9A-E).

There is, moreover, great variation in the amount specific taxes can contribute to the national treasury. It is very difficult to generalize about how important a tax will be without knowing a great deal about the tax base, its rates, and its structure.

Figure 2.9A Property Tax as a Percentage
of GDP, Selected OECD Countries, 1989

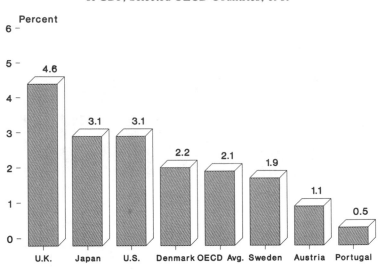

Source: OECD, *Revenue Statistics 1965–1990* (Paris: OECD, 1991).

Figure 2.9B Personal Income Tax as a Percentage
of GDP, Selected OECD Countries, 1989

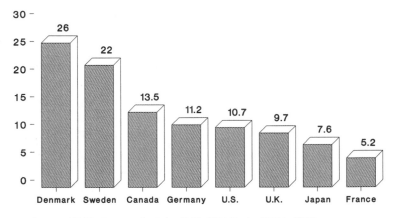

Source: OECD, *Revenue Statistics 1965–1990* (Paris: OECD, 1991).

Figure 2.9C Social Security Taxes as Percentage
of GDP, Selected OECD Countries, 1989

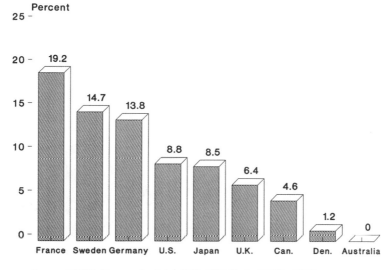

Source: OECD, *Revenue Statistics 1965–1990* (Paris: OECD, 1991).

Figure 2.9D Corporate Income Tax as a Percentage
of GDP, Selected OECD Countries, 1989

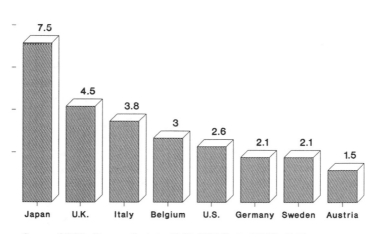

Source: OECD, *Revenue Statistics 1965–1990* (Paris: OECD, 1991).

Figure 2.9E Consumption Taxes as a Percentage
of GDP, Selected OECD Countries, 1989

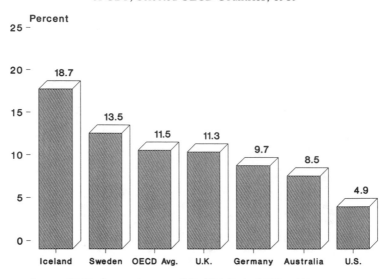

Source: OECD, *Revenue Statistics 1965–1990* (Paris: OECD, 1991).

One does not have to think very long or hard to realize that the more interesting and politically difficult questions about taxes have less to do with how much gross revenue a tax generates and more to do with who pays the tax and how much they have to pay. Revenue considerations are never absent when political leaders create, reform, or abolish taxes. But revenues are far from the only factors involved. The revenue yield of a particular tax is instead a product of a huge set of decisions about the structure and incidence of that tax. A nation's tax system, then, is a product of an even greater number of specific decisions about a whole series of taxes. The amount of money taken in taxes by a government as a whole results from a huge set of decisions about individual taxes, and many of these decisions have little to do with the revenue consequences of these taxes.

Precisely because tax policies are so central to the operation of a modern mixed economy, they are profoundly complex. After spending some time amidst the thorns and brambles of the thicket of complexity, however, one comes to appreciate that not all thickets are alike. In fact, clear patterns emerge, allowing one to distinguish one tax system from another. Tax structures are not random collections of various revenue sources in which each tax differs fundamentally from the others. Instead, a nation's tax system can be distinguished by broad patterns. There are indeed distinct tax systems, not just tax structures which vary from one another in ad hoc ways. Focusing on these broader patterns allows us to examine and compare the tax systems as a whole.

The American Tax System—The Politics of Complexity

The U.S. tax system has become a swamp of unfairness, complexity, and inefficiency. The accumulation of credits, deductions, and exclusions designed to help particular groups or advance special purposes conflict with one another, are poorly designed, and represent no consistent policy. The tax system causes investors to waste resources on low-yield investments that carry large tax benefits, while high-yield investments without such benefits go unfunded. The result is a shrunken tax base that requires needlessly high rates on wages, salaries, and other taxable income. Overall the system undermines the faith of citizens that tax burdens are shared fairly.—Henry Aaron and Harvey Galper, *Assessing Tax Reform*

Most Americans feel that their tax system is unfair (Ladd 1985). Yet a principal distinguishing characteristic of the American tax system is its equity orientation. This statement in no way suggests that the American tax system is, in the end, more equitable than the other systems I examine. Rather, the various attempts to make it equitable define its most outstanding structural characteristics: complexity and low revenue yield.

The American tax system, like all modern tax systems, is confronted with two conflicting equity concepts: vertical equity and horizontal equity. Vertical equity implies that those who have greater incomes should pay a greater percentage of that income in taxes—the system should be progressive. Horizontal equity implies that those who are in different circumstances should probably pay different taxes even if their gross income is similar.[11] In the pursuit of these conflicting goals, American tax policymakers have constructed an immensely complex tax system that typically shuns revenue-rich regressive taxes, has traditionally had a highly progressive rate structure, and allows literally thousands of special exemptions, deductions, write-offs, and special rates designed to accommodate taxpayers' varying ability to pay. One can, of course, question whether the result is a more equitable tax system. "The final and most serious count [against the American tax system]," according to Aaron and Galper (1986, 6), "is that it is just plain unfair." Still, there can be little doubt that the vast majority of individual tax decisions and choices that affect the system as a whole are driven by or at least justified in terms of equity considerations.

A casual look at OECD revenue tables reveals the remarkable fact that America, the land of free-market capitalism and the bastion of individual freedom, relies much more heavily on progressive forms of taxation as percentage of total tax take than any other Western democracy. Congressional tax policymakers have rejected numerous attempts by various presidents and party leaders to impose a national sales tax; we tax corporate profits more heavily than most of our fellow democracies; our wealth tax, commonly known as the property tax, is the heaviest in the world;[12] and finally, the United States has historically collected more revenue from inheritances and gift taxes (as a percentage of total taxes and of GNP) than either Britain or Sweden.

America not only relies more heavily on progressive personal and corporate income taxes, but for most of the twentieth century has also made them nominally more progressive than similar taxes in either Britain or Sweden. It is commonly assumed that the Swedish income tax system is more progressive than the American. The facts, however, tell a different story. Swedish income taxes (and British as well) are certainly more onerous than American, but this does not necessarily make them more progressive. Until the 1980s, at least, American income tax rates were steeply progressive over the entire income scale. Starting rates in the United States have ranged from a high of 22.4 percent (1952–53) to a low of 11 percent (1983–86), and maximum rates have ranged from a high of 92 percent (1952–53) to a low of 33 percent (beginning in 1986). This steeply graduated system, moreover, has consistently exempted large portions of the lower and working classes via the provision of comparatively generous personal, family, and dependent allowances. Additionally, tax thresholds have consistently been higher in the United States than in either Britain or Sweden.

In addition to steeply progressive personal and corporate income taxes, America has had very progressive estate tax and gift tax systems. As George Break and Joseph Pechman (1975, 111) tell us, "The major purpose of taxing gifts and bequests is to reduce the unequal distribution of wealth." Between 1935 and 1981 the U.S. Federal Estate Tax rate rose to between 70 and 77 percent, higher than the 65 percent rate for equivalent taxes in Sweden during these decades.[13]

Finally, in the United States, capital income has traditionally been taxed more heavily than earned income. The opposite is true in most countries. In Sweden, capital income has been so heavily tax advantaged that the government estimates it would actually *gain revenue* if all taxation of capital income were abolished. Since 1986 the United States has taxed capital gains income at precisely the same rate as ordinary income, one of the few nations to do so.[14] In addition, many other countries, including Sweden and Britain, have tax rules that at least partially integrate their personal and corporate income tax systems in order to mitigate the problem of double taxation.[15] Since it is mostly wealthy taxpayers who are double taxed, this type of reform has never been enacted in America, though it has been proposed several times. In short, in the United States, "the corporation and personal income taxes, taken together, impose heavier tax burdens on activities undertaken by corporations than on similar activities carried out by unincorporated entities" (Aaron and Galper 1986, 11). This is not true in most other countries.

If one were to look only at statutory tax rates (the formal tax structure) one would conclude that the American tax system has been extremely progressive for most of the twentieth century, indeed, substantially more progressive than (at least) the Swedish tax system. We know, however, that there is more to a tax system than its formal rate structure.

Tax Expenditures

Effective tax rates do not neatly correspond to formal tax rates because of tax expenditures. Tax expenditures are tax measures designed to reduce the effective tax burden of particular groups, classes, or individual taxpayers. Contrary to popular belief, a large percentage of tax expenditures available in the United States are designed to make the tax system more horizontally equitable. The irony is that these measures also tend to make the tax system less vertically equitable (progressive). For example, of the twenty-six tax expenditures listed by the Congressional Budget Office that lose the most revenue to the Federal Treasury, ten are explicitly equity-oriented tax expenditures, seven can be justified on equity and other grounds (but may serve other purposes as well), and only eight have little or no equity justification for their inclusion in the tax code (Steinmo 1986).

Other measures not normally considered tax expenditures but that affect the real progressivity of the tax code are also consequential.[16] The most notable of these are the generous personal exemptions and deductions for dependents. Additionally, married Americans are given the chance to file their returns jointly, adjusting their income tax burden to their family circumstances. Again, this "equity"-based tax measure substantially reduces the progressivity of the revenue code (Rodriguez and Steinmo 1986).

Some analysts believe that the American tax code is *designed* to be unfair.[17] For them the revenue code is, as Michael Harrington has described it, "a perverse welfare system for the rich." And there are a great many examples of tax measures that purely and simply "derive from private pressures exerted for selfish ends" (Eisenstein 1961, 4). But as Ronald King (1983, 5) suggests, "All tax leakages are not alike." And even those that appear to be classic examples of tax injustices can often be justified on equity grounds— the historical analysis that follows in subsequent chapters demonstrates that. Representative Barber Conable had it right when he said,

> The desire for equity has compounded our tax system. Nobody started out with the idea to make a complex tax system. In the early 1920s, the system was simple and comprehensive. Maybe a lot of things were not taxed, but at least everybody was taxed about the same way. Then we found that we had a complicated economy, and that the tax code was unfair to some people, so we made exceptions, and then we made exceptions and exceptions.[18]

Complexity

> The Internal Revenue Code, indeed, is a remarkable essay in sustained obscurity. It has all the earmarks of a conspiracy in restraint of understanding. The conspiracy never ends because amendments never cease. Tax law has reversed Dr. Butler's celebrated definition of an expert. A tax expert has become someone who knows less and less about more and more.—Louis Eisenstein, *The Ideologies of Taxation*

The result of the thousands of special amendments to the tax code is that the American tax system is by far the most complex system in the world. There are myriad special exemptions, deductions, credits, adjustments, allowances, rate schedules, special tariffs, minimum and maximum taxes designed to affect certain classes, groups, regions, industries, professions, states, cities, companies, families, and individuals. No other tax system in the industrialized world comes anywhere close to the degree of specificity found in the U.S. Federal Revenue Code. All countries complicate their tax systems with equity considerations and through the use of tax structures as instruments of economic and social policy. But no country is nearly as detailed as the United States in its attempts to adjust tax burdens.

Both Sweden and Britain have traditionally allowed vast sums of money to slip through the Treasury's fingers via generous depreciation schedules and other investment stimulative tax expenditures.[19] But in both cases the measures are notable for the degree of flexibility they allow taxpayers (International Fiscal Association 1977). It would be anathema for these countries to write tax legislation that specified firms or individuals. The U.S. Federal Revenue Code, in contrast, attempts to specify in great detail when, where, and to whom specific tax breaks should be permitted. Though proper names are rarely used, it is not uncommon for tax amendments to specify conditions that could apply only to one firm or individual. Some products and goods are also routinely specified in the tax code. It is well known, for example, that the oil and gas industry have their own depletion allowance. It is less known that cement, clay, asphalt, and dirt, to name a few, have their own depletion allowances. Depreciation allowances are even more specific. Christmas trees, railroad boxcars, fruit orchards, cattle, chicken coops, and tuxedos are but a fraction of the hundreds of items that benefit from specific depreciation allowances.

Revenue Yield

The final distinguishing characteristic of the American tax system is its low revenue yield. In 1990 the United States collected less tax revenue than any other OECD democracy except Australia (table 2.4). This low revenue yield is explained by two factors: first, the United States does not have a national sales tax or VAT. Second, the hundreds of tax expenditures discussed in the previous sections make our major revenue source, the income tax, highly inefficient.[20]

It is common to hear the U.S. tax system criticized for allowing the wealthy and rich corporations to pay far less than their statutory tax burdens. But from a revenue perspective it is more significant that the United States taxes the lower and middle classes so lightly. In 1981, a family of four with an average annual income paid 14.3 percent of that income in income taxes in the United States. In the same year, a similar family paid 20.7 percent in Britain and 34.1 percent in Sweden (OECD 1982, 26).

Because of this revenue leakage, the income tax has never generated more than 10.6 percent of GNP, and this in spite of tax rates that ranged from 23 percent on the lowest bracket to 94 percent on the highest bracket (1944–5). Sweden's income tax, by comparison, has generated as much as 20 percent of GNP. Marginal tax rates are now higher in Sweden than in the United States, yet the major factor explaining the differential revenue yields historically has been the level, size, and quantity of tax expenditures available to the average American citizen.

In recent years, tax expenditure losses have grown even larger. The Joint Committee on Taxation reports that in 1986 over $424 billion was lost via tax expenditures. Thus more money was lost via tax expenditures than was generated via federal and state income taxes combined. The Tax Reform and

Table 2.4

Total Tax Revenues as a Percent of
Gross Domestic Product at Market
Prices, OECD Countries, 1989.

Sweden	56.1	Ireland	37.6
Denmark	49.4	United Kingdom	36.5
Netherlands	46.0	Canada	35.3
Norway	45.5	Portugal	35.1
Belgium	44.3	Spain	34.4
France	43.3	Iceland	33.8
Austria	41.0	Greece	33.2
New Zealand	40.3	Switzerland	31.8
Finland	38.1	Japan	30.6
Germany	38.1	Australia	30.1
Italy	37.8	United States	30.1
OECD Average	38.4		

Source: OECD, *Revenue Statistics, 1965–1990* (Paris: OECD, 1991).

Equity Act of 1986 removed some of the most egregious tax expenditures, including in large part those introduced in 1981, but it made only a small dent in the number and depth of tax expenditures available in the federal tax code. Significantly, it did not raise any new revenue.

In sum, the American tax system is distinguished by its equity orientation, its complexity, and its low revenue yield. In the United States, tax equity has been pursued via tax reductions. The rub is that the complexity created by these tax expenditures has undermined the egalitarian impact of the system as a whole. The attempt has been to make the tax system as equitable as possible, but since two competing models of equity (progressivity and horizontal equity) have been championed simultaneously, neither goal has been achieved to the satisfaction of most citizens. The result has been to make the tax system appear unfair to almost everyone.

Sweden—Efficiency

Full employment and low inflation are two necessary conditions for a
more equal and just distribution of living standards. The most
important distributional policies which we can introduce are those
which make it possible to have full employment and stable prices.
—*Finansplanen,* Social Democratic Budget Proposition 1984

Many people expect the Swedish tax system to be the most egalitarian system in the world.[21] The fact is, however, that the Swedish tax system is

Table 2.5

Personal Income Tax Paid by the Average Production Worker (excluding the effects of nonstandard tax reliefs) U.S., U.K., and Sweden, 1984–87

	Single People				Two-child Families			
	1984	1985	1986	1987	1984	1985	1986	1987
Sweden	36.1	35.6	36.1	36.6	34.2	33.9	34.5	35.0
United Kingdom	22.4	22.3	21.6	20.3	18.1	17.9	17.4	16.6
United States	22.9	22.8	19.9	20.0	15.2	15.3	12.4	13.3

Source: OECD, *The Tax/Benefit Position of Production Workers 1984–1987* (Paris: OECD, 1988), table 1, p. 50.

distinguished neither by steep progressivity nor by heavy-handed treatment of capitalist or capital income. Instead, the hallmarks of the Swedish tax system have been its broad base, its stability, and its high revenue yield. The Swedish system, moreover, reaches deeply into the average Swede's pocket but tries to avoid taxing the investment potential out of society's capitalists. "Ironically," Richard Rose and Guy Peters (1982, 99) note, "taxes are least progressive in Sweden (of all OECD democracies examined) because of the high level of tax paid by ordinary workers." Swedish authorities have taxed the working class more and more heavily with each new budget, through increases in invisible indirect taxes, while it has allowed Swedish corporations and capitalists numerous avenues to avoid taxes and accumulate capital.

A few examples are illustrative. Sweden bears the dubious distinction of having the heaviest and most regressive broadly based consumption tax in the world. The Swedish VAT taxes virtually all goods and services at a flat 23.46 percent rate, exempts virtually nothing, not even food or clothing, has no reduced rates, and has no especially high rates for luxury goods.[22] The Swedish income tax, similarly, has a much broader base, higher starting rates, and fewer exemptions or deductions for the average worker than do either the British or American income tax systems. Additionally, the social security tax, which is paid for workers by employers, is almost three times heavier for Swedish workers than for either British or American workers.[23]

Not only does the average production worker in Sweden pay much more in taxes than his equivalent in Britain and the United States (table 2.5) (indeed, he pays more than workers in any other OECD country except neighboring Denmark), but there are few of the generous tax reductions available in most countries for single-earner families and for other dependents. The government has instead decided that it is more efficient to offer direct subsidies in lieu of tax deductions and credits.

The paucity of tax expenditures available to average- and lower-paid workers has broadened the base of the Swedish tax system and thus has augmented tax revenues. As Gustav Lindencrona has observed, however, these same measures have pulled the tax system away from the traditionally valued goal of ability to pay, or what Americans would simply call fairness (Lindencrona 1984).

At the other end of the scale, the Swedish tax system appears less onerous. To quote Rose and Peters (1982, 93–94) again, "In Sweden, tax expenditures are important in making tolerable otherwise extremely high rates of taxation. Thanks to government investment allowances, a company may avoid paying any tax on a gross profit of up to $100 million. Swedes earning a million or more kronor a year may avoid taxes on much of that income by invoking of tax loopholes."

A study conducted in 1974 examined the income tax system in Sweden and found that "the concept of global progressivity has to be qualified by the fact that the distribution takes place mainly between taxpayers in the middle and low income brackets. That is, tax redistribution has affected basically income concentration beneath a certain level. The redistribution process has 'spared' the highest incomes" (Sola 1975, 152).

The taxation of the very wealthy in Sweden differs from the taxation of average income earners in that capital income receives much more favorable tax treatment than does earned income. The taxation of these rich individuals is well illustrated by the British fiscal economist Cedric Sandford. After returning from a study tour of the Swedish tax system, he wrote, "An eminent Swedish economist said to the author in a private conversation: 'Our finance minister is the enemy of the millionaire and a friend of the multimillionaire.' His measure of 'a millionaire' was Swedish crowns, not pounds sterling; so that a sterling paraphrase might be the provisions favored the millionaire but not the man with £100,000" (Sandford 1971, 196).

The above statement should not be taken to imply that the rich as a group do not pay taxes in Sweden. On the contrary, as a group rich Swedes bear a heavier tax burden than do either their British or American counterparts. It is largely the extremely rich (by Swedish standards) capitalists who are able to use tax expenditures to bring down their effective tax burdens. The finger is often pointed at Swedish taxes when entertainers, movie directors, and tennis players emigrate. Owners of large manufacturing interests, in contrast, are much less inclined to leave Sweden because of heavy taxes. Claes-Göran Kjellander tells us, "Some of Sweden's richest businessmen have filed tax returns with Skr. 0 in taxable income in spite of the fact that, before deductions, they earned seven-figure incomes" (Kjellander 1982, 4). Table 2.6 shows the estimated revenue effects of a hypothetical policy of eliminating all capital taxes

Table 2.6
Effect of Abolishing Taxes on Capital
Incomes, 1984, Differences in Paid Taxes

Decile	Taxable Income	(Skr)
1	−22,300	−75
2	22,300–29,700	−839
3	29,700–37,700	−1,110
4	37,700–47,200	−976
5	47,200–58,700	−458
6	58,700–69,500	−978
7	69,500–79,200	+109
8	79,200–90,200	+1,305
9	90,200–108,800	+3,395
10	108,800 and over	+5,065
Top 2.5%	156,500 and over	+7,617
All		+571

Source: Krister Andersson, "Sweden," in Joseph Pechman, ed., *Comparative Tax Systems: Europe, Canada, and Japan* (Arlington, Va.: Tax Analysts, 1987), table 13, p. 90.

and their deductions. As mentioned earlier, the Finance Department projects that it would actually gain revenue through such a move![24]

The key here is that the Swedish tax system is designed to encourage the use of capital because this will contribute to growth and jobs while taxing stagnant wealth, that is, wealth in the form of nonproductive holdings such as large estates, very heavily. The wealthy in Sweden are able to shield their wealth and income from tax authorities by refraining from consuming that wealth and instead placing it in the economy's active working capital stock. In Britain especially, and in the United States to a somewhat lesser extent, the tax system encourages conspicuous consumption by the rich (Kay and King 1983). In Sweden, the taxation of wealth has historically discouraged consumption and encouraged reinvestment.[25]

Swedish corporations are well treated by any standard. "One of the secrets of the Swedish economy is that governments have looked to major corporations to create wealth," Pehr Gyllenhammer, chairman of Volvo and one of Sweden's most powerful industrialists, reported in a recent interview. "There is greater freedom for large corporations in Sweden," he added, "than in the United States" (Lohr 1987).

Though Swedish formal tax rates on corporate profits do not traditionally differ much from those found in the United States and the United Kingdom, effective tax rates for large, successful Swedish corporations are very low by international standards. According to the Swedish Department of Industry, the average tax burden borne by Swedish industrial firms in 1981 was between 3 and 13 percent of profits.[26] Taken together, the numerous tax mechanisms available to corporate investors in Sweden created a bias in favor of expanding profitable firms with large inventories or depreciable assets or both. It has long been the aim of the government to promote successful corporations and to encourage them to stabilize their investment patterns.[27]

In sum, the Swedish tax system encourages the concentration of economic power while it discourages the conspicuous display of wealth. Sweden, in effect, redistributes consumption, not production. The distribution of effective tax burdens for Sweden, then, is the consequence of a politico-economic logic designed to promote stability, economic efficiency, high investment, and growth while concomitantly financing the world's most generous welfare state.

Britain—Instability

The mess into which the present British tax system has drifted has [already] been documented. . . . Anyone who came to it for the first time would regard the present system with some incredulity. There is a maze of taxes on different kinds of income, each tax with its own rules for determining taxable income and liability. The interaction between these taxes is difficult to comprehend, and, because of this, is rarely brought out into the open when tax changes are discussed. . . . No one would design such a system on purpose, and nobody did. Only a historical explanation of how it came about can be offered as a justification. That is not a justification but a demonstration of how seemingly individually rational decisions can have absurd effects in aggregate.—J. A. Kay and M. King, *The British Tax System*

The major distinguishing characteristic of the British tax system is its instability. The British tax system changes faster, more frequently, and more radically than any other tax system I have observed. This instability results in a pattern of fiscal incoherence. Specific tax decisions are often made in an ad hoc manner with inadequate regard for their impact on other taxes and even, at times, with little appreciation of their economic impact as a whole. The instability of the British tax system makes it very difficult to describe the system at any one point in time. As S. James and C. Nobes (1981, 135) have written in their *Economics of Taxation,* "One of the most noticeable characteristics of the British tax system is that it is under continual change. Writing about it is very much like trying to hit a moving target."

In some ways it can be said that the British tax system has taken the middle ground between the American and the Swedish. The United Kingdom is in the middle in terms of overall tax load and the distribution of revenues between various types of taxes. Britain relies heavily on both broad-based consumption taxes and flat rate income taxes, as does Sweden; the British tax code also provides for a number of deep tax expenditures, like the American system. These measures effectively reduce the revenue-generating capacity of these taxes while seriously skewing their effective incidence.

These outcomes have not been the result of any one party or government's choice. Rather, each government has layered new tax provisions, exemptions, deductions, surcharges, and rates on the system. These changes have caused those in the lowest income classes to pay less than the lowest income classes in Sweden (they also get less in terms of social welfare provisions) but markedly more than those at the bottom in the United States. The result has been that very rich individuals have been able to avoid the lion's share of their statutory tax burden even when the maximum marginal tax rate has been as high as 98 percent, as it was in the 1970s.

Britain has not found this middle ground easily. Of course, the state of British taxes is not the result of some rational calculus that shuns radical alternatives. Rather, the British tax system occupies the middle ground because of the waffling to and fro between diametrically opposed perspectives as to what the tax burden should be. As the historical discussion in following chapters will show, the British create, revamp, restructure, or totally remove taxes with remarkable frequency. To take a few examples: capital gains tax (CGT) on short term gains was not introduced until 1962 but was then made a full CGT in 1965. There have been changes made in the CGT in almost every year since it was introduced, and major reforms of note were made in 1972, 1977, and 1982. A classical corporate profits tax was introduced in 1966, and major revisions were made to it in 1973 and 1983. VAT was introduced in 1973, replacing the purchase tax in the same year, and has been reformed four times since then. The selective employment tax was created in 1966 and removed in 1973. Finally, the capital transfer tax (CTT) was introduced in 1976 and reformed to the point of irrelevance in 1980. Additionally, depreciation schedules have been manipulated for companies in at least half of the years since World War II. Taxes on savings, pension incomes, and investments have also had their share of massaging over the past three decades (see Robinson and Sandford 1983; Sandford 1984; Kay and King 1983; Dilnot et al. 1984).

It is not simply the fact that British taxes have been changed frequently which distinguishes the tax system. Rather it is the character of these changes that sets the British system apart. American tax policymakers, as Witte (1985) has shown, are continually changing the American tax system as well. But whereas American taxes change incrementally—except in the most unusual of circumstances—major overhauls of the British tax system are quite normal. Moreover, these changes are not random. On the contrary, they occur with nearly predictable frequency: each time a new government takes office.

The Tax Roller Coaster

The Left in England favors high income taxes largely because it believes that income should be redistributed in society. Labour sees extreme progressivity in the income tax as a key element in its attempts to redistribute wealth. Conservatives, on the other hand, have attempted to mitigate some of the most adverse effects of this system by manipulating both upper and lower rates as well as by providing ample numbers of tax shelters. As a result,

> the redistributive elements in the present tax structure rely heavily on high tax rates on those with large incomes from employment. But high earnings are not an important source of wealth inequality in the United Kingdom, so that these taxes fall heavily on those engaged in productive sectors of the economy without achieving much in the way of true redistribution. The tax system is rightly criticized on both counts; the conflict between equity and efficiency in tax policy appears very acute. Although this trade-off is a real one, preoccupation with rates of tax and concern with the appearance of the tax system rather than its reality have led to excessive emphasis on it; and to a futile process in which political parties have sought to compensate for the deficiencies in the structure of taxation by changes in the rates. (Kay and King 1983, 247–48)

Various governments have changed the rates and exemptions on income from savings, investment, and capital gains (James and Nobes 1981, 66–67; Kay and King 1983, 248). Additionally, special provisions have been included for lower-income individuals via Small Income Relief; Child Relief; Earned Income Credit; Personal Relief; and Old Age Relief. Table 2.7 shows how income tax policies made between 1946 and 1975 have affected the personal disposable income (PDI) of several income groups during this period. PDI statistics are useful because they encompass a whole range of changes in the income tax, including tax rates, exemption levels, and personal deductions.

The data indicate that between 1946 and 1975 tax changes made by both

Table 2.7

Change in PDI by Party in Power,
Single Person, Britain, 1946–75

Government	(Earned income)		(Investment income)		
	£2,000	£5,000	£10,000	£20,000	£100,000
Labour (%)	3.0	−12.0	−25.9	−55.0	−139.5
Tory (%)	20.7	56.2	88.5	83.0	110.6
Total (%)	23.7	44.2	62.6	28.0	−28.9

Source: Morrissey and Steinmo 1986.
Note: Table gives cumulative change in disposable income from 1946 base level,
i.e., total change in disposable income relative to the base year taking all the years
in office of each party into consideration.

parties reduced the PDI of those in the £100,000 income class by 28.9 percent. Each time the Labour party entered office it raised income taxes for this
group, thus decreasing PDI. But Labour's actions were largely counteracted
by Tory tax policies that reduced income taxes for this and all income groups.

Thus despite Labour's dedication to creating a progressive personal and
corporate tax structure, Conservatives have been able to manipulate the character of these taxes so that their redistributive effect is left in doubt. Tax
slippage has been measured in Britain to be second only to that in the United
States. As a result of this slippage, income taxes cannot generate the resources
needed for the British welfare state. Hence excise and consumption taxes
continue to be major revenue producers in Britain. Since the Labour party is
in general opposed to consumption taxes, they are made less regressive via
exemptions (more accurately zero-rating) on a wide variety of products from
food to children's shoes. The result is that despite a VATs rate of 15 percent,
the British VAT does not generate anywhere near the revenue generated by
the comprehensive VAT found in many other countries.

Corporate income taxation has undergone a similarly turbulent history in
postwar Britain. In addition to the changes in nominal tax rates, British companies have been subjected to a large number of changes in the tax treatment
of capital investment. Each successive government seems ineluctably drawn
to introduce, repeal, increase, and/or decrease a wide variety of investment
allowances, initial allowances, and direct grants for investment.[28] According
to the Hansard Society, thirty-eight changes were made in these various forms
of investment subsidies between 1945 and 1972.[29] Mervin King (1977, 5–6)
aptly summarized the history of British corporate tax treatment in 1974 as
follows:

The U.K. experience in the use of taxation to influence corporation behavior is unique. Four major reforms [now five] of the corporate tax system have taken place since the war, the most recent being 1973 [now 1983], and tax rates have been altered at frequent intervals. Most conceivable kinds of investment incentives have been tried, and there have been important changes in personal taxation of income from property. . . . A good illustration of this is afforded by the excitement generated amongst American economists in the 1960s by the investment tax credit and the attempts to assess its effects. A British economist would have shrugged this off as a mere trifle, compared to the changes he had witnessed over the years.

There appears to be no end to the examples of the instability, inefficiency, and absence of fiscal coherence in Britain. Andrew Dilnot et al. (1984, 1), for example, bluntly introduce their examination of the British social security system by calling it "another British failure" owing to the complex interaction of payments and benefits, their incoherence and their inefficiency. They show, for example, that, because of the complex and ill-planned interaction of social security and income taxes in Britain, many low-paid workers in the early 1980s paid marginal tax rates *in excess* of 100 percent. This meant that as their nominal wage rose their standard of living fell.[30] Similarly, the histories of consumption taxation, death taxes, and capital gains taxation have also shown these revenue sources to be tumultuous and unstable.[31] The result is summarized by J. A. Kay and M. King (1983, 18): "The present state of the British tax system is the product of a series of unsystematic and ad hoc measures, many undertaken for excellent reasons—for administrative convenience or to encourage deserving groups and worthy activities—but whose overall effect has been to deprive the system of any consistent rationale or coherent structure."

Thatcherism—Stability at Last?

Over the past ten years a series of reforms have reduced a number of the dramatic inconsistencies in the tax code. This has largely been accomplished through eliminating many of the progressive elements of the revenue system and decisively redistributing the tax burden away from the wealthy and toward the less well off in society. Not only have consumption taxes gone up while income taxes, notably for the wealthy, have been cut, but property taxes have been abolished and inheritance taxes have been reformed into insignificance. Finally, a new head tax, popularly called the community charge, was

Figure 2.10 Effective Tax Rates by Income
Quintile, Great Britain, 1977–1988

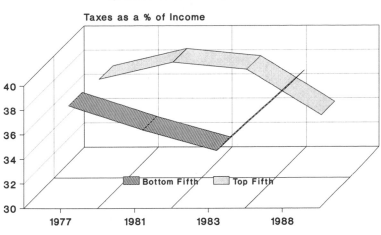

Source: Central Statistics Office, *The Effect of Taxes and Benefits on Household Income* (London: Her Majesty's Stationery Office, 1989).

introduced to replace the local property tax system (called rates). This tax is, however, in the process of being repealed. Still, the British tax system is more coherent in 1990 than it was in 1980. Figure 2.10 illustrates the effects of Thatcher's tax policies for different income classes.

Unsurprisingly, the opposition Labour party has promised to reverse much of what Thatcher did to British taxes once it regains office. Though they do not promise to increase marginal income tax rates to 98 percent, they have promised to raise considerably taxes on the wealthy. Even the Tory government led by John Major has promised to soften the regressivity of the tax reforms introduced since Thatcher took office in 1979. We do not know what a Labour government would actually do to the British tax system once it returns to office, but we can be sure that the system will be reformed drastically and that the roller coaster pattern of British tax policy will continue.

3

The Emergence of
Modern Taxation, 1800–1920

Should foreigners, staring at English Taxation,
Ask why we reckon ourselves a free nation,
We'll tell them we pay for the light of the sun;
For a horse with a saddle, to trot and run;
For writing our names; for the flash of a gun;
for the flame of the fire to cheer the dark night;
for the hole in the house, if it let in the light;
For births, weddings and deaths; For our selling
    and buying;
Though some think 'tis hard to pay threepence for dying;
And some poor folk's crying out, These are
    Pharaoh-like tricks,
To take such unmerciful tale of our bricks.
How great in Financing our statements have been,
From our ribbons, our shoes, and our hats be seen.
By this side by that, in the air, on the ground,
And Act by Act now so firmly we're bound,
One would think there's no room one new impost to put,
From the crown of the head to the sole of the foot;
Like Job, thus John Bull his condition deplores,
Very patient, indeed; and all covered with sores.
           —Anon. English poet, 1784

Classical tax systems were amazingly complicated affairs. They consisted of an array of taxes on virtually every imaginable source. Moreover, as the poem above mockingly points out, there was little consistent logic driving the system as a whole or allowing people to make sense of the choices of one type of tax over another—other than the state's need for money. The worst rub, however, was that these taxes generated very little revenue for the state.

Modern tax systems are, in contrast, remarkably efficient and coherent, though they are by no means all equally so. Not only do a small number of taxes generate massive sums of revenue, but these systems as a whole are meant to abide by a general principle that would have been totally alien to a

Treasury official of one hundred years ago—namely, that tax burdens should be related to the taxpayers' ability to pay. Fairness has always been an important symbol in taxes (when taxes are widely perceived as unfair people have a tendency to revolt against the state—remember the Boston Tea Party). Today it is widely accepted that a fair tax system should tax the rich proportionally more than the poor—be vertically equitable—and that it should take into account people's individual circumstances—be horizontally equitable. As I will point out in subsequent chapters, no modern tax system perfectly accommodates these principles, and indeed they may be moving away from them. Still, these principles have both driven and justified the construction of the kinds of revenue-rich tax systems which have made the modern state possible.

Capitalism, Democracy, and Progressive Taxes

> The individualist town councillor will walk along the municipal pavement, lit by municipal gas and cleansed by municipal brooms with municipal water, and seeing by the municipal clock in the municipal market that he is too early to meet his children coming from the municipal school, hard by the county lunatic asylum and municipal park, but to come by the municipal tramway to meet him in the municipal reading-room by the municipal art gallery, museum and library where he intends to consult some of the national publications in order to prepare his next speech in the municipal town hall in favor of the nationalization of the canals and the increase of Government control over the railway system. "Socialism, Sir," he will say, "don't waste the time of a practical man by your fantastic absurdities. Self-help, Sir, individual self-help, that's what made our city what it is."
> —*London Times*, 23 August 1902, quoted in Derek Fraser, *The Evolution of the British Welfare State*

The transformation of tax systems throughout the world is naturally related to the changing world political economy. Two intimately interconnected and yet distinct forces appear to have been at work at the end of the nineteenth and beginning of the twentieth centuries, forces that explain the transformation from classical to modern tax systems in all three countries studied in this book: one supported political and social equality in society, the other demanded increased revenues on the part of the state, and together these two impulses brought about new tax ideas and structures.

In all three countries, progressive taxation became a major ambition and policy goal of mobilizing working classes. In addition, as industrialization took off, international pressures to lower tariffs intensified; but lowering tariffs meant lowering government revenues precisely at a time when the state was becoming more heavily involved both in protecting individuals from the capitalist market and in constructing infrastructure (Gourevitch 1986). The replacing of tariffs with excises, moreover, could have dire consequences. Many a revolt and even a few revolutions had been sparked by raises in excise taxes. Taxes on land, finally, were exceedingly difficult to raise because landed interests dominated traditionalist legislatures. Eventually, finance officials were forced to turn to new revenue sources and a new principle of taxation: taxes on income and the ability to pay.

All three of the countries studied here had some form of taxation on income well before the turn of the twentieth century, but in each case these were relatively minor taxes that should in fact be seen as excises on income.[1] In no case were these taxes thought of as redistributive. By the end of World War I, however, all three countries had introduced steep taxes on both personal and corporate income. These taxes were not solely revenue-rich tax innovations, but also specifically intended as tools by which the state could intervene in the distribution of wealth in society. They, as Levi (1988, 123) suggests, "fundamentally altered the individual's relationship to the central state."

The process by which each country introduced these new tax principles, however, was critically shaped by the nature of each country's political institutions at the time as well as by each country's position with respect to the two great financial motivators of the times: industrialization itself because of its consequent need for an expanded role by the state in society and World War I because of the incredible expense of waging a modern war in the industrial era.

Britain—Strong Party Government

Britain was of course the first nation to industrialize and, as Bendix (1964) argues, this in itself makes the politics of modernization in this country internationally unique. Both the process of industrialization and the related demands for democratic participation in government evolved more slowly and in many ways less violently than was the case in most of the rest of the world. Because of this peculiar evolution, Britons were able to avoid the kind of cathartic moment of institutional choice and change in which the governing system was fundamentally reevaluated and restructured on the basis of a decisive set of new governing principles. Instead, the right of broader segments of society to participate in national politics was extended quite gradually. Therefore, changes in both ideas and institutions appeared to be the product more of an evolutionary momentum and less of a decisive choice.

This evolution can be traced throughout the nineteenth century as Britain moved away from the traditional "rotten boroughs" system of representation toward a system of more direct representation in Parliament. As the franchise was extended, Conservatives insisted on converting more and more electoral districts from multimember constituencies to single-member districts. Whig and Tory members in Parliament had in the past favored representation by communities and interests rather than a numerically determined fraction of the population. But with the extension of suffrage to the middle classes these interests attempted to gain greater influence with an electoral tactic called the block vote. The Conservatives believed that the best insurance against the electoral successes of the middle classes, then, was via the expansion of single-member constituencies throughout Britain. Thus in exchange for the House of Lords' acquiescence to the extension of suffrage, they insisted that the single-member-district principle be extended throughout the land.[2]

Later in this chapter we shall see that each of the three countries examined here institutionalized electoral measures designed to protect minority (read upper-class) interests against the majority. In each case these measures would profoundly shape the character of the decision-making system in their country throughout the twentieth century. In the British case the decision to create a single-member-district electoral system within a highly centralized political structure had the long-term effect of dramatically concentrating power in the hands of the government. From this point forward, small shifts in the balance of electoral support for one party over another would often result in huge shifts in the numbers of representatives these parties would send to Parliament. This in turn would mean that the victorious party could become a decisive force in Parliament even when it had won a very indecisive mandate from the voters. Though the single-member-district system was originally championed as a measure to protect minority rights, it is far from clear whether in the longer run it has had this effect.

The Income Tax

[The income tax] is a vile, Jacobin pumped up Jack-in-the-Office piece of impertinence—is a true Briton to have no privacy? Are the fruits of his labour and toil to be picked over, farthing by farthing, by the pimply minions of bureaucracy?—From a letter to Parliament written by an irate taxpayer, quoted in B. E. V. Sabine, *A History of Income Tax*

In 1799, faced with a huge public deficit and the growing need to finance the war with Napoleon, William Pitt introduced the world's first progressive income tax. As efficient as this graduated tax was, however, it was much-hated by the wealthy in society, who paid the tax.[3] Pitt thus repealed the progressive elements of the tax after only two years and replaced them with a flat-rate income tax.[4] Even with this moderation, though, the tax continued to be a major irritant to the conservative forces in Parliament throughout the Napoleonic War. The tax was finally abolished after Waterloo in 1816.

Though it was unmistakably a political hot potato, the income tax would not go away for long. In less than thirty years the "temporary tax" was re-introduced by Peel in 1842 to help fight "the growing evil" (that is, the deficit). The problem, according to Peel and the several chancellors who inherited this tax from him, was that modern government demanded greater revenues. Traditional revenue sources, like the window tax, simply would not suffice. At the same time these governments were dedicated to reducing, not increasing, tariffs and customs. Finally, while the government was sympathetic to the philosophical arguments in favor of reduced government, they were also committed to the idea that the state should finance its expenditures through taxation rather than through debt. The governments of the day were plainly caught between conflicting ideological and political pressures. Whatever the current ideological beliefs about laissez-faire, industrialization was creating a need for a somewhat expanded government. Not only was defense becoming more and more expensive in this period, but the growing need for public health and other types of social spending were becoming ever harder to ignore. Capitalism, it appeared, required some expansion in the role of government, and an expanded role for government required an expanded revenue base. The income tax, while certainly not perfect, was, in short, the best of many bad alternatives.

Thus in spite of unwavering opposition to the income tax, chancellors continued to rely on it—indeed, they increased its rates—simply on the grounds that it was too efficient to be abandoned. Although both Liberal and Conservative parties were formally committed to abolishing the tax, the continuing fiscal demands on the Treasury offered the chancellor "no opportunity of allowing the tax to die a natural death" (Sabine 1966, 112). All taxes evoked political opposition, but few taxes generated as much revenue with such small administrative costs.[5] By 1873 the tax stood at two pence on the pound (less than 1 percent) on incomes over £100 a year. Although only a small fraction of citizens were subject to the tax, it generated £5.7 million a year. (The various customs and excises raised £47.5 million at this time.)

As the nineteenth century came to a close, the demands for government spending became more vociferous. The flat-rate income tax proved to be a remarkably elastic revenue instrument and was adjusted nearly annually to meet current fiscal needs. By 1900 the tax had reached 5 percent.[6] Still, successive governments were unwilling to acknowledge the significance of the tax as a permanent part of the revenue system and consistently claimed that it would be abolished as soon as revenue considerations permitted. However, as Levi points out, society was gradually coming to accept the principle that taxation ought to be distributed fairly, though the principle was rarely explicitly acknowledged by the government even as it kept raising this tax. It would take a major political upheaval before this basic principle would be explicitly accepted and used to drive the development of the modern British tax system.

The War Budget on Poverty

I have no nest eggs. I have got to rob somebody's hen roost next year. I am on the lookout which will be the easiest to get and where I shall be least punished, and where I shall get the most eggs. —David Lloyd George, 1908, quoted in Bentley Gilbert, *David Lloyd George*

The general election of 1906 proved to be just such a political upheaval. The Liberal party widened its share of the popular vote only from 44.6 percent to 49 percent, but owing to the now-widespread practice of single-member constituencies, this small shift in popular support led to a massive swing in the party's fortunes in Parliament. The Liberals increased their mandates from 184 to 400 (out of a total of 670 seats). The election was perceived as a decisive defeat for the Conservatives and as a decisive victory for progressive idealism. The massive shift of power in Parliament, moreover, ensured that the new government would have the political authority to translate this idealism into real policies.

One of the first items on the Liberal party's agenda was a thorough examination of the tax system. Herbert Henry Asquith, the new Liberal chancellor, commissioned a study of the income tax. There had been a great deal of political agitation from radicals in the previous century—and now from the young Labour party—in favor of making the income tax more progressive and differentiating between earned and unearned income.[7] The Inland Revenue[8] had argued long and hard that any moves in these directions would seriously complicate the tax, undermine its revenue- generating capacity, and elicit capital flight from Britain. The Liberal party itself had opposed the income tax in the past, but with their apparent mandate for change it appeared to be a good time to reconsider this stance.

In the end, the conflict between the "official view" and the demands for progressivity proved difficult to resolve. The final report of the Royal Commission on the Income Tax rather meekly suggested that graduation and differentiation were indeed possible but should be limited for fear of capital flight and administrative difficulties.[9] Asquith quickly moved to implement these proposals, but apparently out of fear of inciting too virulent an opposition he backed down from introducing either a graduated system or a so-called super tax on capital income. The budget for 1907 thus lowered the rate on earned income slightly but did not move to boost tax rates on the wealthy. It appeared that even with the huge popular mandate that the government enjoyed, there would be only feeble efforts after all to redistribute the tax burden. Many progressive reformers took this as an indication that the Liberals could not be trusted and that a new party, the Labour party, would be necessary to represent the interests of the mobilizing working class.

Upon the death of the Liberal prime minister Henry Campbell-Bannerman in 1908, Asquith was selected to lead the party and thus moved to 10 Downing Street. Asquith chose the energetic reformer David Lloyd George to take his place in the Treasury, despite the fact that Lloyd George had no experience in financial matters and did not appear to be noticeably astute in these affairs. The decision, however, would prove to be a momentous one.

Asquith left Lloyd George with the problem of financing the old age pension scheme that Asquith had introduced in 1908. Incredibly, Asquith had made no provisions to finance his scheme and blithely argued that the budget surplus of 1908 indicated that no special tax increases were necessary.[10] It was doubtful whether the scheme could be covered from current revenues even in the very short run; it was eminently clear that extant taxes would eventually prove inadequate. What happened next was one of the most decisive and crucial political events in British fiscal history: rather than negotiate a compromise among the various interests and ideas within his party and then moderately raise taxes across the board, Lloyd George dramatically and unilaterally decided to embrace not only several new taxes but, more important, new tax principles. In his budget for 1909, he surprised the Parliament and even most of the members of his cabinet by introducing the now-famous War Budget on Poverty.[11] It was learned later that he had devised the plan without consulting anyone but several elite colleagues in the Treasury.

The new plan proposed hikes in a wide variety of taxes, including consumption, income, and land taxes. The most controversial parts of the bill, however, were the proposals to introduce new taxes on the sale of land—a sort of capital gains tax—a capital levy on unused land, and a new super tax of up to 8 percent on annual incomes of more than five thousand pounds.[12] These income taxes applied to both personal and business income. Significantly, though Lloyd George had earlier stated his opposition to graduated income taxes because of their potential negative effects on business and enterprise, his new tax plan made few allowances in this direction and in fact paid little attention to differences in types of business or special circumstances that might apply to individual cases. It would be left to the Inland Revenue's discretion to deal with these issues.[13] The problems with the super tax, however, were politically far overshadowed by the huge controversy evoked by the new taxes on land. Land reform had long been a special interest of many Liberal reformers, and though this tax would probably generate comparatively little revenue it set a fundamental principle for modern taxation: Squeeze the rich.[14]

"The financial details are important," Derek Frazer (1973, 145) notes, "but the general principles underlying them are more so. This budget was frankly and overtly redistributing wealth through taxation. It was seeking to raise revenue by taxing the wealthy few for the benefit of the penurious many." "Here lies the revolution, as opposed to the rhetoric, associated with the Budget of 1909," writes the historian Bentley Gilbert. "The income tax was no longer the financial supplement that since Peel it technically had been. The traditional restraints were now gone. It could be raised to any level" (1987, 369). "The income tax," said Lloyd George bluntly in his budget address, "imposed originally as a temporary expedient, is now in reality the centre and sheet anchor of our financial system." [15]

Lloyd George wished to do two things with this famous budget. First, he was genuinely a social reformer. This budget would allow real social reform. He was seriously concerned about the need to provide a stable and long-term revenue base for the public pension programs to which his party was now committed. "This is a war budget," Lloyd George said in his introduction of the bill in 1909. "It is for raising money to wage implacable warfare against poverty and squalidness. I cannot help hoping and believing that before this generation has passed away we shall advance a great step towards that good time when poverty and wretchedness and human degradation which always follow in its camp will be as remote to the people of this country as the wolves that once infested its forests" (Hansard, April 29, 1909). At the same time, it appeared that this war had an electoral motivation. In introducing these reforms Lloyd George hoped to undercut one of the major planks of the rapidly growing Labour party: the demand for class taxation.[16] As Gilbert (1987, 370) observes, "Balfour's philosophic insight was impeccable. The battle of the Budget of 1909 developed as a war upon the rich. British politics henceforth were to be the story of class politics."

Whatever the motivations for the reform, its consequences both for British fiscal history and British parliamentary democracy were enormous. Indeed the conflict over this budget quickly evoked a constitutional crisis that in the end removed the power of one of the final checks on cabinet authority in British party government: the House of Lords' right to review money bills. Space considerations do not allow discussion of the politics of the battle that ensued over what became known as the People's Budget. But the traditional elite that controlled the House of Lords understood full well the implications of Lloyd George's tax reforms: from this point forward the state would be actively involved in the distribution and redistribution of income and wealth in society. This tax reform not only ushered in a new kind of tax policy, but also, as Balfour noted, revealed the new political realities of British democracy in the twentieth century: "It is very easy for a Chancellor of the Exchequer in a democratic constitution to throw a very great burden on a small number of people who themselves for the very fact that they are a small number of people have very little practical power of making their voice heard." This was something the Lords could not tolerate, he declared. Balfour led the fight for the rights of the Lords against the principle of representative democracy.

The government, of course, equally understood the implications of allowing the Upper Chamber to veto this tax bill. In Lloyd George's view, "Five hundred men accidentally chosen from the unemployed" had no right to block the will of the democratically elected government.[17] Two elections were held in 1910, one effectively on the People's Budget itself and another on the powers of the House of Lords. With the support of the Labour party the Liberals narrowly won both elections. More important, the Lords lost. Following this defeat, the House of Lords was forced to accept the permanent loss of real power in British democracy. From this point forward their veto authority over legislation was reduced to the ability to delay nonmoney bills. Revenue legislation would from this point forward pass automatically.

Social Insurance

At the same time that the two Houses of Parliament were battling over the People's Budget, Winston Churchill and Lloyd George were working out plans for the creation of two new social insurance programs. As with the People's Budget, there was almost no parliamentary involvement in the construction of these two programs. In Hugh Heclo's words, "Parliamentary consideration of the government's [insurance] plan was perfunctory and added nothing of substance" (1974, 89). The two programs, conceived and designed by relatively insulated groups of party officials and civil servants, were not directly the result of pressure from the Left, but rather stemmed from the government's attempts to head off the growing support for socialism generally and the Labour party specifically. Fraser (1973, 152) writes, "As early as

December, 1908, Churchill was advising the Prime Minister bluntly to 'thrust a big slice of Bismarckianism over the whole underside of our industrial system,' and more explicitly a radical Liberal close to Lloyd George urged the 'English Progressive' to take 'a leaf from the book of Bismarck who dealt the heaviest blow against German socialism not by laws of oppression . . . but by that great system of state insurance which now safeguards the German workman at almost every point of his industrial career.' " Though Lloyd George's workmen's health insurance and Churchill's unemployment insurance were conceived and worked out separately, the decision was made to introduce them as a package in 1911. This new program would offer standardized benefits to workers in the event of unemployment or illness and would be paid for by direct insurance contributions made by all workers, their employers, and the state.[18]

Although these initial programs and the taxes levied to pay for them were quite modest by today's standards, they established essential precedents. The most important of these was the principle that they were to be *insurance* systems. The logic was that insurance programs would be politically secure— that is, eliminating the program once workers had contributed to it would be difficult. The insurance principle also distinguished the programs from the old poor law system: "Throughout the poor law's history, the one persistent theme was an effort to discriminate in relief between 'deserving' and the 'undeserving' poor" (Heclo 1974, 87). Under the new systems, benefits would not have these negative connotations. This fact would, in the end, make these programs virtually unassailable politically.

Some five years after being elected to Parliament, the Liberals had built the foundations of the welfare state with national compulsory health and unemployment insurance plans. At the same time, they had introduced two radically new concepts of taxation. On the one hand, they implemented the principle of redistributive taxation, and on the other hand, they created one of the world's first compulsory national insurance systems in which contributions were, in fact, a mandatory tax. From this point forward, taxes would no longer simply be means of generating revenues for the state: they now would also be seen as powerful instruments of social policy. Other countries would follow these models, but in few countries would it be possible to implement programs and taxes like these with as little public discussion, political maneuvering, and policy compromise as was done in the United Kingdom. In both the People's Budget of 1909 and the National Insurance schemes, the Parliament—even the Liberal delegation in the House of Commons—was left on the sidelines.

From War Budgets against Poverty to War Budgets against Germany

Lloyd George frankly admitted that one of the principal reasons he decided to move so abruptly in favor of an expanded and progressive income tax was that the costs of defense were escalating uncontrollably. Britain was already in an arms race with the kaiser, and the new technologies of warfare, particularly the new Dreadnought ships, forced him to choose this new tax precisely because it could have immense revenue potential (Gilbert 1987; Sabine 1966). When the war finally broke out, Lloyd George's foresight in making this prediction proved accurate indeed. Both the expense of the new technological warfare and the amazing amounts of revenues that could be generated via these new taxes went far beyond anyone's wildest imagination.

During the war, in Britain as in Sweden and the United States "a spirit of sacrifice was in the air" (Sabine 1966, 154). World War I, however, was not immediately a popular war, and there was a strong sense, at least among the working classes, that this war was not being fought for them. Working-class agitators insisted that the war was for and between imperialists, but that it would be fought by the workingman. It was workingmen who would spill their blood while the capitalists expanded their profits. These accusations put the Liberal-led coalition government in a bind. The Liberals did not want to lose even more of the working-class vote to Labour, and they did not want to tax the middle class so heavily that it would abandon the party in favor of the Tories. The government thus chose the politically easy way out: it continued the policy of squeezing the rich, although the effort was more symbolic than efficient. The government was thus forced to fill the public coffers with money borrowed from banks. In 1917, for example, the deficit reached £1,625 million, whereas total tax revenues amounted to only £514 million.

Although no one believed that the war could be financed totally out of current expenditures, almost all analysts were highly critical of the extent to which the government went to the banks rather than to the taxpayers. The American financier J. P. Morgan, for example, was alarmed by Lloyd George's recklessness even though he made money on it. "He has no thought for the final bill," Morgan remarked disparagingly. By the fiscal year 1917/ 18, expenditures had risen to nearly £2.7 billion, but taxes had increased to only £613 million, not quite 25 percent of the total.[19]

At the same time, the tax system was made sharply more progressive. Rates of both the income and the super tax were increased as personal allowances were reduced. By 1918 the standard rate of tax had reached an astonishing 6 shillings on the pound (30%) and the highest rate of super tax reached 4s.6d. (22.4%). On the other hand, a series of allowances for dependents, widows,

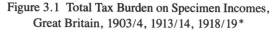

Figure 3.1 Total Tax Burden on Specimen Incomes,
Great Britain, 1903/4, 1913/14, 1918/19*

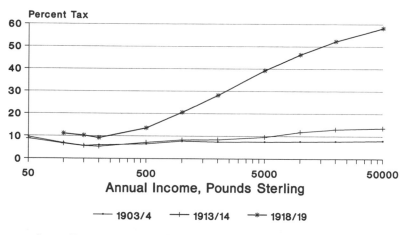

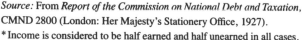

Source: From *Report of the Commission on National Debt and Taxation,*
CMND 2800 (London: Her Majesty's Stationery Office, 1927).
*Income is considered to be half earned and half unearned in all cases.

and housekeepers was introduced in order to minimize the impact of the taxes on those with large families. Consumption taxes moved up as well, but the increased effective tax burden on lower incomes was nominal when compared to the raises suffered by the rich. The combined effects of these tax measures on the distribution of tax burdens in Britain during these years can be seen in figure 3.1.

Business incomes were also subjected to extra war taxes. The excess profits duty (EPD), a special wartime tax similar to that imposed in many other countries at this time, was imposed at a rate of 50 percent in 1914 (raised to 60 percent in 1915 and to 80 percent in 1918) and eventually came to contribute over one-quarter of total government revenue during the war period. To partially offset these very high rates of tax, some compensations were made for the costs of replacing machinery, buildings, and mines. But once again these measures were criticized as being wholly inadequate and inappropriate given the financial situation that many companies suffered from during the war. Rather than legislate specific measures, the government preferred to allow the Board of Referees of the Inland Revenue to rule on the validity and value of particular deductions for particular companies. For many, if not most, companies, such arbitration was highly inadequate, in no small part because of the lack of understanding of business on the part of the bureaucrats who ultimately made these decisions. This solution thus widened businesses' level of uncertainty and made it more difficult for them to plan for postwar expansion.

In sum, the first two decades of the twentieth century witnessed the fundamental transformation of the British tax system. Progressive income taxes, national insurance taxes, and profits taxes were all inventions of this era. The income tax standard rate had risen from 1s. in 1906 to 6s. by 1918; the new top tax rate was now over 50 percent. At the same time, the income tax had been made more progressive through the introduction of a wide series of reliefs designed to further accommodate the principle of ability to pay. Whereas total income tax revenue in 1906 was only £34.2 million, by 1918, income, surtax, and EPD together collected an astonishing £584.7 million. Britain's position within the international political economy and the country's peculiar political institutions each shaped the introduction and character of tax policies developed in this period. As the first industrializer, Britain was also the first country to impose income taxes and then to move decisively toward using taxes as an instrument of social policy—namely, the explicit redistribution of wealth. The centralization of authority in this democratic state allowed the government—once it had made its decision—to impose tax reforms that were as severe as they were decisive. The kinds of compromises with partisan and special interests that (as we shall see below) were necessary for legislative success in both Sweden and the United States were unnecessary in Britain. Whether this allowed the government to act more coherently, however, is a matter of some doubt. To be able to legislate ideologically motivated policy preferences relatively unencumbered by the need to make parliamentary compromises may make political sense. It is less certain whether this makes for good public policy.

Sweden—Bureaucratic Government

At the end of the nineteenth century, Sweden had moved slowly toward developing modern democratic institutions. Not only was the franchise still restricted to a fraction of the citizenry, but the basic principle of legislative supremacy had yet to be firmly established. Reforms enacted in 1866 did remove the feudal estate system and replace it with a bicameral legislature, but the Crown retained effective power over most governmental functions.[20] Heclo (1974, 35) writes, "At a time when politicians in Britain were jockeying for parliamentary majorities to form new governments, the Swedish ministries in fact as well as in form continued to remain in power at the pleasure of the Crown rather than the parliament."

Much like the German states to the south, Sweden well into the twentieth century was dominated by a bureaucratic oligarchy largely derived from the traditional landed aristocracy, and this group, like their Prussian counterparts, ultimately came to side with the forces of modernization (Rustow 1971; Verney 1957; Carlsson 1987). The development of a modern tax system became a significant objective for the interests of modernization.

As in both Britain and the United States, the majority of government revenue in premodern Sweden came from a wide assortment of levies, fees, duties, excise taxes, and charges.[21] In addition to these indirect taxes Sweden had a general property tax (*grundskatt*) and a special levy called the *bevillning*, which was assessed individually by the local sheriff on a wide variety of taxable goods, services as well as income and property. The assessment varied by *kommun* (local district), depended upon the estate of which the individual was a member, and was used as the basis for determining voting rights. The bevillning was deeply resented by the poor. In 1861 this tax was simplified and made a levy on income and property (Garestad 1985; Lownertz 1983).

By the end of the nineteenth century, the bureaucratic elite had recognized that the revenue system was inadequate for Sweden's future revenue needs. Both a strong defense and economic development plainly required greater state revenues, but, for political and economic reasons similar to those in Britain, current revenue sources could not be expanded adequately. Land taxes were politically off-limits owing to the violent opposition of the mighty agricultural interests who controlled the lower chamber of the Riksdag at the turn of the century. Hikes in customs and tariffs would undermine Sweden's export-led industrial vitalization; and increased consumption or excise taxes would work to mobilize the working class.

Indeed, as T. Vallinder (1962, 266) points out, "Taxation's unequal distribution between classes in society was for the suffrage movement an essential example of the evil powers of money and the need for universal suffrage. Aside from the right to vote itself, it is clear that taxation was the most common goal in the movement's attack on existing society."[22]

In 1891 a new kind of Swedish politician, in the person of E. G. Boström, was appointed as prime minister from the First Chamber. Boström, once affiliated with the Center party but now with the New Agrarian party, was unique in both his national outlook and his ability to appease the interests of both the Agrarians and those interested in speeding the process of industrialization. In a daring move to satisfy the demands of the industrialists on defense issues, Boström convened a special session of the Riksdag and convinced his colleagues to support a military draft reform, increase defense spending, and abolish traditional taxes on land. To finance these measures Boström proposed not higher consumption taxes, as had been originally envisioned, but increased taxes on large agricultural holdings and, perhaps even more surprising, a new progressive tax on inheritances. Together, these proposals restructured old political alliances and enmities and were passed into law in 1894.

Bureaucratic and industrial elites soon recognized that Boström's reforms were fiscally insufficient to meet the ever-accelerating revenue needs of the modernizing state. And in the end, the need for new revenue, combined with the political gridlock engendered by the prospect of a rise in traditional taxes, brought the government to seek out an entirely new revenue source, the progressive income tax. The minister of finance introduced a progressive income tax in 1902 with this statement: "There can be no question that future revenue lies in the progressive income tax. We can see this achievement in foreign lands [i.e., Germany] in which this legislation is not inspired by radical tendencies." [23] Thus, although the demand for equity played an indirect role in the introduction of progressive taxation in Sweden, it was not the primary incentive. Instead, the "financial requirements of the state were decisive. . . . Party-political and ideological aspects played a subordinate role" (Rodriguez 1980, 71).

This apparently progressive reform was introduced well before the extension of the franchise to the lower classes in Sweden. Though fear of mobilizing the unenfranchised played a role in these elites' decisions, it could scarcely be argued that progressive taxation in Sweden resulted from anything like the Progressive/Populist pressures that brought this tax forward in the United States in 1896. This is not to say, of course, that the lower and working classes in Sweden did not want these kinds of reforms. Rather, they did not possess the institutional mechanisms necessary to push for them.

It would not be long before these Swedish bureaucratic elites came to see that taxation could be used as an instrument of economic policy as well as for revenue purposes. Again, Sweden was a relatively backward nation at the turn of this century. The modernization of Sweden's economy was not to be achieved by the traditional landed aristocracy; industrialization would instead depend on the success of a dynamic, enterprising corporate sector and capitalist class. In 1910, over the objections of landed interests in Parliament, Finance Minister Carl Johan Gustav Swartz increased progressive income taxes, made interest payments deductible against income for tax purposes, initiated Sweden's first wealth tax, and, finally, structured corporate income taxation into a system designed to consolidate Swedish industry.[24]

These changes did not occur without opposition. In fact, the landed aristocratic class was up in arms against the reforms. Count Ludvig Douglas, an authoritative spokesman for agricultural interests in the Riksdag, denounced the reforms of 1910 as inspired by "a socialist world view" and exclaimed that they were only the toe in the door of more intrusive taxation. Although it was true that the socialist party supported the raising of income taxes and the introduction of the wealth tax, it was far from true that they had the power to push these reforms. At this point less than 10 percent of the Swedish populace was eligible to vote. Bureaucratic interests were the real force behind the introduction of modern tax principles. Income taxes, corporate taxes, and even wealth taxes were not introduced, then, for or by the Left in an effort to redistribute wealth in society, but rather by a bureaucratic elite who believed that the taxes would generate greater wealth and income in society more generally.[25] In fact, the Social Democrats opposed the profits tax policies in the Riksdag on the grounds that they discriminated against small, new companies in favor of the large, export-oriented capitalists.

Bismarckian Social Reform

I described above how in the early twentieth century Liberals in Britain introduced a series of social insurance programs (pensions, unemployment, and health), financed in part through mandatory insurance contributions. Though there was agitation for all of these programs in Sweden as well, only the old age pension program would pass through the Riksdag at this time. In Britain these programs and their taxes were products of both the Liberal elite's progressive idealism and calculated strategic choices aimed at undercutting the growing popular appeal of the Labour party. In Sweden, the Social Democrats were not an electoral threat, but the appeal for greater democratization instilled great fear in the ruling elite. At the same time, many progressive elements within the bureaucracy favored reforming the old age pension system as a matter of principle.

These forces were pulled together by Prime Minister Arvid Lindman when he commissioned a new investigation of the problem of pension relief, the fourth such commission conducted over the past thirty years. Lindman's committee was led by the civil servant Anders Lindsted. It included a variety of interests, among them Social Democrats, farmers, insurance companies, industrialists, and the national employers' federation. The committee examined the old age systems found around the world and eventually proposed the creation of a compromise between the universalistic system found in Germany and a more limited, means-tested system like those in Denmark and New Zealand. The financing of this system, they proposed, should come from general revenues. Conservatives in the Upper Chamber allied themselves with certain Liberals and objected to the financing plan. In the end a compromise was reached in which the basic pension program was to be constructed as an insurance system from workers' pay, but the state would also contribute to the system to make up the revenue shortfall.

The final bill was passed in 1912 with the nominal support of all parties. Two points need to be explicitly noted: First, much as was the case in Britain, "the new departure in Swedish social policy was supported by but scarcely attributable to the advocacy of the political Left" (Heclo 1974, 193). Second, as distinct from the British experience, party political considerations were not a major driving force. Indeed, it appears that the bureaucratic elites were the key actors in the Swedish tax policy. This proved to be a common pattern throughout the twentieth century.

From Industrial Policy to Revenue

Neutrality was one of the few things that the various classes in Sweden did agree upon in the first decades of this century. Consequently, the impact of the Great War on tax structure would obviously be different for Sweden than it was for the combatants in the war. The massive fiscal expenses of World War I demanded new kinds of revenue policies in all European countries. But the burden on the noncombatants was obviously lighter than for those at the center of the war.

Widespread agreement over the basic issue of neutrality in Sweden did not dilute conflict over defense-related issues. First, the issues of conscription and the length of mandatory service continued to plague state policymakers. Second, there was disagreement over how much defense was enough for a nonaligned country and over what types of defense should be constructed and financed. These issues ultimately became intertwined with demands for the democratization of the Swedish political process and in the end forced the Conservatives, who continued to control the Upper Chamber, to accede to constitutional reforms expanding the franchise. These reforms abolished the rule that the right to vote would go only to those who paid both national and communal taxes (e.g., upper- and middle-class men).

Even a noncombatant nation required substantially multiplied state revenues. But the nonpartisan government of Hjalmar Hammarskjöld found itself in the same political dilemma as Conservative and Liberal governments faced earlier. Traditional taxes (land, excise, and customs duties) were either politically stalemated or likely to further mobilize the unenfranchised against the government. Boosts in income taxes were, once again, the most efficient and the most politically expedient alternatives. Rather than increase rates, as was done in the United Kingdom and the United States, Sweden introduced a surtax on high incomes. Called a defense levy and having progressive rates

Table 3.1

Average Wage of Male Industrial Workers
in Sweden, 1900–20, Ore per hour

Year	Ore per hour	Year	Ore per hour
1900	30	1912	42
1902	31	1914	46
1904	32	1916	53
1906	35	1918	94
1908	38	1919	124
1910	41	1920	163

Sources: 1900–13: Stockholm Economic Studies, vol. 2, "Wages in Sweden, Part 1, Table 26"; 1914–20: *Socialstyrelsen lönestatistik.*

of 1–7 percent beginning on incomes over 5,000 Skr., it was placed on top of existing income taxes in 1915.[26] Still, Swedish tax policy was moderate when compared to that of the United States and Britain at the time. As we shall see later, the redistributive fervor in the United States pushed marginal income tax rates up to 75 percent by 1918; the top marginal tax rate in Sweden, in contrast, was only 18.5 percent. Death and gift taxes were similarly moderate.[27]

The Swedish economy was undergoing rapid transformation at this time. Partly because of its ability to trade with both sides during the war, the Swedish economy grew quite rapidly. Though total government revenues surged from Skr 398 million in 1910 to Skr 1,621 million in 1920, the tax share of GDP grew only from 11.8 percent to 12.8 percent in this same period (Rodriguez 1980, 216). Swedes were also rapidly becoming richer. Per capita GNP grew from Skr 567 in 1913 to Skr 1,115 in 1925. In addition, huge numbers of workers were leaving the countryside and moving to the cities, and thus mounting numbers of individuals had money incomes, which could be taxed. The average hourly wage of male industrial workers grew equally dramatically (table 3.1).

These rises in income did not, however, translate into worker complacency, as the Conservative/civil servant governments had hoped. Though the general strike staged in 1909 was considered a defeat for workers, it was also seen as a signal of their deep discontent. Ultimately, fearful of popular revolt, the Conservatives in the Upper Chamber decided to reform the nation's political institutions. The principle of cabinet responsibility to the Parliament rather than directly to the Crown was finally established in 1914 (Heclo 1974, 35; Verney 1957, 185–91). And finally, in 1919, universal male suffrage was introduced. Women achieved the vote in 1920.[28]

Popular support for the Social Democrats grew rapidly among the newly enfranchised, and they soon became the largest party in the Lower Chamber. But owing to the imposition of the proportional representation system created by the Conservative government (I shall discuss this constitutional change at greater length in the next chapter), the Social Democrats were kept out of government until they joined with the Liberal party as minor partner in 1917. Indeed, proportional representation, which was originally promoted as a "Conservative Guarantee" when it was first proposed in 1904, would from this point fundamentally shape Swedish politics generally and the politics of Swedish taxation specifically throughout the twentieth century.

In sum, despite the fact that Sweden had not yet developed democratic institutions, the country followed a tax policy path broadly similar to that we saw in the United Kingdom during this historic epoch. The turn of the twentieth century saw the introduction not only of the principle of ability to pay, but also progressive personal and corporate income taxes. Finally, the basic principle of social insurance was also introduced. These taxes were deeply opposed by traditional interests precisely because they understood their long-term implications. In both cases, their fears were precisely borne out as the cost of defense mandated a search for ever more tax revenues.

The Swedish case differed from the British in important respects, however. First, although the tax system was modernized, the kinds of highly visible and indeed punitive (but relatively low revenue yielding) tax rates experienced in Britain never occurred in Sweden. Second, apparently because these taxes were introduced in Britain by partisan political elites that were cloistered from the very groups who would pay them, they practically ignored the economic impacts of these taxes. In Sweden, in contrast, these taxes were introduced by bureaucratic elites and were consciously designed to bring about specific economic outcomes. Aside from their obvious revenue potential, a key feature for the Swedish elites was that these taxes would be useful in generating wealth in society, not simply redistributing it.

The United States—Divided Government

The limitations imposed by the United States Constitution have, in several cases, an important effect on the scheme of the Federal Income Tax.—Harrison Spaulding, *The Income Tax in Great Britain and the United States*

The men who wrote the American Constitution feared strong government. They saw the extension of suffrage and the creation of a Republic as means to monitor the actions and behavior of those that held the reigns of government.

But the Founders also realized that a representative democracy presented its own dangers. What was to prevent a majority faction from seizing state power and thereby abusing the rights (especially the property rights) of a smaller faction? The critical dilemma for the writers of the American Constitution, then, was, How can we establish a government which has the strength and authority to govern a large and diverse nation, yet protect the interests of the citizens from that very government?

The Federalists' answer to this dilemma was, of course, to fragment authority so that it would be difficult or impossible for any faction to control the state for their own selfish ends. To this end, the Federalists established two national legislatures that represented substantially different constituencies and had radically different terms of appointment, specifically in order to prevent the temporal will of the masses from being translated directly into public policy. Second, executive authority was separated from legislative authority, and the executive was given the power to veto legislative decisions. Third, the Constitution attempted to circumscribe the authority and jurisdiction of the various levels of government within the new federal structure. They were particularly concerned about the national government overstepping its bounds. Finally, a Supreme Court was to act as the final check on the popular will, insuring that the state did not step beyond its authority.[29]

A comprehensive treatment of the Federalists' logic and argumentation is outside the scope of this volume. We are instead interested in the ways in which the constitutional foundation of American politics has affected modern tax policy outcomes. It should be noted, however, that the authors of the American Constitution paid special attention to taxation. In perhaps the most critical document in American political history, Federalist 10, James Madison writes, "The apportionment of taxes on the various descriptions of property is an act which seems to require the most exact impartiality; yet there is, perhaps, no legislative act, in which greater opportunity and temptation are given to a predominant party to trample on the rules of justice. Every shilling, with which they overburden the inferior number, is a shilling saved in their pocket."[30]

Region, Class, and the Income Tax of 1894

The politics of taxation in the United States at the turn of the twentieth century was both a politics of class and a politics of region. For nearly forty years after the Civil War the Republican and Democratic parties were divided more by region than by political philosophy or ideology. This regional division allowed the parties to focus on providing constituent benefits and representing local interests rather than championing divisive political ideologies or explosive policy demands. But by the last decade of the nineteenth century, this system proved incapable of integrating the new political forces and demands evoked by rapid industrialization.

Republicans had dominated national politics since the end of the Civil War and were widely perceived, especially in the South and the West, as representing the monied interests of the industrialist and financier classes of the North and East. The Democrats, however, had scarcely been better at representing the interests of working classes and instead focused on providing patronage and constituent benefits to their supporters. James Sundquist (1973, 109, 110) writes, "The national leadership of the two parties undertook nothing that can be called courtship. . . . The party platforms were empty, backward looking documents . . . [and] almost indistinguishable. . . . The parties were not seeking issues, they were avoiding them." The result was that the system essentially stagnated, with established elites dominating the electoral process in the constituencies and often using their influence within the parties to stymie demands for reform and change.

Popular discontent grew slowly at first, but when the Republicans introduced their famous McKinley tariff in 1890, frustration with the system turned into a firestorm. It was widely believed that the massive economic changes the U.S. economy was experiencing at the turn of the century were not benefiting the working class. Instead "economic royalists" and "the plutocrats," especially in the northeast, were swindling the nation of millions while their representatives in Washington were imposing stiffer tariffs and thereby raising the cost of living for the great masses.[31] The McKinley tariff poured fuel on this fire, mobilizing large numbers of farmers and workers to join a populist revolt and support politicians who demanded cheap money and redistributive taxes. An income tax on the very wealthy and a profits tax for corporations quickly became rallying cries for populists both within and outside the Democratic party.[32]

Despite an extremely heated and ideologically charged campaign against the proposed "confiscation," which Republicans charged was a product of "socialism, devilism and communism,"[33] the demand for justice could not be stopped.[34] Though at first "[the Democratic party] appeared to have taken no cognizance at all of the farmers' revolt" (Sundquist 1973, 122), by the election of 1892 they embraced a variety of Populist demands including the demand for fairer taxes.

The Democrats were indeed rewarded—if only temporarily. But this had as much to do with the vagaries of the American single-member-district electoral system as it did with popular conviction in favor of the Democrats. In the election of 1892, America's first-past-the-post electoral system worked decisively in the Democrats' favor.[35] Democrat candidates for the House of Representatives received a smaller percentage of the popular vote (46.1 percent) than they had just two years before, but they won 71.1 percent of these seats in Congress.[36]

The key to understanding these curious outcomes, of course, is to remember the institutional bias that the single-member-district electoral system lends established parties. Though the populist People's party and other third parties won nearly 1.5 million votes (12.7 percent of total votes cast) in House elections, they sent only 9 (out of 332) members to Congress in 1892.

The Democrats attempted to capture the moment and moved quickly to steal the platform of the Populists, promising to introduce a series of populist policies including tariff reform and a national progressive income tax. The young Democratic reformer William Jennings Bryan described the Democrats' new position in the following way:

> To-day the Democratic party stands between two great forces, each inviting its support. On the one side stand the corporate interests of the nation, its moneyed institutions, its aggregations of wealth and capital, imperious, arrogant, compassionless. They demand special legislation, favors, privileges, and immunities. . . . On the other side stands that unnumbered throng which gave a name to the Democratic party and for which it has assumed to speak. Work-worn and dust-begrimed, they make their sad appeal. . . .
>
> This army, vast and daily vaster growing, begs the party to be its champion in the present conflict. (Congressional Record, August 16, 1893)

With the Democratic/Populist landslide and the party's newfound radicalism, it seemed certain that redistributive taxes would soon become an integral part of the Federal tax system. Within two years Congress passed the nation's first permanent progressive income tax—though it was not signed by President Grover Cleveland it was allowed to pass into law. Still, it would be nearly twenty years before the United States would actually put an income tax into place. There were two reasons for this delay. First, the Supreme Court chose to exercise its role as watchdog over the Constitution and in 1896 ruled the act of 1894 unconstitutional. Second, the radicalization of the Democratic party frightened many middle-class voters, who shifted their support decisively in favor of the Republican party (Burnham 1970; Hayes 1957). In the election of 1896, the Republicans, led by William McKinley, sponsor of the infamous tariff, routed the firebrand Bryan, whose faction had now seized the Democratic party.[37]

Had the United States had a parliamentary system, it would have been the first of the three nations discussed in this study to enact a permanent progressive national income tax.[38] In fact, it became the last. In many ways the decentralization of the American federal system allowed political institutions to adapt to the new ideas and the new political demands sweeping the nation without breakdown or constitutional crisis. But at the same time, the fragmentation of authority built into this constitutional system allowed established interests to stymie the income tax and to absorb the political forces that championed it.

In the United States, those who opposed the income tax had an institution for blocking the legislation that was not available in parliamentary democracies: the Supreme Court. Opponents to the tax quickly went to work pressuring the Court to rule the new law unconstitutional. Joseph Choate, one of the most eloquent of the team of corporate lawyers who argued the case, went directly to the quick of the matter. He began his address to the Court by denouncing the income tax as "defended here upon principles as communistic, socialistic—what shall I call them?—populistic as ever have been addressed to any political assembly in the world." He warned the Court of the "the communistic march" of increasing tax rates that would go on indefinitely. He ended his speech with an appeal to the Court's sense of power, class, and role in history:

> I do not believe that any member of the Court ever has sat or ever will sit to hear and decide a case the consequences of which will be so far reaching as this. . . . [Precisely because the] passions of the people are aroused on this subject . . . [and because] sixty million citizens may be incensed by the decision, it is vital to the future of the country that this Court declare . . . that it has the power to set aside an act of Congress in violation of the Constitution, and that it will not hesitate to exercise that power, no matter what the threatened consequences may be. (Ratner 1942, 200)

Choate's arguments against the new tax were persuasive. In what Jerold Waltman (1985, 4) has described as specious logic, the Court attempted to justify its decision to block the tax on the grounds that it was a direct tax and that the Constitution specified that a direct tax had to be apportioned according to each state's population. Apparently, because some states had more rich people than other states, the tax was illegal. The Court did not specify what it meant by a direct tax, but it was sure about the intent of its decision: Justice Stephen Field argued that the income tax was in fact class legislation and was no different from the English law of 1641 that taxed Protestants and Catholics at different rates. He put the issue most bluntly when he wrote, "The present assault upon capital is but the beginning. It will be but the stepping stone to others, larger and more sweeping, till our political contests will become a war of the poor against the rich; a war constantly growing in intensity and bitterness" (Concurring Opinion, 157 U.S. 429).

Committee Government

Justice Field was wrong; the war between rich and poor did not escalate to the massive national class confrontations that he feared. The strong class-based parties like those emerging in Europe at the time continued to be weak in the United States. These different outcomes were largely the product of different institutional structures through which these new political forces were channeled. Although there were many similarities in the general political demands of both middle- and working-class interests in Europe and the United States, the institutions through which these demands had to be expressed differed radically.

In Europe industrialization evoked demands for the extension of the franchise to the working class and the middle classes. But in the United States, male suffrage had already been extended; as a consequence, the bitter political fights evoked by the economic changes of the era took a peculiar turn. In all three countries under study in this book, reformers at the turn of the century believed that a means for redressing the economic injustices of the modernizing economy was political reform. They argued that political power was held by a ruling class of economic elites and that this concentration of political and economic might was both illegitimate and unjust. European reformers concluded that the way to redress this problem was through the extension of suffrage and the construction of mass-based political parties that could seize the reins of government and use political authority for the benefit of all citizens.[39]

In the United States, however, political parties were often perceived to be obstacles to democracy rather than agents of its implementation. The ever-larger middle class was fearful of the potential for demagoguery in mass-based parties. The political agenda for democratic reformers in the United States, then, required the dismantling of these obstacles to democratic accountability rather than their strengthening (Hays 1957; Burnham 1970). Progressive reformers thus demanded and eventually won a series of measures designed to reduce the power of political parties and their leaders. Some of these measures included the introduction of the nonpartisan Australian ballot, the direct primary, the direct election of U.S. senators, the initiative process, and manipulation of voting qualifications and requirements (Burnham 1970, 72–90).[40] These reforms worked. They reduced the authority of party elites and weakened political parties generally. They would ultimately have profound consequences for the character of tax policy making for the rest of the twentieth century.

Within the halls of Congress there were also demands for "democratic" change. Reformers believed that the centralization of political authority in the hands of party elites, most notably under the near-autocratic leadership of Speaker Joe Cannon, undermined the democratic principles that the nation was founded upon. Speaker Cannon had tried to hold together his splintering Republican party by controlling appointments to congressional committees. But his control did not last for long. Insurgent Republicans and Progressives joined forces and revolted. The reformists not only deposed Speaker Cannon from the speakership in 1911, but also instituted a series of reforms designed to protect themselves from the will of their party leaders. The most consequential of these for our purposes was the institutionalization of seniority selection for committee chairmanships (Polsby 1969). From this point forward, individual members of Congress would dramatically expand their individual sphere of influence and thus become truly freer to steer their own policy course—even when opposed by party leaders or the president.

The Right to a Class Tax—The Sixteenth Amendment

The politics of the income tax in the early decades of this century were shaped by these institutional realities. The Republican party victory in 1896 began what is commonly seen as one of the major partisan realignments in American political history. Still, the Republican party was unable to prevent the introduction of the income tax, largely because the rule changes of 1911 yielded greater autonomy to individual congressmen. Though the Republicans were strongest in the Northeast, those who represented districts outside this region found little electoral incentive to fight the issue. Tax policy increasingly pitted one region against the rest.

The Republican party was also deeply divided between its Progressive and Conservative wings. Insurgent and Progressive Republicans were committed to both political reform and an expanded role for the federal government. Expanding government would require new revenues, but, given the public's response to the McKinley tariff, Republicans were leery of any suggestions to increase tariffs. In addition, many Progressives had come to accept the new principles of fairness and ability to pay.

Somewhat surprisingly, then, it was the Republican president William Taft who sponsored the idea for a constitutional amendment permitting a federal income tax. The demand for an income tax as well as demands for political (democratic) reforms was a wedge that threatened to split the party. Taft prepared what he thought was a brilliant strategy to undermine the movement to legislate such a tax in Congress. Knowing how difficult it would be to pass a constitutional amendment, Taft felt certain the amendment would fail. It had, after all, been nearly forty years since any amendments to the Constitution had passed. Unfortunately for Taft, his strategy backfired. As he predicted, the current income tax legislation quickly died, but the amendment to the Constitution enabling Congress to impose an income tax was signed into law in just four years. Little did Taft know that by forwarding the constitutional amendment he would undermine the last bulwark against the so-called socialist scheme his supporters so bitterly opposed.[41]

By June 1913, forty-two states, six more than the two-thirds necessary, had ratified the Sixteenth Amendment, which provided that "Congress shall have power to lay and collect taxes on incomes, from whatever source derived, without apportionment among the several states, and without regard for any census and enumeration." The Federal Income Tax Act followed ratification very quickly. This tax imposed a "normal" tax of 1 percent on all individual incomes over three thousand dollars or family incomes over four thousand dollars, and a "surtax" that rose from 1 to 6 percent was levied on incomes over twenty thousand dollars. Only a tiny fraction of citizens were affected by the new law.

The process of putting the income tax proposal up before each state legislature, however, had its costs. In their efforts to build support for the amendment, proponents promised a variety of tax exemptions to hesitant supporters in exchange for their acquiescence. Cordell Hull, the author of the 1913 law, subsequently disparaged it in the following words: "A possible danger to the successful and permanent operation of an income-tax law, as is true of all tax laws, is the disposition of its friends to insert additional exemptions here and there and to add liberal qualifications, thereby opening many doors to those who would evade or avoid their full share of taxes" (Waltman 1985, 79). As the amendment went from statehouse to statehouse, the fear that the new tax might weaken the revenue-generating capacity of state governments began to grow. In an attempt to assuage this fear and ensure the amendment's passage through the various statehouses, proponents of the tax promised the introduction of the first explicit tax loophole. It was agreed that interest from state and local bonds, which was becoming an indispensable source of revenue for these governments, should be exempted from the new federal tax. It was understood not only that this would provide an incentive for wealthy individuals to buy these bonds, but also that these same individuals would be able to use the bonds to protect their income from the federal taxman.

In sum, even in the very first stages of the construction of the modern tax system, America's unique political institutions shaped both public ideas and public policy. The fragmentation of political authority in Washington as well as the division of responsibilities among levels of government due to federalism in the United States shaped both the development and structure of our national tax system. At the very outset, the federal income tax was forced to open itself to specific loopholes in order to wind its way through the institutional labyrinth created by the U.S. Constitution. After this inauspicious beginning, it would not be long before the doors swung wide open.

The Institutionalization of Progressive Taxation—Finance and War

By 1913 the United States had finally passed national taxes on both personal and corporate income. Soon these taxes were transformed into precisely the kind of political weapons and financial honey pots that their opponents had feared. Within five years, tax rates would shoot up to 77 percent on the very wealthy; in less than ten years, these two taxes would generate more revenue for the federal government than all other taxes combined (fig. 3.2).

The primary explanation for the immediate transformation in these taxes was, of course, World War I. There was a great deal of isolationist sentiment in Congress at the time, but little support for being unprepared. The new income tax, it was quickly discovered (in the United States as in Europe), could be a strikingly efficient revenue source. The tax came at a particularly convenient time because of a precipitous decline in tariff revenues. Moreover, the political logic of raising taxes paid by the wealthy rather than those paid by the soldier or his family was no less potent in the United States than it had been in Britain at this time. Few congressmen were openly willing to defend the interests of those who were amassing huge riches from the war and raise taxes paid by the people who spilled their blood in this rich man's war. In the words of John Witte (1985, 86), "During the war years the cries of 'ability to pay' and 'war profiteering' drowned out pleas for defense against 'class legislation.' In effect the income taxes were class legislation—a fact explaining some of their appeal."

The maximum income tax rate was increased to 15 percent in 1916, to 67 percent in 1917, and finally to 77 percent in 1918.[42] The number of individuals subject to this tax rocketed from 362,000 in 1916 to 5,518,000 in 1920. This was still a small percentage of the workforce, however, which was estimated at more than 41 million in 1920 (Witte 1985, 86).

Figure 3.2 Personal and Corporate Income Taxes as a Percentage
of Total Revenue, United States, 1900–85

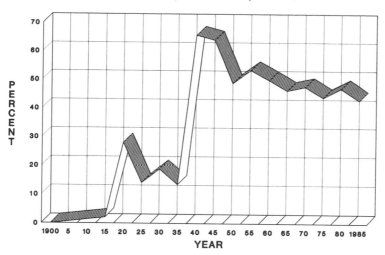

Source: U.S. Bureau of the Census, *Historical Statistics of the United States
from Colonial Times to the Present* (Washington, D.C.: Government Printing
Office, 1975), various series and tables.

The income tax was, however, becoming a real burden to politically powerful interests. It did not take long for these interests to begin their campaigns
for tax reductions. In the context of the strongly Populist/Progressive/Left
climate after the war, the lack of coherence in Congress, and the reasser-
tion of Congress's strength vis-à-vis the president, it was politically unfea-
sible to reduce tax rates significantly. This did not necessarily mean that it
was impossible to get narrow tax breaks for specific interests, however. The
very autonomy given U.S. congressmen through the congressional reforms,
combined with their traditional allegiances to local interests over and above
national ideological or philosophical interests, gave them both the incentive
and means to offer specific tax breaks to specific constituents. At first there
were breaks for "worthy causes," whose political appeal was difficult to resist:
but it would not be too long until others followed suit.[43]

Seeing the early erosion of the tax base, President Woodrow Wilson introduced what was probably the first presidential effort at tax reform in 1918. His
proposals, which included both rate hikes and measures to close certain loopholes, failed. Congress was lobbied heavily (Waltman 1985, 4) and agreed to
increase tax rates, but rather than close existing loopholes, Congress opened
new ones for many of the nation's most dominant forces.[44]

Jerold Waltman's superb study of the politics of the early income tax summarizes the revenue politics already in force:

> We have already alluded to how the question of rates was sidestepped by affected interests. . . . What they could press for, however, was special treatment of some items of receipt or expenditure. Lowering income by either of these expedients could mean substantial savings on one's tax bill. Congress was to be faced from this point on with pressure from various economic interests to alter this or that section of the tax code. Of course, once such an exception was granted, others presented themselves pressing analogous arguments, frequently with some justice. . . . The result is not only a panoply of interest groups pleading that their business is different from and deserving of some special treatment; it is also that the code itself becomes more complex. This very complexity creates its own anomalies, which means more attempts must be made at rectification. This in turn begets more complexity, leading to an unbreakable circle. (Waltman 1985, 78)

The turn of the twentieth century witnessed the transformation of revenue systems in all three countries studied here. I have only hinted at some of the political dynamics that would help explain why these nations seemed to move in such similar directions despite their very different political systems at the time. To fully examine the issues surrounding this era of political history and the relation between the emergence of democracy and the principles of social and economic justice obviously requires a much deeper treatment than is offered here. For now I will leave this for other scholars to explore.

The broad commonality in outcomes notwithstanding, it is important to note the extent to which the political institutions through which this historical transformation was legislated profoundly affected both the timing and the structure of the tax systems that were developed. In Britain, tax policy became a major political tool with which the Liberals attempted both to impose their vision of a more just society and to undermine the growing popularity of the rival Labour party. Given the very strong position of the government vis-à-vis the legislature, the government was able to essentially dictate its tax policy preferences to the Parliament, often without even consulting its own backbenchers. The tax policies that were developed, then, were highly charged political events that tended to exacerbate class tensions rather than ameliorate them. The tax policies that came out of this process, moreover, were very vague and, from many points of view, poorly designed.

Sweden did not fully democratize until after World War I but also moved to introduce progressive taxes based on the principle of the ability to pay. In

Sweden's case these taxes were less efforts to buy off working-class discontent than they were fiscal instruments to be used by the bureaucratic government to bring about economic change. Though the bureaucrats were not able to hold onto power much longer, both the tax system and the electoral system they created in their last decades of rule would continue to influence the direction of Swedish politics for many years to come.

Finally, battle over tax policy in the United States took on elements of both regional and class conflict. In many ways the demand for progressive taxation was the most virulent in the United States. But just as the fragmentation of political authority inherent in the U.S. political system stifled and slowed the introduction of progressive taxation in the United States, this same fragmentation made the tax process very difficult to control. In the end the United States had the most nominally progressive, indeed punitive, tax code; at the same time, it had already begun to create the most porous tax system of the three examined here.

4

The Historic Compromise, 1918–1945

A compromise is the art of dividing a cake in such a way that
everyone believes that he has got the biggest piece.
—Dr. Ludwig Erhard

In the decade following the Great War, bourgeois parties appeared to dominate the political agenda in Sweden, Great Britain, and the United States
as well as in a great many other industrial democracies. Marginal tax rates
on both the wealthy and corporations were reduced; the heavy wartime defense duties and levies were abolished while consumption taxes and custom
duties were increased. In no case, however, could the Right dictate its policy
preferences. Instead, they were forced to compromise with the recently enfranchised working class. Though capitalists demanded that elected officials
repeal or drastically reduce income and corporation taxes, these officials were
forced to accept another political reality: the majority of citizens would be
angered by a dramatic redistribution of the tax burden—and now the vast
majority of the citizens could vote.

The Great Depression tipped the political scales away from bourgeois
interests, evoking mass discontent with both capitalism and the politicians
who defended it. The Social Democrats in Sweden, the Labour party in Britain, and the New Deal Democrats in the United States swept into office and
promised a fairer deal for those that elected them. Somewhat surprisingly,
however, in none of these cases was there an immediate turnabout in tax
policy. The political reality that framed the bourgeois policies of the 1920s
also framed the Left's tax policies in the 1930s. Whether they fully understood it or not, and whether they had the structural capacity to institutionalize
the new political reality, neither side of the political spectrum could hope to
ignore the interests of the opposition and stay in office for very long. In each
case, policymakers acted not only as arbiters between competing interests
in society, but also according to their perception of their own self-interest.
Given the political realities of the interwar years, this meant searching for,
and sometimes finding, new bases of compromise from which the political
agenda could move forward.

In short, though neither the Left nor the Right was able to dictate their tax
policy preferences in the 1920s and 1930s, they were not defeated. The key
to understanding tax policy development during the interwar years and after-

ward, then, is to appreciate that the representatives of capital and labor were each strong enough to protect their interests in their respective legislatures but lacked the power to dictate their agenda.

As common as this general pattern is, the paths followed in each nation were often quite different. The simplest and most well documented example of the basic historical compromise of this era is, of course, Sweden. This chapter begins with Sweden's story, demonstrating how the country's unique political and economic structure biased policymakers toward the institutionalization of this compromise. In the American case we shall also see the institutionalization of the basic compromise; but in the United States the separation of powers between the executive and legislative branches complicates the story considerably. Though some neocorporatist institutions were in fact constructed, the looming stalemate facing the polity more often led to policy solutions that accommodated politically influential groups through particularistic policy compromises.

Britain presents the most difficult case. Given both the decisive power and extreme electoral vulnerability of British governments, institutionalized compromise has been difficult to come by. In many ways the British inability to institutionalize compromises before World War II is quite surprising, given the fact that coalition governments held office for most of this period. However, these political coalitions differed from their Swedish counterparts because they lacked the electoral stability that framed the basic strategic choices of all participants in the Swedish case. Given the vagaries of the British electoral process, all participants knew full well that small shifts in voter preferences could bring about huge changes in Parliament and government. The incentive, therefore, to institutionalize compromise solutions was limited in Britain. Still, governments were aware of their electoral vulnerability and, as we shall see, legislated accordingly.

In all three countries, the crisis of World War II forced the feuding parties to pull together. The fiscal crisis and immediate demands of fighting (or, in Sweden's case, staying out of) the war forced cooperation and compromise. The new technologies of war drove up its price beyond anyone's wildest imagination. The consequence for tax policy was quite simply that taxes—all taxes—had to go up.

Sweden

As I noted in chapter 3, the modern Swedish tax system at the turn of the century was a product of the ruling bureaucratic oligarchy's desire to generate revenues with which to build Sweden's infrastructure. None of the major innovations described (e.g., the introduction of progressive income, wealth, death, or corporation taxes) resulted directly from demands made by the working or lower classes. Universal adult suffrage was not achieved until 1921. But at the same time, these elites were responding to widespread social and economic changes and in part attempting to use tax policy as an instrument to ameliorate working-class discontent.

This ruling elite held authority as long as it could, but by the first decade of this century it was clear that the forces of democratic participation could not be resisted forever. In defense of their interests, given the radical changes the society and the economy were undergoing, the ruling elite conspired to change the Swedish electoral rules. Although modestly broadening the franchise in 1907, Prime Minister Lindman introduced the Conservative proposal that Sweden should move to a system of proportional representation rather than the then-current first-past-the-post system. This change was proposed and defended as a "Conservative guarantee" with the explicit intention of protecting the influence of the traditional elites in politics despite their obvious numerical inferiority when compared to the middle and working classes (Castles 1978).

Proportional representation would, moreover, be extended to both the Upper and Lower Chambers of the Riksdag. Rather than fully democratizing the Upper Chamber and making its members directly responsible to the citizenry, the Conservatives who still controlled this house insisted that the only reform they would accept would be proportional representation. The Conservatives had already been driven into a minority position in the Lower Chamber (whose members were directly elected), and it was unavoidable that they would be pushed into an equally weak position in the Upper Chamber. Because only one-eighth of Upper Chamber representatives were elected each year and because of the relatively long eight-year tenure of each representative, the move to proportional representation was seen as a way of protecting the Conservatives' interests for both the long and the short term (Verney 1957).

Proportional representation had originally been proposed by the Liberal party earlier in the decade, but the Liberals now only grudgingly approved on the grounds that the Conservatives would not otherwise extend the franchise to propertyless males. The Social Democrats, however, resisted the temptation to support the constitutional change and categorically opposed the measure. The party's leader, Hjalmar Branting, argued that the measure was a trick designed to keep power in the hands of the rich and that the bill would ensure that one-seventh of the people would retain 90 percent of the power (Verney 1957, 164–65). The electoral reform was passed, however, in exchange for the partial extension of the franchise.

The move to proportional representation and the maintenance of this peculiar two-chamber system are crucial to my explanation of the subsequent developments in Swedish tax politics. Although the traditional elite would never achieve authority again after the introduction of universal suffrage, the new electoral system virtually ensured both that no party would be able to rule with a majority in both houses of Parliament and that small shifts in electoral outcomes would bring about only small shifts in Riksdag representation. Compromise became a necessary prerequisite of governing in Sweden.

The demand to democratize the Upper Chamber was thus subverted by the traditional and bureaucratic interests, who saw democracy as a fundamental threat to their interests. The maintaining of this institution's power profoundly affected the basic tenor of Swedish politics until the early 1970s, when the Upper Chamber was abolished. The effects of these institutional reforms can be seen almost immediately as suffrage was extended to broader and broader segments of the population throughout the early 1900s. For example, though the Social Democrats won 36.4 percent of the popular vote in the second national election of 1914, their share of Riksdag seats rose to only 8.6 percent in the Upper Chamber (13 of 150). Their share of Lower Chamber seats more accurately reflected popular will, giving the SAP 32 percent of the chamber's 230 seats. The Conservative party, on the other hand, won 36.5 percent of the vote but retained 57 percent of the seats in the Upper Chamber and 37 percent of the seats in the Lower Chamber (table 4.1).

Even after the election of 1917, in which the Conservative party popular vote dropped to approximately 24 percent, the Conservatives continued to control the Upper Chamber, holding 86 of the total of 150 seats. By now, however, the king could scarcely ignore the changing political realities of the Swedish electorate, and he chose a coalition Liberal/Social Democrat administration even though this coalition could be out-voted in the Upper Chamber.[1] Table 4.1 shows the effects of this system when divided into Conservative and Socialist block votes.

It is, of course, impossible to know exactly what the outcomes would have been if Sweden had either maintained the first-past-the-post system or neutered the Upper Chamber's legislative powers, as was done in Britain during the first decades of this century. One can see, however, how participation in a coalition government affected Social Democratic tax policy positions over time. For example, though Branting was the minister of finance in the first of many coalition governments in the interwar era, the Socialists were never able to enact tax policies that even faintly resembled the radical policies suggested in their early campaign rhetoric.[2] By the late 1920s, the party's position on tax policy, like its positions on a variety of issues, was muted.

Table 4.1

Percentage Distribution of Votes Cast in Swedish National Elections,
1912–32, for the Conservative and Socialist Blocs;
Percentage of Seats in Each Chamber of the Riksdag held by these
blocs in the year following each National Election.

| | | | Parliamentary Seats in % | | | |
| | Votes Cast in % | | Upper Chamber | | Lower Chamber | |
Year	Con. Block	Soc. Block	Con. Block	Soc. Block	Con. Block	Soc. Block
1914R	63.6	36.4	90.7	9.3	62.2	37.8
1917R	60.8	39.2	88.7	11.3	57.8	42.2
1920R	63.9	36.1	64	36	64.3	35.7
1921R	56	44	64.7	35.3	53.9	46.1
1924R	53.8	46.2	64.7	35.3	52.6	47.4
1928R	56.5	43.4	64.7	35.3	57.4	42.6
1932R	49.3	50	60.7	39.3	51.3	48.7

Source: Sverige efter 1900 (Stockholm, 1981), tables 1c, 2a.
R = National Parliamentary Election to elect representatives directly to the Lower Chamber.
Vote percentages may not equal 100 percent owing to the existence of fringe parties.

There appear to be two complementary explanations for the change in SAP tax policy positions. On the one hand, the Socialists began to appreciate the limits of their working-class electoral base (Tingsten 1941). On the other hand, the practical experiences of participating in government, as both coalition partners and members of investigatory commissions, educated key SAP elites in the economic realities of managing a liberal capitalist economy. In the words of Diane Sainsbury (1980, 256), "More subtle and varied meanings were also attached to socialization . . . more importance was expressly assigned to increased production in eradicating poverty. It was held that poverty could not be wiped out solely by equal distribution, that greater production was a precondition."

Heclo (1974, 41) notes in his study of social policies in Britain and Sweden that "even Socialist Ministers would necessarily be recruited into the practical formulation of social policy." This is even more clearly evidenced with respect to tax policy. For, while the working-class grassroots were still undergoing a phase of radicalism and activism in the early 1920s, the Socialist elite was sharing in the responsibilities of the government.

I do not mean to suggest that the SAP leadership had betrayed the ideals or goals of their party. Rather, the Socialist elite's understanding of how they could best champion the interests of the working class was changing. First, if their experiences between 1917 and 1932 taught them nothing else, it taught them that they needed to gain a stronger electoral base in order to do their core constituents much good; for this, they needed to soften their rhetoric. In their attempt to reach out for broader electoral appeal, the rhetoric of class conflict common to the language of the 1920s began to give way to two separate concepts: The people versus class and cooperation versus conflict (Sainsbury 1980, 32–33). Second, the elite's position on what they should do once they attained power was undergoing change. Rather than nationalize industry and fundamentally redistribute wealth,

> the Party's task was the administration and/or development of the welfare state; its method was to find a further basis for its policies in strata not belonging to the working class, through readiness to make compromises; its ideology was to maintain the market economy, to set its limits through a legislative framework, to counter its shortsighted fluctuations through anti-cyclical policies, and to neutralize its negative effects through social and fiscal policies. The rallying cry was full employment, economic growth, fair division of national income, and social security. (Meidner 1980, 344–45)

Thus, the very concept of socialization of the economy was beginning to have new implications. Replacing radical redistributive and nationalization policies, Social Democratic elites gradually came to perceive that the interests of their working-class constituents lay in economic planning and economic growth (Lewin 1970). Taxation, one of the tools at the disposal of government, was to be the advance troop in the new economic planning game. Importantly, the right of private ownership was no longer seriously questioned, at least not by SAP elites. Rather, its economic ill effects were to be brought under control (Sainsbury 1980; Lewin 1970, 32). The question was gradually becoming, as Erik Åsard (1980, 381) has put it, "How can we abolish the negative effects of capitalism without, at the same time, injuring the laws and mechanisms of the system itself?"

Socialists in Government

By the early 1930s the peculiar two-chamber parliamentary system began to work to the advantage of the SAP. Because the D'Hont parliamentary representation system selected early in the century gave an electoral advantage to the largest parties,[3] the Social Democrats were becoming ever more dominant. The SAP share of the popular vote climbed steadily after the election of

1928 (see table 4.3). More important, owing to the staggered system in effect in the Upper House, the Socialists would be the strongest party for some time *even if their electoral fortunes declined temporarily.*

The Social Democrats had spent several decades declaring that once they held the reins of government they would use their strength to radically redistribute wealth via taxes. Taxation had been a key part of the party's electoral program from its inception. It would, then, be quite reasonable to expect the SAP to at least have increased income taxes on the wealthy once they reached office in 1932. Tax radicalism, however, was not the course taken by the party at this time.[4] Indeed, despite the long-standing commitment of Ernst Wigforss, the SAP's leading economic policy spokesman, to correct Sweden's "unjust" tax burden, when he finally took the post of finance minister in 1932, he felt compelled to raise consumption taxes—but not income taxes.

Carl Uhr (1977) convincingly shows that the unexpected moderation in the new Socialist government's economic policy can at least partially be explained by the fact that Wigforss was influenced by the writings of a small group of young economists from the elite Stockholm School of Economics. Wigforss served on the influential Unemployment Commission of the late 1920s with members of this group (especially Erik Lindahl, Gunnar Myrdal, and Bertil Ohlin) and had come to value their expert opinions. Not one of these men was noted as being partisan, but all were committed to addressing the issue of unemployment and asking what types of public policies would be most appropriate to deal with it.[5] Wigforss took to the Stockholm school's ideas readily and asked Myrdal to write an addendum to his budget of 1933 that argued for the limited expansion of make-work programs. Myrdal's tract explicitly rejected the notion of permanently expanding the size of the public sector and recommended only "self-liquidating" work projects. Equally important, Myrdal argued strenuously against steep increases in income taxes.[6]

On the other hand, Wigforss could find no economic logic that prevented hikes in wealth and death taxes: "One can have divided opinions on the weight of the objection to economic inequality. That it is not lacking in importance should be fully realized. But the conclusion that great wealth should be left untouched is a bit sloppy" (Wigforss 1980, 134).[7] In 1933, Wigforss thus submitted proposals to introduce an estate tax modeled after the British form of death duties. He failed to get the necessary support in committee that year, but as a part of the package of deals struck with the Farmers party, Wigforss was able to bring part of his tax reform legislation to life in 1934.[8] Still, in comparative perspective the Swedish taxes were quite moderate (table 4.2).

The 1930s did not elicit the kinds of radical redistributive policies that many expected or feared, yet they were nonetheless immensely significant for

Table 4.2

Top Tax Bracket Rates, Sweden,
1910–39 (selected years)

Year	%	Year	%
1910–1911	5.00	1927–1928	29.85
1917–1918	11.57	1929–1930	30.24
1918–1919	19.00	1932–1933	34.92
1920–1921	25.06	1933–1934	36.46
1921–1922	24.56	1934–1935	35.97
1922–1923	24.94	1937–1938	36.58
1926–1927	25.28	1938–1939	44.08

Source: Swedish budgets, various years.

Table 4.3

SAP Popular Vote Percentages in Elections,
1928–40, and Percentage of Seats Held by SAP in
Each Chamber in the Year Following
Each National Election

Year	SAP Vote Totals, %	SAP Seats in Upper Chamber, %	SAP Seats in Lower Chamber, %
1928	37	34.7	39.1
1932	41.7	38.7	45.2
1936	45.9	44	48.7
1940	53.8	50	58.3

Source: Sverige efter 1900 (Stockholm, 1981), tables 1a, 2c.

the future shape and direction of the Swedish political economy generally and tax policy specifically. In the election of 1936, the SAP won a solid 48.7 percent of seats in the Second Chamber (112 out of 230) and continued to inch toward assuming control of the First Chamber (by 1937 they held 66 of the 150 seats). This election convincingly demonstrated that the Social Democrats, though still unable to form a majority government, would continue to be the dominant force in Swedish politics for many years to come. This electoral reality shaped the strategic orientation of all concerned and ultimately helped redefine their tax policy preferences (table 4.3).

Saltsjöbaden

Employers and labor unions alike were worried that the government would legislate some form of national incomes policy or otherwise usurp the labor market organization's independence (Hadenius 1966, 54; Söderpalm 1980, 38–44; Micheletti 1984, 8). Apparently, the Swedish Employers Federation (SAF) and the major trades union congress (the LO) therefore agreed to several meetings beginning in May 1936 in which they would discuss means of addressing the problems of labor unrest.[9]

These meetings, held in a hotel in the resort city of Saltsjöbaden, were immensely significant for the development of the Swedish political economy. The Saltsjöbaden agreement helped redefine the labor market and push the polity toward a substantial centralization of political authority. On the labor market side, the LO and SAF agreed to accept responsibility for labor peace, upon which continued SAP political fortunes depended. Several specific mechanisms for resolving labor market disputes were also institutionalized (Swenson 1989). Moreover, the LO agreed to the right of employers to make management decisions according to market principles. Finally, the SAF agreed to not use strikebreakers or mass lockouts in wage disputes. As a consequence of these agreements, workdays lost because of labor stoppages decreased from 2,141 million in 1931–35 to 564 million in 1936–40.

The political implications of the historic compromise were even more significant because, as Söderpalm (1980, 39) suggests, "the cooperation between the government and these organizations increased the influence of the interest organizations at the cost of the Riksdag and the parties." These interest organizations not only came together in a forum that facilitated labor market/ state cooperation, *but also accepted responsibility to act in the broader public interest.*

The labor market organizations, notably the SAF leadership, saw that, given the likely dominance of the Socialists over partisan politics, it would be in the employers' interest to cooperate rather than obstruct:

> Söderlund [head of SAF] clearly saw that the power structure had changed and that this fact demanded a new strategy. Social Democrats had very good prospects to hold power, but at the same time the new quasi-corporativist "Organized Sweden" began to take form. This was a situation which opened up new possibilities for political influence, but on the condition that Swedish business organizations retained their neutrality and separated expert technical work and party politics in such a way as to give them access to the decision making process and facilitated working together with other organizations. (Söderpalm 1980, 40–41)

The tax reforms instituted in 1938, the year of the Saltsjöbaden agreements, appear to justify the SAF's new strategy. During the period of the Saltsjöbaden negotiations (1936–38), the Swedish Federation of Industries (Industriförbundet) submitted a series of proposals for reform of the corporate tax system to Finance Minister Wigforss (Lewin 1970, 169). These proposals were modeled after suggestions made by the economist Erik Lindahl in his *1928 Commission on Direct Taxation* and were designed to promote corporate rationalization by giving tax breaks to large successful companies (e.g., SAF members), to the disadvantage of smaller, newer, and less successful enterprises.[10]

No direct connection can be proven, yet it is quite reasonable to postulate a link between the Saltsjöbaden agreements and the substantial changes made in the corporate tax system in 1938.[11] Sven Anders Söderpalm, in his *Employers and Saltsjöbaden Politics* (1980, 39), puts it this way:

After the 1936 election the Social Democrats went into coalition with the Farmers' Party and secured their parliamentary standing, but this did not prohibit the Socialists from engaging in extensive cooperation with big corporations and their organizations. While Farmers' support depended on social policies, employment and prosperity depended on industry and export. . . . The Industriförbundet agreed to informally report to the government about the investment plans of its members. The government showed its willingness to cooperate with the reform of the corporate tax system and other measures which favored the rationally managed and profitable large corporations.

It would be wrong to assume, however, that these corporate tax measures were instituted simply to buy off big business. Instead, Swedish economist/academic/civil servants argued that these measures would contribute to the rationalization of the Swedish economy. Social Democratic elites were far from hostile to the rationalization idea, but it was the continuous argumentation of both the bureaucratic and corporate elite that appears to have moved the minister of finance to legislate the rationalization measures.[12]

The corporate tax expenditures of 1938 are significant not only because they reveal the degree of cooperation developing between the Ministry of Finance, academic/bureaucratic advisers, and big business, but also because they show the remarkable influence the minister of finance had developed over tax affairs vis-à-vis his own party. These measures proved to be a major, if largely unnoticed, victory by Wigforss over socialist members of Parliament in the Parliamentary Ways and Means Committee (Bevillningsutskott) (Kung. Major. Proposition 258, 1938). These corporate tax reforms were opposed by all eight socialist members in the Ways and Means Committee. In their reservation against the socialist government's proposition they argued that these reforms would reduce revenues to municipalities and discriminate against low-profit companies.

It cannot be known today whether these members of Parliament missed the point of the proposals or whether they were substantially against the economic logic inherent in the new corporate tax system. At any rate, the Parliamentary Yearbook (Riksdag Årsbok) of 1938 reports that the free depreciation system particularly was considered a major victory for business interests (Bjerlow 1938, 448). Owing to the rule of party discipline on the floor of the Riksdag, however, it was left to a Communist member of Parliament to make this biting comment: "Minister Wigforss has earlier declared that this has been a long-standing desire for business. That is correct, they have had this goal for nearly twenty years. Now the Right can be very pleased with their triumph" (Parliamentary Yearbook 1938, 67).

The integrated character of Swedish political economy in general and tax policymaking specifically are also well illustrated in the reforms of 1938. Though union elites had long advocated structural rationalization, it could scarcely be argued that they advocated generous corporate profits.[13] Wigforss was able to get at least tacit support for these tax measures because LO elites were confident that they would benefit in the long run. As Pontusson (1986, 17) points out, the LO's willingness to cooperate must be seen "as an expression of the belief that Social Democratic control of the government would ensure that economic rationalization and structural change conformed to the interest of labor."

During this period in the United States and the United Kingdom, labor elites held fast to their deep commitment to the notion that anything that was good for capitalists was bad for workers. The argument that one should give tax benefits to already successful companies would have been rejected as pernicious, trickle down theory. Given the fragmentation of economic policy making in the United States and the fact that the Tories would inevitably return to power in the United Kingdom, skepticism toward this type of policy was certainly understandable.

The LO's trust in their government was justified. Though corporations did very well in 1938, some of the wealthy who owned those corporations were not necessarily pleased. Along with the corporation tax expenditures initiated in this year, Wigforss increased income, wealth, and inheritance taxes.[14] But, more crucial from the LO's institutional point of view, the Social Democrats not only passed laws that favored large corporations, but also continued to push measures that favored large organized unions. For example, in 1934 the

Social Democrats struck a deal with the Liberal party, creating a new unemployment insurance scheme based on the Ghent system. The basic point of this new system was that it would give the labor unions control over the administration of unemployment insurance and thereby provide a forceful incentive for workers to join unions. Though it was technically feasible to join the insurance funds without being a union member, the Ghent system made this both impractical and expensive for the individual worker. Indeed, Gustav Möller, the Socialist minister of social affairs who introduced this scheme, argued that the unions should support this scheme because "it would force workers into the unions." [15]

World War II

The politics of taxation in Sweden during the war years were uneventful—even though all taxes rose markedly. As in Britain and the United States, politicians and interest group elites alike focused their attention elsewhere. Although no one wished for tax increases, few were willing to sacrifice preparedness for personal gain. The war period was notable precisely because of the high degree of cooperation among business, labor, and state that the crisis elicited. As a result of the Historic Compromise of the 1930s, Sweden was positioned much better than most to forge a successful relationship among these partners. The war cemented the relationships that Saltsjöbaden had formed.

Swedish wartime tax policy followed a pattern broadly similar to that followed in Britain and the United States. Taxes, all taxes, went up. Tax revenues more than doubled between 1937 and 1945. But because Sweden was able to remain neutral during the war, the tax revenue needed by the government for defense was considerably less than that needed in either Britain or the United States.

The Social Democrats put together a national coalition government (*samlingsregering*) and attempted to confront these difficult times with as much consensus building as possible. Having their attention focused elsewhere, all parties seemed to agree that raising sufficient revenue for defense was the fundamental objective for tax policy at the time.

In 1939, a war profits tax (*krigskonjunkturskatt*) was placed on all business incomes. As in the United States and the United Kingdom, excess profits taxes were intended to limit war profiteering. Sweden's version of this tax differed from that of other countries, however, because of the generous tax expenditures offered to big business. These tax expenditures were explicitly designed to allow Swedish companies to use war profits to build their industrial base after the war. It was widely agreed among academic, industrial, and Finance Ministry elites that heavy war profits taxes should not create difficulties for companies when the war was over. Tax policymakers remembered the last war, in which some companies had many of their war profits taxed away, leaving them in a position of poor liquidity when it was time to retool for non-military production (Kuylenstierna 1973, 53). A special wartime defense levy was also imposed on incomes over three thousand kronor. Rates ranged from 5.5 percent to 23 percent in 1940 and were raised to 7 percent to 31 percent in 1942. Finally, Sweden, like Britain, introduced a special wartime sales tax as well. Though the LO was hardly happy about this last measure, they accepted it with the promise that the end of the war would be "harvest time."

World War II and Technocracy

A profound effect of the continuous and cooperative communication among elites over economic policy and defense readiness was the strengthening of the power of these elites vis-à-vis their organizations. For example, at the Congress of 1941, the LO pushed through a rule change that radically restricted the member unions' independence. The LO's national organization strengthened its control within the association and got the right to stop all strikes that created difficulties and affected more than 3 percent of the association's members (Söderpalm 1980, 50).

This centralism also implied the expanding power and influence of these organizations' technocratic elites. In order to communicate and cooperate with the Ministry of Finance over the details of economic and tax policy, these organizations had always needed a degree of technical expertise. As the level of cooperation intensified, so did their need for sophisticated analytic capabilities. Influence over policy depended on access to information, and the need for information led to broader research and research capacity. This ultimately increased the influence of the technocrats over the positions and perspectives of the organizations' constituent units. At the same time, the concentration of power within the labor movement and the business community gave the Social Democrats the opportunity to cut deals with these large organizations and more fully institutionalize a Historic Compromise with them. As we shall see in chapter 5, tax politics in Sweden was largely depoliticized in the 1950s and 1960s. Such a move was possible largely because of the institutionalized relationship among technocratic elites and the amount of influence they had gained over the tax policy agenda during World War II.

By the end of World War II the Social Democrats had held government office six times, but always in coalition or as a minority government. The peculiar constitutional/electoral structure extant at the time put the Social Democrats in a unique political position vis-à-vis their tax policy positions. On the one hand, because Sweden had moved to a system of proportional representation, their consistently strong electoral performances were never translated into majority control of the Swedish Riksdag. Their minority status thus prevented them from enacting radically progressive tax policies in line with the redistributive positions taken up to the 1930s. This was a political reality that the Social Democrats, their various coalition partners, and the opposition understood very well. On the other hand, the existence of pro-portional representation for the Lower Chamber combined with the indirect and slow-to-change electoral system for the Upper Chamber meant that the SAP would be in a dominant position in the Riksdag for a long time, even if they temporarily fell out of favor with the electorate. This conclusion was understood by all participants in Swedish politics. The tax policies formulated during this decade reflected these political and institutional realities.

The United States

Between the two great wars, the American economy went through the best and the worst of times. The rate of economic growth in the late teens and twenties was unprecedented, and the United States was quickly becoming the world's richest and most potent country. While perhaps not apathetic, citizens were content with politics and did not agitate for radical changes. The Republicans' campaign for a return to normalcy under Warren G. Harding in the election of 1920 seemed to capture the mood of Americans of the day.[16] The continued economic expansion of the twenties, moreover, built faith in the capitalist system and its successes. "The business of America is business" proved to be a successful Republican campaign slogan (Sundquist, 1973: 167–182).

Thus, in the first postwar election (1920), the Republican presidential can-didate, Harding, smashed his Democratic opponent, James Cox, winning over sixteen million votes against his opponent's nine million. In light of this decisive victory and President Harding's subsequent decision to appoint the financier Andrew Mellon as treasury secretary, it would have been reasonable to expect that the progressive taxes introduced over the previous several years, and particularly high marginal tax rates on the wealthy, would be immediately abolished.[17] Reasonable expectations, however, are not always realized.

By the 1920s, the committee system had become firmly established in Con-gress, and the practice of seniority appointment to committee chairmanships was equally firmly ensconced. These institutional reforms not only weakened political parties and professionalized the national legislature, but also further debilitated an already weak executive. Though there were attempts at recentralizing power during the second Woodrow Wilson administration, both the Democratic and Republican parties were still effectively split between progressive and conservative wings. As a consequence, "party cohesion and majority rule through the caucus gave way to majority rule in the House based on a powerful cross party alliance which supported and maintained the seniority system. . . . [Therefore] decentralization took a major leap forward" (Polsby 1969, 802). This institutional reality would shape tax policy in the United States at least until World War II.

Initially emboldened by the electoral successes of his party in 1920, Finance Minister Andrew Mellon introduced tax legislation designed to radically redistribute the tax burden downward. Responding to intense lobbying from corporate interests, he proposed abolishing corporate profits taxes, cutting the top marginal income tax rate from 75 percent to 20 percent, and replacing these revenues with a national sales tax. None of these proposals would come to pass.

Neither Mellon nor the president had the influence to force congressional votes. Congress writes tax law, and congressmen were representatives of regional interests and local constituencies more than they were members of any individual ideological grouping. The income tax, notably the high surtax rates on the super wealthy, continued to be seen as a tax paid mostly by the "economic royalists" of the Northeast;[18] Republicans from the Midwest— sometimes called Insurgents, but called "wild asses in the desert" by Secretary Mellon—were not eager to cut these taxes. Equally, farmers, small producers, retailers, and unions opposed the introduction of sales taxes, especially since sales tax revenues were intended to offset tax cuts for the rich. Thus despite intense lobbying from business interests, essentially all of Mellon's tax proposals failed.[19] The sales tax proposal failed on the Senate floor by only one vote, however, in 1921. Although continued support for some type of sales tax was evident throughout the early 1920s, no bills were successful in Congress.[20]

Unable to abolish the corporate profits tax or even to radically reduce the income tax rates paid by the very wealthy, lobbyists went to work pressuring for specific measures that would benefit their special interests. This route, they soon discovered, could be much more successful. Members of Congress (even Republicans) were loath to so blatantly give the rich an obvious victory. Democrats above all, but many Republicans as well, were more interested in reducing taxes on lower- and middle-income taxpayers as a group than capitalists as a group. But being opposed to capitalists or the rich rhetorically did not necessarily mean that the representatives were opposed to the interests of employers and prominent supporters in *their* districts. Democrats as well as Republicans found it more appealing to pass amendments to the tax code that benefited specific constituents than to give breaks to broad classes of wealthy individuals. The Senate alone added 833 amendments to the tax bill of 1921.[21] Cordell Hull described the politics of this "tax reform" as follows:

> It was most unfortunate that the attempted revision legislation of 1921 degenerated measurably into a wrangle between champions of large income taxpayers and those of smaller taxpayers each striving to see which could unload the largest amount of taxes first. The legislative situation thus became so confused and demoralized that but scant opportunity for consideration and comprehensive scientific tax revision was afforded. (Witte, 1985, 91–92)

Though Mellon was opposed to punitive taxation, he also had the institutional responsibility to protect the national economy from the short-term interests of politicians in Congress. Traditional economic theory held that the budget must be balanced and, given the high defense spending that continued after the war, high tax revenues continued to be necessary.[22] If the Congress would not introduce a national consumption tax, it was the administration's responsibility to ensure that the taxes that remained in place could provide sufficient revenue to meet expenses. The Congress, however, was systematically undermining the fiscal integrity of the government's main revenue source, the income tax. Mellon also believed that a loophole-ridden tax code created economic incentives that undermined the health of the national economy.

Mellon was furious at his Republican colleagues, who he believed ought to have supported the president's proposals, but who in fact often abandoned the president and pressed for narrow tax breaks for their constituents. In a book he published in 1924 Mellon quotes the Yale economist T. S. Adams, who wrote that Congress assumed that "four or five years from now, when we get around to the task of patching up holes in the income tax, we shall have the kind of income tax that can be patched up." In reality, however, "the probability is strong that in four or five years the income tax will, as a matter of practical politics, be past patching" (Mellon 1924, 85–86).

Academic and administration warnings notwithstanding, the fantastic economic growth of the early 1920s more than compensated for the tax breaks handed out by Congress. By 1922 federal spending had been reduced to $4.2 billion, while federal revenues had been reduced to $4.6 billion. The continued economic expansion meant that taxes could be cut. The question was, however, Who would receive the lion's share of the benefits? While the Democrats and Insurgent Republicans continued to win tax victories in the early

1920s, the smashing electoral victory of Calvin Coolidge over John Davis in 1924 (15.7 versus 8.4 million popular votes, with 4.8 million going to the Progressive party candidate, Robert La Follette) appeared to give an unmistakable mandate for the Republican policy of tax cuts focused on the wealthy. Almost immediately, Mellon began pressing for more tax cuts for the rich. He was, by and large, successful. Mellon was now finally able to fulfill his long-standing ambition of slashing marginal tax rates on the very wealthy. By 1926 the top rate was reduced to 25 percent. Even during this heyday of Republican conservatism, however, the administration was forced to make a large number of compromises over its tax policy ambitions. Though marginal income tax rates were scaled back for the rich, taxes on the poor were also pushed farther back than the administration wished. Mellon was also unsuccessful in his attempts to drastically cut back death taxes. Finally, the administration fought vociferously against new loopholes for congressional constituencies. Here especially the most powerful treasury secretary in twentieth-century American history was most often rebuked.[23]

The Great Depression and the Great Compromise

The Great Depression forced a reevaluation of the political strategies of both the Left and the Right in America. In particular it promoted a reevaluation of revenue policy on both sides. The Right, still firmly committed to traditional economic theory (Salant 1989, 27–52; Weir 1989, 53–86), believed that in this crisis the government's first responsibility was to balance the budget. The Left was perhaps less committed to this principal but insisted that tax increases must not be borne purely by the poor. A fundamental compromise was necessary.

After eleven straight years of surplus budgets, the Treasury reported a deficit of $461 million in 1931 and predicted a deficit of $2 billion in 1932. To meet the fiscal crisis, Secretary Mellon proposed boosts in excise, inheritance, and income taxes in 1931. Although the administration once again did not get all that it asked for, Congress did agree to increase dramatically marginal income tax rates to a maximum of 63 percent. Still, less than 3 percent of citizens had incomes large enough to qualify them for the income tax, and thus these rate hikes did not provide the revenue needed to meet the administration's central objective of balancing the budget.

By 1932 it was widely agreed by economists, at least, that the government needed to raise more revenue. Indeed, the federal deficit exceeded the Treasury's estimates and climbed to $2.9 billion in 1932. In response to the economic crisis, the Democratic leadership and the Ways and Means Committee proposed a new form of national consumption tax called the Manufacturers Sales Tax. It was widely predicted that the bill would pass early in the legislative session (*New York Times,* February 26, 1932, March 2, 1932, March 6, 1932). Yet once again neither the executive nor the congressional leadership was able to guide a consumption tax through the legislative labyrinth. As we saw in chapter 3, the reality of American federalism is that U.S. representatives fundamentally represent local constituencies, even while they are members of the national legislature. As a result, local and state government interests have a national voice that is quite unavailable in more centralized countries like Britain and Sweden. Even when there is broad national agreement over principles (e.g., the need for new revenues at the national level), local interests can kill specific national policies. The Manufacturers Sales Tax was just such a specific national policy. Thus, subjected to criticisms that the new taxes they propounded would be too regressive and too complex and would usurp a growing state/local revenue source, several proposals died on either the floor of the House or the Senate.[24] Following the failure of these measures, the deficit jumped to 5 percent of GNP in 1932–33, but neither Hoover nor Roosevelt once he came to office seemed able to convince Congress to raise taxes sufficiently.

In light of the massive legislative mandate given the Democrats in 1932 and again in 1934, one might have expected Roosevelt to move decisively on the tax front—to radically redistribute the tax burden, to impose heavy new taxes on the rich and on corporations, and to close major loopholes in the porous revenue system. But, as Stein (1969, 75) notes, "Roosevelt and the business community were suspicious of each other but still recognized that they needed each other." As a result, the administration did not use its electoral mandate to push tax issues. The budget of 1933 did, however, introduce three measures of note: a 5 percent tax on corporate dividends paid to individuals; a 0.1 percent annual tax on the adjusted declared value of corporate stock; and an excess profits tax of 5 percent on corporate incomes in excess of 12 percent of declared values of a corporation's capital stock. These measures, while obviously opposed by the Republicans and by capitalists, were in fact relatively mild when compared to the many proposals put forward by progressives and radicals within and outside the Congress at the time. Moreover, they were more the work of agitators such as La Follette and Huey Long than initiatives of the administration.[25] The budget of 1934 was also quite moderate: it closed some loopholes, made the income tax more progressive, and increased estate tax rates.[26] Once again, the administration was not the principal mover and shaker in these reforms; in fact, Congress felt that the administration was more against them than for them.[27] It appeared, temporarily at least, that Roosevelt would be a moderating force against the more radical elements in his party. "The forces demanding change [had] captured the Democratic Party. And even after Roosevelt's election, they, more than he, controlled the direction of the party and the government. If Roosevelt led his party and the people, he was also led by them" (Sundquist 1973, 196). But it was not the case that the early 1930s were an era of unmitigated domination by the Left. Indeed, the legislative landslides of 1932–34 led by Roosevelt had the perverse effect of further entrenching conservative southern Democratic chairmen in both the Ways and Means and Senate Finance committees.

Roosevelt, however, was soon to change his political colors. He and his administration became quickly committed to a series of public programs designed to help the nation deal with the economic crisis it was facing.[28] These New Deal programs did not come cheap. The conservative Democrats who now controlled the revenue committees in Congress definitely would not go along with big tax increases on corporations or the wealthy. Faced with this political reality, Roosevelt apparently decided not to fight a two-front war. It is impossible to know now the extent to which the political realities of taxation led to the acceptance of Keynesian economic thinking in the United States or whether the new ideas justifying deficit spending simply allowed the government to ignore a political battle it probably could not win. We do know, however, that in the first three years of his administration, Roosevelt did not push tax issues. Though revenues increased, these were largely the result of the tax policies introduced in the last year of the Hoover administration. The deficit rose to almost $5 billion by 1936.

At several levels the politics of this era in the United States appear notably similar to those of Sweden at the same time. The Left had finally come to power and, perhaps surprisingly, acted more moderately than many expected. To push the comparison even further, many sectors of the American business community, like their Swedish counterparts, explicitly recognized the need for compromise and conciliation with the administration. "After the overwhelming Democratic victory in the 1934 Congressional elections, the [Chamber of Commerce] leadership had decided on a policy of getting along with the administration. They had called for cooperation between business and the government in the promotion of economic recovery" (Stein 1969, 79).

But the American and Swedish economies differed, and so, therefore, did the options available to political and economic elites. Whereas the need for cooperation in Sweden led the SAF to agree to the famous Saltsjöbaden agreements, in the United States business was less well organized and therefore had little to offer for such cooperation. America's business interests were far more fragmented and decentralized than those of late-developing Sweden, so the

United States had no institutional equivalent to the Swedish SAF. Indeed, the National Association of Manufacturers never accepted a policy of conciliation and accused the Chamber of Commerce of "pussyfooting and kowtowing" (Stein 1969, 79).

By 1935, frustrated by both business and congressional opposition to his New Deal programs, Roosevelt finally decided to face the Right and the business interests head on. As if rejecting his former conciliatory approach, Roosevelt now decided to outflank La Follette and Long and proposed an astonishing Share the Wealth budget in 1935. In the same budget, however, he introduced what would turn out to be a fundamentally more important policy initiative: the Social Security plan.[29]

In short, Roosevelt appeared to move down two contradictory tax policy paths in 1935. On the one hand, he proposed a regressive scheme for financing his new Social Security plan.[30] On the other hand, he launched a vigorous attack against corporations and the wealthy in what was subsequently called the Wealth Tax Budget of 1935.[31] The regressive funding of the Social Security system was a surprise to many and a disappointment to others.[32] Roosevelt later justified the "contributory" system on the grounds that it would remain politically invulnerable. He presented his argument on this point to a visitor to the White House who complained about the regressivity of the tax: "I guess you're right on the economics, but those taxes were never a problem of economics. They are politics all the way through. We put those payroll contributions there so as to give the contributors a legal, moral, and political right to collect their pensions. . . . With those taxes in there, no damn politician can ever scrap my social security program" (Derthick 1979, 230).

But another consideration almost certainly contributed to Roosevelt's strategic choice: he was losing his influence over Congress. Given the entrenched position of conservative southern Democrats in Ways and Means and Finance, he did not want to undermine the entire Social Security program by insisting on taxes the conservatives in his own party would fight.[33] Roosevelt thus overruled the Committee on Economic Security—the cabinet-level committee that designed the Social Security plan—at the last minute, insisting that they rely exclusively on regressive payroll taxes rather than on general revenues.[34]

After the passage of the Social Security Act, Roosevelt continued to take aim against what he called "economic royalists," but the administration's relations with Congress began to deteriorate even though many congressmen had come to office on Roosevelt's coattails in the election of 1936.[35] For example, the Treasury decided to use the 1937 budget to take aim at many of the obvious tax loopholes used by the economic royalists in legally avoiding their fair share of the tax burden. A modified version of the administration's bill did pass through Congress but, as Ratner notes,

> The 1937 Revenue Act was a step forward in closing some of the loopholes in the income tax laws, but it failed to deal with such important tax avoidance devices as tax-exempt securities, undistributed profits, capital gains, single premium life insurance policies issued by fictitious companies, pension trusts, community property laws, percentage depletion, and multiple trusts for accumulating income. . . . Tax attorneys still saw plenty of ways for their clients to escape paying the price for civilized society. (Ratner 1942, 478)

After 1937, Roosevelt's influence in tax matters continued to decline to the point that he could not realistically hope to gain any of his increasingly radical tax policy goals. Rather than raise taxes on the wealthy to finance more public spending and to redistribute wealth as Roosevelt proposed, the Congress cut effective tax rates for most individuals and introduced (or sometimes reintroduced) tax loopholes for their influential constituents.[36]

Though Roosevelt returned to a more moderate stance on taxation in the last years of the decade, his relationship with the taxing committees deteriorated even further as the decade came to a close. Indeed, the acts of 1938 and 1939 were passed over the administration's objections that they overturned many of the progressive tax policies, however compromised they had already become, of the past four years.[37] Congress was coming under heavy fire from the president, the Treasury, and academic analysts for ignoring the continuing deficit and for using the tax code as a political plum to pay off their constituents. But their incentive structure led them to listen to their constituents, not to academics or presidents. In their text *The Federal Income Tax* (1940), Roy and Gladys Blakey describe the passage of the 1938 tax bill in the Senate with more than a small amount of frustration: "As the clerk speedily read the bill for amendments, the chairman punctuated his steady flow of words with the formula, 'Without objection amendment agreed to,' spoken as though it were one long word. At the end of twenty minutes Vice President Garner turned the gavel over to Minton with the remark that they had already passed 224 pages of the measure" (Witte 1985, 105–06). An already high deficit of $1.44 billion in 1938 was increased to $3.6 billion in 1939, partly through the generosity of Congress.

In sum, during the interwar period essential changes were made in taxation policy in the United States, but these changes were not as dramatic as many hoped they would be. Neither the Right in the 1920s nor the Left in the

1930s was able to implement their tax policy goals in spite of huge electoral victories at the national level. In the twenties and thirties these interests were forced to accept an implicit compromise over both the details of federal tax policy and the general principles that should guide the future development of the American tax system. Republicans accepted the idea that taxes should be based on the principle of ability to pay, and Democrats accepted the principle that expansion of new public programs could not be financed exclusively, or even mostly, through increases in taxes on the rich. Again, broadly similar compromises were struck in both Sweden and Britain. Though an explicit and institutionalized compromise is most obvious in the Swedish case, in all three cases the foundation is the same: Both the 1920s and 1930s demonstrated that neither side could achieve its policy goals without fundamentally conceding to some of the demands and interests of the opposition.

In the American context, however, representatives of both the Left and the Right in Congress could agree to a large number of particular measures designed to benefit constituents back home. The Treasury as well as presidents from both parties fought the Congress over these amendments, but in the United States, Congress, not the president, writes tax law.

War: Sacrifice, Yes—Coalition, No

It did not take long after the outbreak of hostilities in Europe for national political elites in America, much like their counterparts across the Atlantic, to realize that massive new amounts of revenue were necessary. It was evident to all by then that it would be impossible to simply pass the burden on to opposing interests: war preparation would have to be financed through *mutual* sacrifice. Still, the government had significant problems to surmount in translating this general agreement into specific tax policies. One major problem for the Roosevelt administration was convincing the nation that the war required the massive extension of the income tax. For decades the Democrats had argued in favor of this tax as a class tax levied on the economic royalists; now they had to convince average workers that everyone should pay it. The government mounted a massive propaganda campaign with the aim of legitimizing the extension of this tax to the middle classes and working classes and their representatives.[38]

The government's campaign was largely successful. As in both Sweden and Britain, the tax base was extensively broadened at the same time that tax rates on both income and profits were radically increased. Whereas in 1939 only 6 percent of American workers paid income taxes, within six years over 70 percent of workers had been brought into the income tax net.[39] Income tax rates paid by the rich were also raised massively. By 1944 the tax rate on incomes over $200,000 reached 94 percent.[40] Corporate income taxes were also increased and an excess profits tax was reintroduced. Again, when American workingmen were spilling their blood on foreign shores it seemed only fair that those who were making huge profits in the war should have to pay heavy taxes.

The government, however, was far from wholly successful in achieving its wartime tax objectives. The institutional fragmentation of American politics did its work even during the wartime crisis. Whereas the European parliamentary systems allowed for coalition governments, in the American case the administration could neither formally invite its antagonists into the government—and thereby share the glories and defeats of government—nor could it suspend popular elections, as had been done in Britain between 1935 and 1945. As Edwin Amenta and Theda Skocpol (1988) point out, both business interests and Republicans were free to sit outside and criticize the government in ways that were quite impossible in Britain or Sweden. At the same time, not formally including these interests in a governing coalition had the effect of preventing them from gaining a stake in the policies developed during the war. Rather than building support for the administration and its reformist ambitions, the war in many ways had the effect of undermining the New Deal coalition. The election of 1942, above all, was a serious setback for reformists. Not only did the Democrats lose forty-six seats in the House and nine in the Senate, but, more important, the election strengthened conservatives within the party and weakened the position of liberals.

Thus, while Roosevelt's tax policy objectives were in fact similar to those of the British and Swedish administrations at the time, the tax policies actually legislated were sometimes quite different. The most crucial difference was, of course, the American government's inability to impose a national consumption tax. The administration fought hard for a national spendings tax early in the war, but the Congress could not be convinced that such a measure was needed, even though it was widely agreed that additional revenues were needed,[41] and it was commonly assumed that some form of consumption taxation would in fact be passed. Owing to the fragmentation of authority within Congress, no specific proposal could wind its way through the legislative labyrinth. Each was met with a different objection; some were too regressive, others were too complicated. In the end, none could generate broad enough support to move through both Houses. A Treasury official, Randolf Paul, described the fate of the administration's spendings tax proposal: "The spendings tax foundered on the rocks of administrative intricacy. There was the perennial dilemma. When a revenue proposal is presented in general terms,

Congressmen want to know how it will be implemented. When the particulars of a proposal are immediately offered, the mass of details makes it seem too complicated. The Treasury was impaled on the latter horn" (Paul 1947, 103).

A second difference between American and British and Swedish wartime tax policy had to do with the number of tax exemptions offered to certain industries and interests. In spite of broad agreement that taxes needed to be raised, there were powerful forces demanding special treatment. These forces often had friends on the revenue committees. As a result, Congress agreed to steep income and excess profits taxes but also opened a plethora of loopholes to some of the very industries whose profits expanded because of the war.

Finally, in part owing to the special provisions offered by Congress to particular taxpayers, the American tax system was becoming infinitely more complex than its European counterparts. The revenue act of 1942 alone, for example, devoted 42 pages to "clarifications" and "definitions." Of its 208 pages, 162 (78 percent) were devoted to "corrective" measures. Randolf Paul (1947, 318) described the 1942 law with distaste: "The rate structure had reached the point where loopholes resulted in drastic loss of revenue, and where inequities and discrepancies threatened to be not only troublesome, but even disastrous to taxpayers." John Witte (1985, 118) bluntly states, "The complexity of the bill was overwhelming."

As the war progressed, resistance to high taxes and congressional catering to special interests became even more pronounced. In 1943, with progressive forces in the Democratic party weakened by the previous year's election, Congress essentially ignored the tax bill sent to it by the administration. The law finally passed by Congress was so littered with special provisions that Roosevelt, in vetoing it, labeled it "not a tax bill, but a tax relief bill." This was the first revenue bill ever to be vetoed by an American president   and it was the first time a veto of a revenue bill was ever overridden by Congress. *Yet Congress was still controlled by the Democratic party when it overrode Roosevelt's veto.* In the parliamentary systems of Britain and Sweden, a conflict over revenue policy of this magnitude would not only bring down the government, but might also provoke a constitutional crisis. In America, the conflict between the president and the Congress over tax policy had by now become routine. Rather than bring down the government, it was becoming commonplace for the president/Treasury's tax measures—designed to champion the broad national interest and take away tax privileges from the special and local interests—to be fundamentally rewritten by a Congress that had other tax policy objectives in mind.

Table 4.4

British Political Parties: Percentage Popular Votes and
Seats Won in Parliament, 1918–29

	1918		1922		1923		1924		1929	
	(v)	(s)	(v)	(s)	(v)	(s)	(v)	(s)	(v)	(s)
Con.	39.5	54.0	38.5	55.9	38.0	42.0	47.6	67.5	38.1	42.3
Lib.	13.3	5.1	18.9	10.1	29.7	25.7	18.2	7.2	23.5	9.6
Lab.	22.5	8.6	29.7	23.1	30.7	31.1	33.3	24.6	37.1	46.7

(v) = popular votes (s) = seats won in parliament
Source: Mackie and Rose, 1991: tables 23a–d, 24a–d.

Great Britain

At the end of World War I, each of the three main political parties in Great
Britain was split over whether it should remain in a coalition government.
Though some Labourites essentially defected from their party and stood for
office as Coalition Labour,[42] and though some Conservatives did not stand on
their party's Coalition Unionist ticket, the vast majority of Labour voted to
stay out of the coalition while the majority of Tories voted to stay in. For the
Liberals, the election of 1918 proved to be a watershed; the party literally split
in half. This political misfortune was, moreover, exacerbated by the vagaries
of the British electoral process (table 4.4).[43]

Immediately following World War I, then, there appeared to be substantial potential for compromise solutions to many of the political issues facing
Britain, including tax issues. Though the core of the Labour party continued
to argue for quite radical redistributive tax policies (e.g., the abolition of all
indirect taxes), their demands were effectively shut out by the electorate. In
contrast, half of the Liberal elite and, most important, Lloyd George, the
architect of progressive taxes in Britain, decided to deal and compromise with
the Tories. Most commentators have focused on this decision as the death
knell for the Liberals. It is important to recognize, however, that the Tories
also moved to the center. A coalition was imaginable precisely because the
Conservatives had come to accept many of the basic premises pushed by the
Liberals over the previous twenty years.

Balancing the Budget

The linchpin of the governing coalition's agreement at this time was that Britain's first fiscal requirement was to balance the budget and only then to work
toward paying off the national debt. By 1917 the public debt had skyrocketed

Table 4.5
British Debt Service and
Budget Balance, 1913–23

	Debt Service		
	Amount	% of Budget	Current Balance
1913	23	14	−1
1918	248	11	−1,331
1919	310	22	−427
1920	320	34	+54
1921	303	31	+10
1922	307	36	+24
1923	315	41	+38

Source: Silverman 1982, 120.

to 64.6 percent of GNP! The traditional Treasury view in Britain, as in the United States and Sweden, held that deficit spending could be justified in wartime but could not be tolerated in peace.[44] Thus, despite the Liberal and Conservative parties' resolve to lower the postwar tax burden, their common commitment to retiring the debt prevented the kind of wholesale tax cuts favored by many of their supporters (table 4.5).

Significantly, every coalition government chancellor (all of whom were Conservatives) was committed to maintaining not only high revenues, but also broadly constant *tax distributions*. Even though these chancellors were under heavy pressure from Conservative party supporters to redistribute the tax burden away from the wealthy and corporations, they bluntly and consistently refused.

Wartime taxes almost never cover wartime expenses. In wartime, countries must find other, extraordinary sources of revenue. In the twentieth century the favored source has been government bonds. But bonds have to be paid back even after the war has been won. Thus in the first peacetime budget (April 1919), Chancellor of the Exchequer Austen Chamberlain announced a budget designed to bring back fiscal integrity and confidence in the pound sterling. Rather than announce tax reductions he announced cuts in public spending and continued high postwar taxes. The central point of his budget speech was later paraphrased and immortalized by President John Kennedy: "Until the time comes when the ordinary man, instead of asking himself, 'What can I get out of the State?' will ask himself, 'What can I do for the State?' we shall never be able to put that drag on Governments which is absolutely essential in the interests of sound finance" (Silverman 1982, 67).

Notwithstanding great pressures exerted on Chamberlain by the business community, he refused to abolish the EPD or even to reduce marginal income tax rates. He instead *increased* death duties as well as taxes on beer and spirits. The chancellor also considered the argument of some of his advisers and members of the academic community that he should abolish the EPD and replace it with a more permanent and coherent corporate profits tax system; but he concluded that whatever the merits of such an idea, the plan was at this point beyond the capacities of his administration: "As regards the EPD, my original intention had been to abolish the existing tax and to impose a new tax of permanent character on what I call the excess profits of business . . . but the time at my disposal was not sufficient to devise a new form of taxation which would operate fairly as between one business and another" (Silverman 1982, 68). He did, however, find it possible to reduce the EPD rate from 80 to 40 percent.

Capitalists in Britain, like those in Sweden and the United States, argued that the best way to pay the war debt would be to lower taxes and thereby heighten the incentive to save and invest. Productivity increases, they argued, would pay off the debt much faster than high taxes ever could. But the government, under the heavy influence of Treasury officials, rejected these arguments in favor of traditional fiscal policy. This meant, given the economic recession of 1920–21, that new revenues would have to be found. The Treasury "considered every conceivable tax on every conceivable item and transaction" (Silverman 1982, 76). Two that were considered but then rejected indicate the degree to which British politics, much like Swedish and American politics, had become a standoff between the interests of capital and labor. The first tax considered was a capital levy, which surprisingly was narrowly rejected by the chancellor on the grounds that it would induce capital flight from the country. The second major alternative rejected by the government was a kind of indirect tax called a turnover tax, which was much like a tax proposed in the United States at the same time. This option was thrown out by the government for fear of the working classes' reaction to such a move. The Treasury argued against these taxes on the grounds that "the Treasury might take in a little more revenue, at the cost of a major struggle between capital and labor. Given the new-found power of the unions, capital would probably lose. The working class would simply demand and obtain higher wages, ultimately shifting the cost of a turnover tax to the industrial classes and middle-class consumers."[45]

In this light, the chancellor decided in his budget for 1921 to raise the EPD rate back to 60 percent (from 40 percent) and introduce a new corporate profits duty of 1 percent on all corporate profits. The business community was predictably outraged. But Chamberlain would not be deterred. He was determined to put the wartime deficit spending behind him and not only balance the budget, but begin retiring the national debt. When told by the National Union of Manufacturers, "We shall have to take our factories, our ability, our industries, abroad," the chancellor retorted, "Have you picked your country yet?" Later Chamberlain declared to another delegation of industrialists who had argued for boosting indirect taxes in order to finance profits tax cuts, "I can always get suggestions from delegations to tax somebody else," he complained. "I have not asked for that. . . . Assuming that the same classes are to produce an equal amount of money, is there some other way in which they would prefer to produce it?" (Silverman 1982, 83, 85). Again, the government was committed to the notion that the budget had to be balanced; this, combined with the fear that dramatic redistributions of the tax burden would lead to spreading social strife (and thereby contribute to the electoral fortunes of the quickly rising Labour party), meant that new revenues would have to come out of old pockets.

Not until 1922–23 did the government feel financially secure enough to begin reducing taxes. In his first budget, Chancellor Sir Robert Horne cut the income tax standard rate from 30% to 25%. But even in this budget, which was attacked as a rich man's budget by the opposition, Horne refused to abolish or meaningfully reduce either surtax rates or profits taxes. Noting that capitalists "have conducted and are still conducting an organized campaign throughout the whole country against its burden," the chancellor bitterly complained that these interests were in effect reneging on a "tacit agreement" struck during the war to finance much of the wartime expense through borrowing rather than through increased taxes on the wealthy (Silverman 1982, 92).

Labour in Power

Many feared that even tacit agreements would become null and void when and if the Labour party finally achieved office. Labour had been gaining ground more or less steadily since before the war, and while there was obvious conflict within the party over the real meaning of socialism, the party continued to use the rhetoric of class conflict and socialization. Phillip Snowden, for example, argued, "In view of the failure of the capitalist system to adequately utilize and organize natural resources and productive power, or to provide the necessary standard of life for vast numbers of the population . . . legislative effort should be directed to the gradual supersession of the capitalist system" (Mowat 1955, 154).

Finally, when the Conservative government, led by Stanley Baldwin, announced its decision to fight unemployment with protective tariffs and go to the polls to build support for its decision in 1923, Labour won its opportunity at government. The Tories were surprised to find that Baldwin's strategy, which he had hoped would split the Liberal party and isolate Labour, did not work—at least in the short run. Once again, the vagaries of the British single-member-district electoral system dramatically skewed electoral results. For example, even though the Conservative party's share of the national vote barely declined between the 1922 and 1923 elections from 38.2 percent to 38.1 percent, the Conservatives gave up 87 seats in Parliament and lost their majority. The Liberals presented a more united front in 1923 and actually gained 43 seats despite the fact that their share of the vote in fact declined marginally.[46] The big winner in this election was Labour, who, with an increase of just 1 percent of the national vote, from 29.5 percent to 30.5 percent, gained 49 seats in Parliament (the party now held 191). Labour was now plainly the second largest party, and, given the Liberal and Tory divide over the tariff issue, the logical choice was to form a minority government.

Corporatism Averted

Why did no Liberal/Labour coalition government emerge at this time? In Sweden this would have been the obvious solution to the dilemma. The answer seems to be that the striking dissimilarities between the two electoral systems framed the strategic choices for all participants in quite different ways. All parties in Sweden could see that even if there were sizable shifts in the electoral support for one or another party from one election to another, the proportional representation system for both houses, combined with the staggered and incremental elections for the Upper House, meant that the partisan composition of the Riksdag was most likely to remain stable for some time. The rational calculation for British party elites was, of course, different. The last election was just the most recent example of how very small shifts in popular support could have stupendous effects on parliamentary control. To enter a coalition with Labour could all too easily taint the Liberals as socialists and push voters back to the Tory camp. For its part, Labour declared self-righteously that it would govern alone or it would not govern at all. Labourites apparently were determined to demonstrate that they were not the fire-breathing Communists the bourgeois parties and the press made them out to be. If they governed in coalition, the moderation of their policy proposals could easily allow the Liberals to take the credit for whatever clearheadedness resulted in the government.

Labour, then, was allowed to form a minority government. This in itself had its strategic appeal to both the Liberals and the Tories. Asquith noted in December 1923 that as the largest antiprotectionist party, Labour should be given a chance. As a minority government, its chances to act on its socialist rhetoric would be limited. The Conservative Neville Chamberlain "privately reached similar conclusions [to Asquith's]; a 'merely tactical' alliance to keep Labour out would only strengthen it in the future, whereas in office, 'it would be too weak to do much harm but not too weak to get discredited' " (Mowat 1955, 169). These strategic calculations proved to be both right and wrong. In their nine months in office, Labour did not introduce any radical proposals. But the Liberals' decision not to side with Labour against the Tories proved to be a fatal miscalculation for the Liberal party.

The leader of the Labour party, J. R. McDonald, in an apparent attempt to assuage middle-class voters and to enhance the party's electoral position for upcoming elections, chose a cabinet dominated by moderates. In spite of vociferous complaints from radical elements of the party, McDonald's cabinet consisted of middle- and upper-class members of Parliament and new, more moderate recruits to the party. In fact, only five of twenty-five members of the first Labour government were trade unionists. Phillip Snowden was selected as chancellor of the exchequer. Despite his long-standing interest in taxation and his reputation as the archcritic of "right-wing finance," he was, in truth, unprepared. He had, after all, only three weeks to construct his first budget, and, "with the Financial Secretary at his elbow to nudge him if he made a slip," he had no opportunity to introduce a "Socialist Budget" (Sabine 1966). Perhaps most surprisingly, the budget of 1924 continued the policy embarked on by the previous Conservative government and abolished the corporation tax. Snowden, faced with a substantial surplus of £38 million was able to move, albeit in small steps, toward the Socialist ideal of reducing indirect taxes. He also extended the allowances for housekeepers. In the words of B. E. V. Sabine (1966, 166), "In relieving indirect taxation he was certainly following a Labour (and Liberal) ideal. But there was no 'national scheme of productive work' as promised by the Labour Party manifesto; no nationalization; no capital levy; no schemes for tapping 'the unappropriated incomes of the very wealthy.' . . . Certainly there was a marked difference between Snowden in opposition and Snowden in office."

Perhaps Snowden and his government would have moved to more socialistic tax policies if they had had more time to prepare or if they had been able to present additional budgets in the following years. This, however, was not to be. A conflict over a proposed loan to Bolshevik Russia and a minor scandal within the government led to a vote of no confidence in Parliament. Then, just four days before the national election, the *Times* published the famous

Zanoviev letter and a reply from the government that appeared to authenticate the Russian's claim that the proposed treaty and loan to the Soviet Union were linked to a plan to bring about armed conflict, class war, and revolution in Britain. The effects of this letter were as devastating as the government's defense was weak. Labour lost 40 seats (but less than 3 percent of the total vote), while the Tories returned to their majority position, going from 38.1 percent to 48.3 percent of the vote and gaining 161 seats in Parliament. The Tories gain, moreover, was mainly the Liberals' loss. They were routed, dropping to only 17.6 percent of the vote and retaining only 40 seats in Parliament.

Winston Churchill, who had by now abandoned the Liberal party and joined forces with the Conservatives, became the next chancellor of the exchequer and held this position for five years. Churchill was uninterested in taxation, and the nation had broadly accepted the outlines of the existing tax system. A compromise had been reached.

Though income tax rates were reduced under the Conservative governments in the 1920s, even the right wing Tories had at this point accepted the principle that the overall tax burden ought to be based on the ability to pay. Budget debates in Parliament became ritualistic conflicts between the two sides of the House. Labour consistently railed against the Tories' "rich man's budgets," arguing that income taxes ought to be ever more progressive. "The taxation of the rich is really a payment which has been made by the poor who have been exploited," for example, was one of Snowden's common themes (Sabine 1966, 148).

As to the yearly confrontations, Snowden is recorded as having said that they were "the best show in London." Despite the tempo and temper of these rhetorical confrontations, by the 1920s income taxes and, more generally, the principle of ability to pay had become thoroughly ensconced in the British tax system. The Inland Revenue, once the strongest opponent of the graduated system, came to be one of its major defenders. The forecasted revenue flight had not occurred, and the Conservatives, afraid of alienating potential swing voters, retained the highest brackets on super tax, though they reduced the rates on those with middle-range investment income. Taxes on the wealthy were somewhat lowered in the 1920s, but these formal tax reductions were rather insubstantial. Public spending continued to be high, and the Tories were first and foremost dedicated to keeping a balanced budget.

Company Taxation

Interestingly, the impact of taxation on industry was apparently not an issue that either the government or the civil service took seriously at this time. The reader will recall the attention given by tax policymakers in Sweden to the general interests of productive capital and to Swedish efforts to use tax policy to promote the rationalization of the economy. American tax policymakers also were deeply concerned with the effects of taxation on capital and corporations during the interwar years, but in this case concern was as often focused on particular companies and industries as it was on the economy as a whole. Yet in Britain, the government appeared to be cavalier about the effects of taxation on British industry. A major review of the tax system conducted in the late 1920s, the Colwyn Committee Report, for example, "which might have been expected to have considered this question in some detail, limited itself to the statement that the heavy tax burden had to some extent affected . . . industry . . . although we regard it as of minor importance compared with more general difficulties affecting our foreign trade" (Middleton 1985, 71). Though some (especially industry) argued that high marginal rates of tax were destructive to the economy, neither the Colwyn Committee nor the Balfour Committee on Industry and Trade, which issued reports between 1927 and 1929, accepted these arguments. The Colwyn Committee argued, for example, that the personal income tax "had no important effect on their [individuals'] work and enterprise," although it did acknowledge that, for higher income groups, high personal income tax rates reduced savings. Both committees also denied the argument made by the Confederation of British Industries (CBI) that the real incidence of the corporate business tax was on consumers. Undoubtedly, these reports reflected the views of the Treasury (Middleton 1985, 71–72).

British industry "neither shared nor concurred with this view or the assumptions underlying it," maintaining instead that high tax rates depressed business confidence (Middleton 1985, 73). Industrialists went so far as to argue that a reduction on income tax was the primary means by which the government could assist economic recovery. Their pleas, however, fell on deaf ears. The Treasury, as has often been noted, has historically been insulated from industry in Britain (Shonfield 1965; Zysman 1983). In the United States, the Treasury was headed by the great financier and industrialist Andrew Mellon; in Sweden academic economists moved in and out of both the Finance Department and research organizations funded by industrialists. In the United Kingdom, however, Treasury officials were surprisingly cut off from the needs and interests of capital. Churchill, the chancellor of the exchequer from 1924 to 1929, was, as mentioned, uninterested in tax matters. Finally, the "cleavage between business and official opinion suggests that the task of facing the inter-war budgetary authorities was not solely one of acknowledging the necessity for Keynesian demand management, but that there was also a need for a more intelligent appreciation of distributional questions. The papers of the Treasury and Inland Revenue reveal their extreme amateurism in this latter respect" (Middleton 1985, 72).

Labour Forms Government—Again

Not until the Left regained power in 1929 was there much motion on the tax front. The election of 1929 enlarged Labour's share of the vote from 33 percent to 37.1 percent and brought 132 new Labourites to Parliament. Though still not a majority, Labour was the largest party in the Parliament.[47] But the final product of Labour government tax policies was far from the radical redistributive policies that the Left had gallantly promoted over the years. Even though Labour's fiery tax spokesman Phillip Snowden became the chancellor, the new socialist government moved slowly indeed.

As might be expected, maximum rates on the super tax, now called the surtax on investment income, were raised somewhat (to 37.4% in 1929 and to 41.25% in 1930–31). But in moving up tax rates on the richer families, Snowden only partially fulfilled his commitments to redistribute the tax burden in Great Britain (see table 4.6). Indeed, measured against the specific tax commitments in the so-called Socialist Budget (for example, the proposal to abolish indirect taxation in favor of exclusively direct progressive taxation) the reforms of 1929–31 must be considered a U-turn.

The central explanation for Labour's apparent change of heart over its tax policy has to do with what Heclo describes as the "practical formulation of policy." Specifically, Snowden, faced with the practical constraints of managing the budget, had changed his mind about how best to promote workers' interests via the tax structure. No longer, he concluded, was pure income redistribution a sufficient policy. Keith Middlemas (1979, 315–16) suggests that the explanation for Labour's failure to implement its radical reformist ambitions in 1929–31 lies in its (especially Snowden's) "tacit acceptance of Treasury and Bank of England's authority in questions of Finance; and the consequent growth of cross-party thinking and practice." In other words, as Parliamentary Labour party (PLP) elites took office, they ceased to become the opposition and suddenly found themselves to be Her Majesty's Government.

As both Heclo (1974) and Weir (1989) point out, virtually all party elites accepted traditional economic theory, which argued that Britain must stay on the gold standard and that it must maintain a balanced budget. Severe economic downturns, then, required cuts in public spending. The conflict that eventually brought down the Labour minority government was over what to do in the context of the decline. Heclo (1974, 118) writes, "As the depression advanced, the major roadblock to policy adaptation was a continuing adherence to old truths rather than any lack of political power. New ideas were available, but the Labour Cabinet, with the help of the Treasury and the Bank of England, remained transfixed by orthodox economic convictions."

Instead of either increasing taxes or abandoning the commitment to balance the budget, the Labour cabinet agreed on August 21, 1931, to cut spending by £56 million, of which £48.5 million was to come from cuts in unemployment insurance benefits and greater contributions.[48] The Bank of England declared that such a reduction was not enough, "particularly from the point of view of foreign interests concerned" (Heclo 1974, 120). But when Snowden and McDonald came back to the cabinet on August 23 requesting £22 million more in cuts, the Labour cabinet split. Though the chancellor won the vote, eight or nine members threatened to quit the cabinet. McDonald saw no alternative but to tender his resignation to the king.

McDonald and Snowden effectively left the Labour party and joined the Conservatives under the label National Labour party (Skidelsky 1967). The Labour party moved back to the left and repudiated the policies of the Labour government of 1929–31, attempting to generate support on traditional labor/ socialist appeals and rejecting the class compromise of McDonald and Snowden. This proved to be a disastrous strategy for the party. The party not only lost two million popular votes, but was reduced from 289 to 46 seats. The left wing of the party suffered the worst. Only one of Labour's ministers retained his seat. As Heclo (1974, 122) put it, "When the voice of democracy was heard, it overturned not the restrictive social policy but that policy's Labour opponents."

Historic Compromise?

Why did the government not attempt a neocorporatist solution to the nation's political and economic problems? The answer requires an institutional explanation. One might have expected the new government to reach out to extra-parliamentary groups, as happened in Sweden. But parliamentary elites were simply unwilling to give up their ideal of parliamentary sovereignty. McDonald's encounters with the Trades Union Congress (TUC) in February 1931 provide an excellent example of this point. In the words of Middlemas (1979, 243), "As the crisis developed he [McDonald] was not unwilling to negotiate the terms of a tri-partite political concordat, but only on party terms; and the

Table 4.6

Distribution of Tax Burdens,
United Kingdom, 1913–38

Income	£100	£200	£500	£1,000	£10,000
1913–1914	5.4	4.0	4.4	5.2	8.0
1918–1919	9.9	7.9	10.2	16.9	42.5
1923–1924	14.1	11.8	8.0	14.1	37.1
1925–1926	11.9	10.2	6.2	11.0	31.2
1930–1931	11.0	9.6	4.5	9.7	35.8
1937–1938	10.4	8.4	5.6	11.8	39.1

Source: Pollard 1982, 206.
Note: Death duties and corporation taxes have not been included
in this table. The high burden of taxation on those at the lowest
income levels—considerably below income tax thresholds—is explained by relatively heavy excise taxation on tea, tobacco, beer,
wheat, and coal.

Cabinet's almost contemptuous rejection of TUC's claims to participate in
solving the August crisis can be seen as the high point of party delineation
against institutional power."

In the 1920s and 1930s the stability of the Swedish electoral system led
opposition parties and capitalist interests alike to realize that they were better
off cooperating than fighting. But in keeping with the institutional heritage
and position of the sovereign cabinet in Britain, ministers there were less
willing to yield authority and power to nonparliamentary elites. At the same
time, the obvious electoral vulnerability of any government in Britain prevented consideration of the kinds of stable parliamentary coalitions that were
becoming obvious in Sweden. Why compromise if you felt that you could win
outright?

The failure to institutionalize compromise solutions does not necessarily
mean, however, that government can or will make radical policy choices. In
fact, for the remainder of the 1930s, the tax front was relatively quiescent, the
Labour party devastated by the election of 1931 and the Tories in control of
the national governments. From a policy perspective, this decade was marked
only by its lack of innovation and the sustenance of the status quo. In C. W.
Mowat's (1955, 413) words, "The history of the National government was
one long diminuendo. From its triumph in 1931 it shambled its unimaginative way to its fall in 1940." As table 4.6 indicates, the trend toward more
progressive taxation, far from being reversed, continued.

Such policy lethargy was not simply the result of unimaginative politicians complacent in their positions of authority over the state. It was instead a product of Britain's awkward means of addressing the historic compromise. By the 1930s there was no doubt in any of the three countries that neither capital nor labor would win an all-out struggle. In Middlemas's (1979, 243) words, "This change had not been imposed from above, but had been brought about by the multiple responses to circumstances, and to each other, of the governing institutions. The state of equilibrium was not static but protean, continually transmuting itself into new forms. The corporate triangle between government, employers and unions was not a system, as the corporate theorists of the thirties defined systems, but a tendency, or bias, central to the evolution of modern government."

In Britain this bias, however strong, was more difficult to realize than in either Sweden or the United States. The British electoral system provided the Tories with a huge governing majority in Parliament and thus muted those who saw the need for institutionalizing basic historical realities. It would take the crisis of war to finally build the "social contract" (Beer 1965).

The Return to Wartime Finance

Toward the end of the 1930s there was a growing realization that defense would be the primary aim of fiscal policy. In his last budget speech in 1937 Chancellor Chamberlain declared, "The national finances must continue to be dominated and governed by the vast expenditures of defense."[49] Still, as late as the last budget before Dunkirk, the government had failed to fully tackle the fiscal implications of a nation at war. Battles over fiscal policy continued to be "ritualistic conflicts" (Sabine 1970) between the Left and the Right over the distribution of the tax burden and specifically over the reliance on direct versus indirect taxes. Even in the last years of the decade, taxes were increased, but the government continued to be timid (Sabine 1970).

Dunkirk changed Britain. The government was forced to bring out a second budget, one that more fully accounted for the realities of the war. This budget required sacrifice from all sectors of society. Though both the unions and the Labour party historically opposed any increases in indirect taxes, believing instead that a capital levy was preferable, they also believed that sacrifice at this time of crisis would work in their interests after the war. Workers and unionists were not the only ones, after all, called upon to sacrifice by increases in taxation; moreover, increased taxes were not the only sacrifices. The unionists agreed, for example, to a wartime ban on strikes, strict arbitration procedures for labor disputes, and limitations on industrial freedom of speech. The unionist Ernst Bevin, minister of labor in the new coalition government, justified the sacrifices in the following way: "I have to ask you . . . virtually to place yourselves at the disposal of the state. We are Socialists and this is the test of our Socialism. It is the test whether we have meant the resolutions which we have so often passed. . . . If our Movement and our class rise with all their energy now and save the people of this country from disaster, the country will always turn with confidence to the people who saved them" (Middlemas 1979, 275).

At the same time Conservatives and industry also recognized the need for compromise and sacrifice. They realized that labor was the "ultimate scarce resource," notes Beer (1965, 212). "The cooperation of the unions and their members was indispensable and was given unstintingly. Yet labor did not accept these heavy burdens without receiving and indeed demanding major concessions from other groups in society." Thus in this context the Treasury was forced to move away from much of its traditionalism and finally adopt "a fiscal bargain to match the tri-partite wage system" (Middlemas 1979, 279).

Thus the excess profits tax that was introduced in the first budget of 1940 at a rate of 60 percent was raised in the second budget to 100 percent. The standard rate of income tax was increased to 8s. 6d. Allowances were decreased, bringing a great number more workers into the income tax net. Surtax rates were raised to 9s. 6d. Now the top rate of tax on personal income stood close to 90 percent.

Indirect taxes were also raised substantially. The most consequential innovation was the introduction of a new sales tax called the purchase tax. This new tax was defended not only as an instrument of economic management in that it would help dampen demand in the economy but also as a major source of new revenues. Assessing 16.66 percent on basic commodities and 33 percent on luxury goods, the tax promised success on both fronts. To all these burdens the response from both industry and labor was "muted and conventional" (Sabine 1970, 127).

As the financial demands of the war economy grew, so did Britain's commitment. The historic budget of 1941 increased revenues massively through a host of changes. The standard rate of income tax was raised to 50 percent, and even the so-called reduced rate on low incomes was increased to 32.4%; earned income relief was lowered by one-tenth, and all other allowances except that for children were reduced. Finally, surtax rates were raised to the point where the maximum marginal rate stood at an astonishing 97.5 percent. As a consolation, these extra taxes were to be repaid in the form of a postwar credit at the end of hostilities.

By 1942, even TUC and CBI opposition to the pay as you earn system of tax collection had been surmounted, and the system whereby income taxes were deducted at source on a cumulative basis (eliminating the need for a year-end tax return for the majority of taxpayers) was introduced in this year.[50] Chancellor Kingsley Wood was quoted as saying, "What I need is cash and cash out of current income" (Sabine 1966, 196). To this there could be little argument.

The period leading up to and including World War II transformed modern democratic states. In Sweden, Great Britain, and the United States it was necessary to find some compromise between the basic interests of labor and capital—of the Left and the Right—and to build policy structures that could accommodate these interests. Where tax policy was concerned, this meant that the Left would abandon its goals of socialization and the radical redistribution of wealth; for the Right, it meant the acceptance of both the ability to pay as the basic principle of a modern tax system and the growth of an increasingly large state.

Table 4.7 illustrates the extent to which the principle of progressivity had been brought into British and American tax systems by the end of the war. Not thirty years before, there had been deep divisions in society over whether taxes should be based on the ability to pay at all; by now this principle defined modern tax systems.

One of the biggest winners in this compromise was, of course, the state itself, which, by the end of the war, had gained new importance for society. In the past three decades the state had taken on more than its traditional responsibilities of defense, order, and contracts. By the end of the war it was clear that the state was now responsible for both management of the economy and, to a somewhat lesser extent, the distribution of social justice as well.

Despite broad commonalities among the three nations, each came into and out of World War II in quite different institutional and policy positions. In Sweden and Britain, the war cemented a social contract, the state provided the forms into which this cement had been poured. In Middlemas's (1979, 273–74) words,

> The country could not afford the luxury of argument about voluntary obligation, and as a result, when more open debate began about the amelioration of poverty, unemployment and unfair distribution of wealth, it took place on the basis of two or three years' experience of state activity which had *already* profoundly changed the social relationship between classes. It was not party which benefited, but the image of government; government which had run, fairly and efficiently, if often without inspiration, such mundane areas of potential friction as food

Table 4.7

Individual Income Tax: Marginal Rates of Tax for the
United States (including New York State) and United
Kingdom, Married Person with No Dependents, 1945

Net income[1] before personal exemption[2]	United States, incl. New York State[3]			United Kingdom[4]		
	Total tax liability	Post war credit[6]	Net tax liability	Total tax liability	Post war credit[7]	Net tax liability
800	1.6%	0.6%	1.0%	6.5%	6.5%	—
1,000	2.4	1.0	1.5	11.1	6.1	5.0
1,500	6.7	1.4	5.3	18.7	6.3	12.3
2,000	11.0	1.6	9.4	25.3	6.4	18.9
4,000	18.8	1.9	16.9	35.1	4.8	30.3
8.000	26.0	2.1	23.9	41.3	3.3	38.1
10,000	28.7	2.1	26.6	45.1	2.6	42.5
20,000	40.0	2.2	37.9	56.2	1.3	54.9
60,000	61.4	1.7	59.8	76.0	0.4	75.5
100,000	70.7	1.0	68.7	84.1	0.3	83.8
400,000	87.9	0.3	87.6	94.1	0.1	94.1
600,000	90.0	0.2	89.9	95.3	[5]	95.2
1,000,000	90.7	0.1	90.6	96.2	[5]	96.1
5,000,000	90.7	[5]	90.7	97.2	[5]	97.2

Source: Treasury Department, Division of Tax Research, Washington, D.C., 1946.
Notes: Because of rounding off, items may not add to totals.
[1] For the U.S. and U.K., maximum earned net income is assumed. In excess of $30,000 is assumed to be investment income.
[2] Before deduction of the New York State tax.
[3] Includes the Victory Tax.
[4] Pound converted at $4. New York State tax takes into account reduction applicable to taxes paid in 1943.
[5] Less than .05 percent.
[6] Maximum postwar credit was $1,000.
[7] Maximum postwar credit was $260.

supply, evacuation and labour exchanges. Slowly but inevitably, the
state came to be seen as something vaster and more beneficent than
the political parties, under whose temporary management it rested, as
the real guarantor of reform and reconstruction, which parties could no
more pledge themselves to fulfill.

In the United States, the war did not cement this deal. Instead, it in many
ways undermined some of the basic thrust of the New Deal. The historical

facts that encouraged compromising solutions were present in all three countries during the war. But in the United States, the administration proved unable to construct continuing institutional foundations for national compromise. Absent these broader national institutions and experiences, congressional tax policymakers reverted to the defense of local and special constituency interests. In Britain and Sweden economic and military crises brought about formal coalitions that in turn educated both the Left and the Right, in Heclo's terms, and allowed for the conception of new programs to be implemented after the war (Heclo 1974). Noting the differences between British and American social policy developments during the war, Amenta and Skocpol (1988, 109) argue, for example, that these institutional differences were decisive: "The formalization of a bipartisan coalition opened the Conservatives to reforming influences. Labour Party leaders were brought into the wartime Cabinet and, more importantly, were placed in key Ministerial positions." In the United States, the basic institutional conflict between the executive and the Congress inhibited the formalization of such a coalition. Instead, the relations between Congress and the presidency deteriorated even further during the war. Ultimately, the government lost its grip.

In sum, these three nations faced remarkably common problems and in many ways muddled their ways toward remarkably common solutions during this period. To understand these commonalities we must look to the broad historical trends faced by all modernizing capitalist democracies; to understand the policy differences we look to the institutional differences. As the next chapter will demonstrate, the institutional and policy structures become even more important as these states build on the foundations laid in these earlier years.

5

Postwar Tax Policy—
More Revenue Gain, Less Political Pain

> When people became accustomed to paying taxes as they had
> always paid for automobiles—on the installment plan—
> Congress and the president learned, to their pleasure, what
> automobile salesmen had learned long before: that installment
> buyers could be induced to pay more because they looked not
> at the total debt but only at the monthly payments. And in this
> case there was, for the government, the added psychological
> advantage that people were paying their taxes with not much
> resistance because they were paying with money they had
> never even seen. The term "take-home pay" now entered
> the language.—David Brinkley, 1988

To understand the development of modern taxation over the thirty years following World War II, the most elementary factor to keep in mind is that the
means of generating government revenues was transformed during the war.
Not only was the tax base radically broadened in the 1940s, but also the
administration of the personal income tax was changed forever by the pay-
as-you-earn withholding system. Instead of paying taxes yearly or quarterly,
taxpayers found their taxes being deducted from their paychecks each pay
period. And, as David Brinkley wryly notes, this forever changed the fiscal
possibilities available to the state.

Neither the British nor the Swedish nor the American governments, no
matter which party or which political ideology was dominant, acted on their
wartime promise to dramatically scale back taxes once the war was over (Peacock and Wiseman 1961). Each government did cut back some, but over
the preceding decades governments had come to accept a wide array of new
responsibilities for the economy and the society, and these responsibilities
required both funding and instruments with which to affect these outcomes.
Taxes—specifically, high taxes—offered governments both the needed revenue and the public policy instruments.

Sweden is often cited both in the comparative politics and comparative
economics literature for its success in balancing the demands for expanded
social welfare spending and the heavy tax burden this implies with the need
for an efficient economy and healthy capital sector. It has often been held up

as a model for other nations to follow. A unique mix of political and economic factors made it possible for the Swedes to develop an enviably efficient and revenue-rich tax system in the 1950s and 1960s—yet this model was not destined to live forever. Changing political demands combined with basic changes in the Swedish constitution and electoral laws have undermined the Swedish model and with it this country's reputation as the premier example of the Middle Way.

As for developments in the United States, here too institutional changes have decisively shaped tax policy outcomes: The most particularistic and complex of the three tax codes studied here becomes even more complex as the responsibility for tax policy is further decentralized. In Britain, institutional changes are less significant, but drastic shifts in tax policy have nonetheless occurred over the years. These shifts result from the unique electoral/constitutional structure that puts British governments in absolute political control of tax policy and offers governments incentives to act decisively and radically, but at the same time constrains them with the political and economic realities of governing in a capitalist, democratic polity.

Sweden—The Politics of Compromise

By the end of World War II, Sweden had moved farther than Great Britain and the United States toward institutionalizing a basic compromise between the dominant political and economic interests in society. By the 1950s and 1960s, Sweden had indeed become internationally famous for having worked out a compromise that seemed both rational and efficient. The state had taken a decisive role in bringing social and economic forces together while building the foundations of agreement and mutual cooperation. In so doing they had virtually abolished industrial strife, eliminated poverty, and maintained very high rates of economic growth. Political scientists and economists alike flocked to Sweden to discover the secrets of the Middle Way.[1]

The accomplishments and the degree of political consensus found in Sweden for most of the postwar era have indeed been impressive. These successes have been the product of skillful political choices and even some luck, but they have also been possible because of a unique set of political institutions that were peculiarly well suited for the tasks at hand. The combination of Sweden's two-chamber Riksdag with proportional representation elections created an incentive structure that favored compromise and political conciliation. Though the Social Democrats were the dominant political force—and were certainly going to remain the dominant political force for some time to come—they could not monopolize the political process. Thus the basic historical context that framed politics in all advanced capitalist democracies in the postwar era found a decidedly congenial institutional environment in Sweden.

The politics of taxation for most of the 1950s and 1960s mirrored the political climate of Sweden. It was depoliticized. Taxation became the domain of technical experts who manipulated taxes to produce both sufficient revenues for the expanding welfare state and the desired economic outcomes. The efficiency and sophistication of Swedish tax policy became the envy of economists the world over.

Nothing in politics lasts forever. By the late 1960s, under intense pressure from all sides of the political spectrum, the Social Democrats were forced to admit that the peculiar two-chamber system yielded them an unfair political advantage. The Social Democrats then came to believe that the very stability of the system could be turned against their interests, as social and political demands matured in the 1970s. Sweden thus reformed its political constitution in 1970 and abolished the two-chamber system. This institutional change has had profound effects on the character and development of the Swedish tax system and indeed—though I will not develop this point fully in this book— marked the beginning of the end of the Swedish model more generally.

Immediately following World War II, it was widely expected that the Social Democrats would finally act on the redistributive pledges they had made during the preceding forty-plus years. It was commonly held that the tax burden on the lower classes had increased heavily during the war years, while that on the wealthy had increased much less significantly (Elvander 1972, 27). It was felt that during and after the war the wealthy benefited from the international demand for Swedish products, while workers, who were prohibited from striking for higher wages, were asked to pay for defense. This state of affairs was perhaps excusable during the wartime emergency, but the end of the war would surely bring about a reorientation of Swedish policies. The Social Democratic Congress announced the following program for 1944: The goal of Social Democracy is to reformulate the economic organization of bourgeois society so that the right to determine production is placed in the hands of all citizens; so that the majority is freed from dependence on a minority of capitalists; and so that a social order built on economic classes gives way to a community of free and equal citizens.

The Communists, though they ultimately endorsed the postwar program drawn up by the LO and the SAP, used the opportunity to criticize the Social Democrats for having sold out. They used this attack to good effect, and in the election of 1944 widened their share of the vote to 10 percent, raising their Lower Chamber representation from three to fifteen. The Social Democratic party, in contrast, reversed its steady post-1932 electoral successes, losing nineteen seats in the Lower Chamber.[2] The Communists were also making headway in grassroots union organizing. In 1945 they led a metal-workers' strike that shook both the LO and the SAP's confidence in their own leadership. In the election of 1946, Communist strength continued to grow, reaching 11.2 percent, while the SAP share of the vote declined to 44.4 percent. More important, the Communists took 32 percent of the working-class vote in Stockholm and 40 percent in Gothenburg. "Such percentages kept alive Social Democratic fears that the Communists might succeed in splitting the working class in half" (Sainsbury 1980, 116; see also Hadenius 1966; Lewin 1970).

Faced with these changing electoral conditions, the Social Democrats moved to head off the Left. The comparatively radical tax reforms they introduced must be seen in this context. It is difficult to determine whether Wigforss was personally leaning toward a more redistributive view—his public rhetoric would certainly support this notion—or whether he simply felt driven by electoral considerations to move to the left.[3] Whatever the exact explanation, the Socialists, under the personal stewardship of Finance Minister Wigforss, embraced a new tax strategy. The strategy was new not only because it was more progressive than tax policies pursued in the past fifteen years, but also because it was confrontational.[4]

In a flurry of activity during the Riksdag session of 1947, several major pieces of reform legislation were pushed through. The most consequential tax measures included the elimination of the despised sales tax, steep rises in income taxes paid by the very wealthy, and the introduction of an additional form of death taxes based on the estate tax used in Britain. In addition to these tax initiatives, a series of spending programs was introduced in this legislative session.[5]

Criticism of Wigforss for introducing these reforms dominated public debate for fully six months (Elvander 1972). But faced with the SAP majority in the Upper Chamber combined with the SAP/Communist majority in the Lower Chamber, there was little the bourgeois opposition could do. In spite of the "socialist block" majority in the Riksdag and the intense criticisms of the Socialists' rediscovered radicalism, the tax reforms were in fact quite moderate compared to those in effect in Britain and the United States at the time. We saw above that top marginal income tax rates in both the United States and United Kingdom reached the high 90th percentile by the end of the war. In Sweden, however, they never exceeded 80 percent average tax and only rarely exceeded a marginal tax rate of 80.75 percent.[6] The estate tax evoked a virulent storm of criticism, but in reality it was not as onerous as the same tax in effect in Britain and the United States at the time.[7]

The Social Democrats' relative radicalism did not last long. Soon economic problems—notably inflation—and the need to reassure voters in the
middle overshadowed the desire for more redistributive reforms. By the election of 1948, the Communists had fallen back to 6 percent of the electoral
vote. The Socialists' biggest electoral threat now came from the political
Right (Sainsbury 1980, 116–21). Harvest time was over. The tempering of the
radical ambitions did not imply a full-scale retreat from the reforms of 1947–
48, but it did mean that new policy initiatives would have to wait. It was now
time to consolidate.

Technocratic Rationalism

The politics of taxation in the 1950s and 1960s can largely be summarized
in one word: boring. This was the height of technocratic management of
the economy by officials both within and outside of the Social Democratic
party. The government expanded the traditional Swedish practice of bringing in academic and interest group technical experts to consult, and in many
cases design, government policy. At the same time, the Social Democrats
continued the wartime practice of incorporating major interest organizations
(among the most influential were the LO and the SAF) into the design and
implementation of public programs. During the war, the government created
a series of so-called crisis commissions that were intended to deal with administrative problems brought up by the wartime emergency. In most cases,
representatives from the major interest organizations were given seats on the
commissions that directly affected their interests. The most obvious effects
of this incorporation were the moderation of government policy, on the one
hand, and the commissions' remarkable ability to arrive at technical compromises that seemed to accommodate the interests of all major participants
in the policy-making process, on the other. This policy-making system had
evolved so far that by the mid-1950s it sometimes became difficult to determine exactly whether the key policy-making officials were Social Democrats
or not.[8]

For taxation policy in particular it is clear that technical experts did more
than implement policies handed down to them by their political superiors;
they were actively involved in designing the future direction and scope of the
Swedish tax system. There were, of course, some vital political battles during
these years, but taxation was generally left to the realm of the administrative
elites, who used the tax system as an instrument of macro and micro economic
policy. A comparative study of national tax systems conducted by Harvard
University provides a typical example of how international fiscal policy ex-

perts have evaluated the Swedish tax system of the late 1950s. Heralding the efficiency of the various revenue instruments in place, the Harvard report glowingly notes that Sweden had developed "an arsenal of revenue devises unmatched elsewhere in the world." [9]

Harpsund Democracy

In the early 1950s, Finance Minister Per Edvin Skjold, who served from 1949 to 1955, began a series of semisecret meetings with SAF leaders that came to be known as the Thursday club. In these meetings, government and business could frankly discuss current economic issues and usually agree on measures to deal with them. Inflation/recession were the chief economic interests of the time, and since taxes had become the major countercyclical instrument, tax policies were high on the agenda. Ultimately, the Thursday club was replaced by a somewhat more public set of meetings known as Harpsund (named after the prime minister's retreat where the meetings took place). Participants in these meetings included the ministers of Finance, Transport, Trade and Commerce, and "certain selected spokesmen for organized business and labor market organizations. . . . Once again the parties of the opposition were not included" (Michcletti 1984, 15).

During these years, a number of tax reforms were implemented. Practically every tax reform implemented during these years was technical in nature and involved little or no public controversy. Such indifference is in itself remarkable, for these same reforms would have evoked huge protests in most other countries (or even in Sweden at most other times). The reforms included changes in capital gains taxation (1951), the restructuring and dramatic liberalizing of the Investment Reserve System (1955), the introduction of a special investment tax in 1952–54 and again in 1956–57,[10] and reform of the property tax system in 1955. Even the government's decision in 1957 to abandon the estate tax, which had been so controversial when introduced only ten years earlier, was "depoliticized." Nils Elvander characterizes this reform as follows: "There was a change from ideologically motivated argumentation to a technical discussion" (Elvander 1972, 102). Finally, surplus budgets and the desire to stimulate the economy led to cuts in income tax rates in 1952 and again in 1956.

The technocratic nature of Swedish policymaking during these years did not, however, make everyone happy. Many were beginning to question the nature of a democratic political system in which many of the most difficult and controversial issues of the day were, in fact, settled behind closed doors by unelected representatives of interest organizations and technocrats. Not surprisingly, the opposition parties were the most displeased. *Dagens Nyheter,* a major news daily connected with the Folk (Liberal) party, complained about the private meetings with the following comment: "Parliament is in reality regulated to the sidelines, even if a bill in question is formally deliberated by the normal political organs . . . the new development that is taking place is that organizations and interest groups which do not have political connections with the Social Democrats are increasingly favoring direct contact with the government rather than making known their demands and wishes in public debate" (Hancock 1972, 162).

Against these criticisms, the government argued that the characterization raised by the opposition was incorrect; that the extraparliamentary meetings between the SAP and the interest organizations were not decision-making meetings but were instead simply consultative. Few people really believed them, especially after the finance minister, Gunnar Sträng, slipped up in commenting after a Harpsund meeting with insurance companies and bankers that "we had never promised so much before" (Micheletti 1984, 15).

The Social Democrats had not simply sold out. The years of cooperation and dealing with representatives of business and labor over technical issues of economic management had led both sides effectively to conclude that they did indeed have common ground. In short, *their policy preferences changed.* The Harpsund discussions later became more formalized when LO elites were included in the meetings. The socialist desire to use tax policy to socialize the economy and fundamentally redistribute wealth, for example, had been replaced by the desire to use tax policy to fine-tune and rationalize the capitalist economy, on the one hand, and to finance public programs, on the other.

Even the LO, which had consistently been more populist in its policy ambitions than the SAP elite, ultimately agreed with the new policy paradigm. Their congressional program for 1961, for example, accepted a report from their research department that discussed corporate taxation in the following terms: "The job of company taxation must first and last be to promote the long-term evolution of the economy toward higher productivity and growth. Arguments about equity and justice must come later, for example, through capital gains taxation and higher inheritance taxes on the owners of business firms" (LO Congress Program 1961, 86).

Sales Taxes Reintroduced

The single most important exception to the depoliticization of tax politics during this period was the reintroduction of a national sales tax.[11] Still, this story brilliantly illustrates both the degree to which technocrats influenced political decisions and the way in which the delicate balance of power established by Sweden's political institutions shaped strategic choices made by policy actors. At the end of World War II, one of the most significant concessions demanded by the Left generally and the LO specifically was the abolition of the sales tax. Opposition to consumption taxation had long been a symbolic position of labor in Sweden, just as it had been in the United States and Britain. But just as the government was moving to repeal the sales tax in 1948, two economists from within the LO concluded that the sales tax could be a useful tool for generating more revenues in the long run.[12]

Though skeptical at first of the reasoning behind the economists' proposal to reintroduce sales taxes, Finance Minister Sträng eventually came to see the merits of the idea. In his view, the increasing of income tax rates would alienate the middle-class voters that the party was continuing to attract, while the increasing of corporate taxes would unnecessarily anger Swedish capitalists and undermine this tax as a tool for managing the economy. To raise taxes on this sector of the economy would have been akin to killing the goose that laid the golden eggs.

Thus, by the late 1950s, Sträng came to agree with the LO economists.[13] If the government was going to finance a continued expansion of Social Democratic public programs, it would be necessary to reintroduce the bane of the LO, a national sales tax. But LO union officials, the majority of union members, and the majority of Social Democratic voters opposed the reintroduction of a sales tax. Indeed, only 34 percent of SAP voters supported the tax in polls taken in 1959 (Sarlvik 1967, 116).

It was not the Social Democrats, however, who presented the most difficult political problem for the government: whatever the Social Democratic party members' personal preferences, they would support the government in the final Riksdag vote. This was not true, however, of either the opposition bourgeois parties or the Communists. Seeing that the new tax would provide the revenues needed for the expansion of the public sector, the parties of the Right were hostile to the proposal and did not believe that the new revenues would be used to cut income taxes.[14] The Communists, for their part, opposed the new tax as regressive. They argued that the government should act on its traditional party platforms and impose steeper inheritance, wealth, profits, and income taxes.

When it finally came to the Riksdag vote, the Communists at first refused to support the measure in the lower chamber and thus provoked a governmental crisis. At this point, Prime Minister Tage Erlander made a strategic

Table 5.1

Sales Taxes, 1960–83, Sales/VAT

Percent of Purchase Price

Year	Percent	Year	Percent
1960	4.2	1972	17.65
1961	4.2	1973	17.65
1962	6.4	1974	17.65
1963	6.4	1975	17.65
1964	6.4	1976	17.65
1965	6.4	1977	17.65
1966	10.0	1978	20.63
1967	10.0	1978	20.63
1968	11.11	1980	20.63
1969	11.11	1981	23.46
1970	16.28	1982	21.51
1971	17.65	1983	23.46

Source: SAF, *Facts about Sweden's Taxes*, 1983, 10.
Note: In 1969, a "technical" reform was made replacing the sales tax with the more comprehensive VAT.

choice, believing that the Communists would prefer to abstain from the vote on the new tax rather than bring about the fall of the Socialist government. The Communist party had done terribly in the election of 1958, the total Communist vote having fallen to its lowest level in their electoral history.[15] It was thus very possible that a new election would drive the Communists from the Riksdag.

Erlander thus declared that the vote over the new sales tax was to be equivalent to a vote of confidence. The strategy worked. The Communists, fearful of the electoral backlash if they, in Erlander's words, "acted irresponsibly," decided to abstain. The new tax was thus allowed to pass into law. This was neither the first nor the last time the Communists were cajoled into accepting a proposal inimical to their philosophical position on the simple grounds that to fail to do so would likely bring about an even more terrible fate: a bourgeois government.

Those who opposed the sales tax (which was converted into a VAT in 1969) because of its potential for raising revenue were soon to have their fears borne out. Though the tax was initially set at a seemingly modest 4.2 percent, the government quickly boosted the rate (table 5.1).

Table 5.2

SAP Popular Vote Percentages in
Elections, 1940–68, and Percentage of
Seats in Each Chamber of Riksdag
Held by SAP during this Period

Year	SAP Vote Totals	SAP Seats in Upper Chamber	SAP Seats in Lower Chamber
1940	53.8	50	58.3
1944	46.7	55.3	50
1948	46.1	56	48.7
1952	46.1	52.7	47.8
1956	44.6	52.7	45.9
1958a	46.2	52.7	48.1
1960	47.8	50.1	49.1
1964	47.3	51.7	48.5
1968	50.1	52.3	53.6

Source: Sverige efter 1900 (Stockholm, 1981), tables 1a, 2c.

Reforming the Constitution

If tax policy was depoliticized in the 1950s and 1960s, it was in large part because authority for revenues (and for most policy issues) had slipped from the Riksdag to the government. "In theory the Swedish political structure still approximates to the separation of powers," wrote Douglas Verney (1957, 244), "but in practice it has leant first towards legislative supremacy and, in the last twenty years, increasingly towards a more powerful executive." Although this concentration of authority proved to be quite efficient, some began to question its representative legitimacy.

It had long been understood that the system of selecting representatives to the houses of the Riksdag discriminated against smaller parties and in favor of the larger parties. The Upper Chamber, with its system of indirect elections of one-eighth of the chamber each year, was markedly biased in favor of the SAP. This bias can be seen simply by comparing the SAP mandates in the first and second chambers. In the lower, directly elected chamber, the SAP held a 50 percent majority only twice from 1932 to 1968. In the first chamber, by contrast, the Socialists held a majority in every year after 1940 (table 5.2).

The process for selecting members of the Upper Chamber also contributed mightily to the stability of Swedish electoral politics.[16] Because of the virtually perpetual SAP majority in the Upper Chamber, the government could always count on legislative victory in at least one house of the Riksdag and could predominate in the joint legislative sessions. Swedish governments, then, never found themselves in the situation familiar to American presidents, in which after a long, hard-fought battle in the House, a proposal could be totally changed or even tabled by the Senate (or vice versa).[17]

Questions about the legitimacy of this system were voiced throughout the 1950s and 1960s. As we saw in chapter 3, the Riksdag had, early in this century, fought for and apparently won the principle of parliamentarism and the right to exercise power over the government. Now, in midcentury, this principle was waning as the Riksdag's influence seemed to be ebbing. As a result, the pressure for reform intensified in the 1960s, with the Liberal party leader Bertil Ohlin leading the charge. Ohlin claimed that citizens should have the right to "determine the composition of the Riksdag and the government of the country in one and the same election" (Stjernquist 1987, 238). Their central demand, in short, was either democratize the Upper Chamber or abolish it.

Eventually the SAP, spurred on by losses in the local elections of 1966, agreed to a revamping of the Swedish constitutional structure. A new Commission on the Fundamental Laws was formed, and in 1967 it recommended abandoning the indirectly elected Upper Chamber. Erlander, the Social Democratic leader and prime minister, decided to go along with these proposals and introduced the requisite legislation to the Riksdag in 1968 and again (after the 1968 election) in 1969.[18]

The Social Democrats did not want this change but felt they had no electoral alternative. First the Liberals, then the Moderates, then the Center, and finally the Communists in 1964–65 attacked the SAP for clinging to the old electoral system. The election of 1966 went badly for the SAP, in part as a consequence of their intransigence over the constitutional issue (Von Sydow 1989). Thus a standoff developed between the four opposition parties and the SAP. The opposition parties dominated the lower chamber, and the SAP held a majority in the Upper Chamber. According to Björn von Sydow, "The Social Democrats were forced to leave a Constitution which they understood better suited their interests." He explains: "Had the 1966 election gone better for the SAP there would still have been a Constitutional reform, but it would have favored the SAP more than this one did. . . . So, the Social Democrats acted rationally. The Constitutional reform can be explained by the immediate self-interest of the parties." [19] In short, the Social Democrats accepted constitutional reform knowing that it would make their position in government more difficult to maintain, but without fully recognizing its longer term implications.

The impact of this modernization of the constitution has been both subtle and profound. The most obvious effect, of course, was to allow the non-socialist parties to form a government in 1976, when they increased their share of the vote to 50.8 percent of the electorate. This was not the first time that the bourgeois parties had received a majority of popular votes—but it was the first time that this popular majority could be directly translated into a new bourgeois majority in the Riksdag (180 out of 349 seats).

The long-term impacts of these constitutional changes have been less obvious but far more significant than the bourgeois victory in 1976. First, the constitutional change eventually evoked a change in the political strategies of all political parties. Before, the SAP hold on the government was widely seen as unshakable;[20] now the party was decisively more vulnerable to shifts in electoral support. On many occasions in the past, the bourgeois parties had concluded that they could get more by cooperating with the Socialists than by fighting them. Now the calculation had changed. If the parties of the right could actually reach and hold the reins of government, it made sense for them to pursue their policies aggressively.

Second, the constitutional changes evoked changes in the political strategies of organized interests in Sweden. Before 1970, strong interest organizations were built up and balanced by strong government. After 1970, the government was weakened, but the interest organizations remained strong. The effect of this imbalance was a massive expansion of spending by the state. The government no longer had the institutional power to withstand the pressure for more health spending, welfare spending, educational spending, industrial subsidies, and so on. In the new institutional context, the government (no less the bourgeois government of 1976–81 than the socialist) was unable to hold back demands for greater spending and had no alternative but to increase taxes.

The Social Democrats had, of course, also instituted a tax system with massive revenue potential. Taken together, these two factors go a long way toward explaining why Sweden moved from being a country whose citizens carried an average tax burden (as a percent of GDP) to being the most heavily taxed nation in the world (fig. 5.1).

The End of Social Democratic Hegemony?

By the mid-1970s, the cooperative relations among labor, business, and the state were tightly strained. There was still a large measure of contact among

Figure 5.1 Total Tax Revenue as a Percentage of GDP,
Sweden and OECD Average, 1955–89

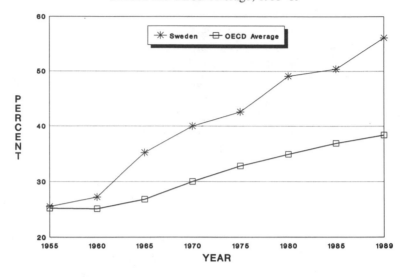

elites and experts, but their position had weakened in the face of broadening ideological strife. The LO became more active in demanding specific public policies from the government—most important, the wage earner funds—and the SAF also took a more activist partisan position (Åsard 1978; Pontusson 1992). Olof Ruin (1981, 149–50) described what he saw happening in Swedish politics with great uneasiness: "At the parliamentary level the most important development in the 1970s, parallel to the new constitution, was the weakening of the executive. . . . Strong government is taken to mean an ability to take unpopular decisions, an ability to distance itself from special interests, and an ability to formulate long term plans." He goes on to argue, "Swedish parliamentarism, during the past decade, showed itself to be significantly less successful in providing strong government in at least two important dimensions; majoritarian government, and a degree of cohesiveness and integration in the policy field. This adverse development coincided with the country's difficult economic problems. In addition . . . bureaucracy continued to expand and special interests strengthened their role in the policy process."

The consequence of these changes was that by the mid-1970s, Swedish politics became more confrontational and compromise more difficult. There continued to be contact between the elites of the government and those of the major interest organizations, yet the climate of Swedish politics was changing. Having lost the Upper Chamber, the government saw its power vis-à-vis both the Parliament and interest groups begin to wane. Indeed, the very character of Swedish democracy was undergoing a transformation. In December 1970, several prominent conservative newspapers carried the following banner headline: GOVERNMENT CAN BE FORCED OUT BY THE MAJORITY (Malmström 1970). One wonders what British citizens would have thought if the *London Times* had published this headline. Certainly they would have been puzzled—obviously, the majority can force the government out; that is how a democracy works.

It was not long before these predictions came true. In 1976, the Socialists were forced to give up their control of government after forty-four years of continuous rule.[21] The bourgeois coalition government promised a new beginning, and, of course, all three parties agreed that taxes and spending should be reduced; but whose taxes and whose spending was quite another matter.[22]

Essentially, now that they were in government instead of being in the opposition, the three parties could not agree on what to do. As any British ex–cabinet minister can testify, it is easier to complain that the current government is doing everything wrong than it is to act out policies that are all right. During the bourgeois parties' six-year tenure, Sweden's economic situation also deteriorated. This basic economic fact, which was only in part a consequence of the government's economic leadership, complicated the task of governing.[23]

Though all three parties had made the reduction of income taxes a critical theme in their attacks against the Socialists over the preceding two decades, it was not until 1979 that reductions were actually legislated, and even then, marginal tax rates were reduced only from 1 to 7.1 percent, depending on the income bracket. Differences in interests (farmers and environmentalists versus small business, middle classes versus big business) and strategic electoral positioning by the three parties inhibited their ability to work out acceptable compromises.[24] Unable to strike general compromises, Swedish tax policymakers began to act more like their American counterparts. Dozens of new tax expenditures were opened up for, among others, farmers, small businessmen, and the self-employed. Social security taxes were reduced by 1 percent, but the VAT had to be increased by 3 percent. Public expenditures rose at roughly the same rate during the new government's tenure as they had during the previous five years—in other words, very rapidly. By 1982, the annual deficit had reached 13 percent of GNP![25]

In short, by the early 1980s the dynamics of Swedish politics had undergone astonishing changes. These new politics reflected both changes in Sweden's economic position (I shall examine the changing international economy in the next chapter) and reforms in Sweden's domestic political institutions. The worsening economy not only made political decisions more difficult to reach, but created a climate in which it made political sense for political parties and interest groups to be obstructionist—even when they were part of the ruling coalition. In Hadenius's (1981, 199) words, "The parties were not only fighting against the common enemy (social democracy); they competed also among themselves. None of them had anything against taking votes and mandates away from the others." Since they were jockeying to be in the public eye as well as for policy positions, voting against a compromise decision and maintaining the status quo was often strategically more appealing than supporting another party's initiative.

By the end of the 1970s, criticism of the Swedish tax burden reached crisis proportions. Swedes were not only increasingly upset about the by-now internationally infamous tax loads, but also more and more aware of inequities developing in the system. The intellectual and administrative elites had also become critical of the Swedish system. Within a remarkably short period of time, Sweden had changed from being the star of the fiscal policy world to the international pariah. Whereas in the 1950s and 1960s tax policy experts from around the world went to Sweden to study its excellence, by the late 1970s Swedish experts were traveling around the world decrying its excesses.

To sum up, the wartime crisis institutionalized a set of formal arrangements between the government and the major interest organizations in Sweden, and these arrangements developed in the postwar years to become an efficient extraparliamentary policy-making system. The gears of this system were oiled by the fantastic revenue growth provided by taxes passed during the war. Until the 1970s, the system was managed by a technical and administrative elite of representatives from both the state and interest organizations. Sweden provides the clearest case of the development of a successful postwar compromise.

But the success of Sweden's postwar compromise was possible only because of a particular distribution of power between the government and the Parliament. The government could not dictate to the Parliament its preferences without finding coalition partners and striking bargains with (and perhaps coopting) interests outside the government; at the same time, the government was a hostage neither to these interests nor to the Parliament itself. The Social Democrats could dominate Swedish politics but not always predominate. Following the constitutional reform of the early 1970s, this balance of power changed. Parliamentarism shot down the Swedish model. With it, the political harmony and policy efficiency for which Sweden had become so famous was critically wounded.

Minority governments do not always lead to compromise and consensus building. Neither do Swedish political elites compromise simply because they are culturally predisposed to consensus politics: they compromise when it is in their strategic advantage to do so. The Swedish model depended upon a particular economic and institutional context. By the early 1980s this context had changed.

The United States

The fragmentation of political authority in the United States has shaped America's tax policy development. President after president has attempted to reform the tax system by eliminating loopholes, broadening the tax base, and introducing national consumption taxes, yet their efforts have repeatedly been rejected by Congress. During World War II, however, the centralizing forces of wartime emergency in some ways countered the decentralizing tendencies built into American political institutions.[26] In the United States, as in Europe, a form of compromise emerged. The end of the war presented an opportunity to institutionalize compromise. The challenges of managing a complex economy, combined with incredible revenue growth provided by the mass taxes imposed in the 1930s and 1940s, might have overwhelmed the fragmented nature of political power in the United States. The following discussion shows why this did not happen.

Rather than a continuation of the trend toward centralized power in the United States, the postwar decades witnessed two separate sets of institutional reforms that reinforced and indeed exacerbated the institutional antagonisms between the legislature and the executive. During both of these periods of reform, first in the late 1940s and then in the 1970s, Congress reasserted the authority of congressional committees to act as decision-making units. Unfortunately, these reforms also undercut the strength of the party leadership and thus further decentralized power *within* Congress. As a result, the United States developed the most potent and least disciplined legislature in the democratic world. This double fragmentation of political authority dramatically shaped the politics of taxation in the United States in the postwar years (Dodd and Schott 1979, 86–92).[27]

At the same time that Congress attempted to wrest power from the president the national government was taking on new responsibilities. In both the United States and Europe, state revenues and responsibilities grew immensely during the war. The role of taxation and the responsibility of tax policy committees grew correspondingly.[28] As Stein (1969, 194) points out, "The developments of the war, the opportunity provided to reflect on the experience of the 1930s, and the further digestion of Keynes led to a convergence of thinking on two points. The first was that the government must take responsibility for the maintenance of full employment, however defined—or, more commonly, not defined. The second was that active fiscal policy must be a major instrument, perhaps the major instrument, for discharging that responsibility."

Fiscal policy, moreover, meant tax policy. "The chief policy implication of the progress of fiscal theory during the war years was to focus economists' attention more on taxation as a variable instrument of fiscal policy" (Stein 1969, 181). Stabilizing the economy and maintaining full employment meant adjusting the tax system not to fiscal requirements but to the demands of full employment. In short, postwar attitudes toward tax and fiscal policy in the United States were similar to those in Sweden. The government had taken on new responsibilities for economic management, and tax policy was seen as a major instrument to discharge these responsibilities.

In the United States, the question of who exactly should have responsibility for these new tasks was far from settled. The history of postwar tax policy can be understood only through an appreciation of the indeterminacy of this issue. The Reorganization Act of 1946, for example, "did little to resolve the fundamental problems of Congress. In their attempt to protect fundamental personal prerogatives, members of Congress failed to take the really difficult steps that might have helped resolve structural problems within Congress. They left party leadership as weak after the act as before, ensuring that central party leaders would offer no threat to committee autonomy; congressional leadership and accountability remained weak" (Dodd 1977, 286).

Postwar Tax Policy

Immediately following the war, there was widespread agreement that tax rates should be reduced: the first postwar budget, which eliminated the excess profits tax, reduced excise taxes, and cut personal income taxes, was passed with little controversy. Within a year, however, the apparent consensus over tax policy evaporated. There was no fundamental conflict over the aims of tax policy or over the long-term goal of reducing the overall tax burden on society. Congress and the executive fundamentally accepted the notion that taxation should be a major instrument for managing the economy, and both agreed that tax burdens should be lowered. But questions remained. First, who should benefit the most from tax reductions? Second, how and when should taxation be used as an instrument of social and economic policy?

A major battle over tax policy erupted within months of the end of the war. The Republicans had made tax cuts a major platform of their electoral strategy for 1946 and with this banner won a massive electoral victory and finally retook control of the Congress. President Harry Truman remained intransigent, however. He felt that the nation's best interests would be served by maintaining high tax rates in order to restrain demand and balance the budget. He also believed that tax cuts should be focused on society's less well-off rather than on the wealthy. Unwilling to yield on the tax issue, President Truman vetoed three successive tax cut bills before he was finally overridden in 1947. Though the veto override was an important and frustrating defeat for the president, his opposition to the tax cut did have an effect on the final bill passed. Although the Republicans had an impressive 246 versus 188 majority in the House, their 51 to 45 lead in the Senate ensured that the president could maintain his veto unless the Republicans persuaded a sizable number of Democrats to support the tax cut. To gain this support, Republicans broadened each subsequent version of the tax cut bill so that more groups would receive tax benefits— ultimately including the lower and middle classes as well as the rich.[29]

The "standard view of economists was that the tax bill was a mistake" (Stein 1969, 217), but the Republicans argued that the bill was necessary to stimulate the economy in the face of the oncoming recession. It was not known whom these politicians had consulted; as A. E. Holmans later noted, "At the time nobody who analyzed the situation in terms of compensatory fiscal policy had a good word to say about it."[30] According to Stein (1969, 219), "An objective view in 1948 would probably have been that the Republicans were being politically astute in pushing the tax cut, but economically irresponsible. . . . For example, before voting in favor of the tax cut Senator Morse delivered a long speech explaining that he felt obliged to represent his constituents' desires in this matter, even though he doubted their wisdom."

The same pattern was repeated over most of the next four decades: When new tax legislation was desired, whether by the president or the congressional leadership, the Republicans or the Democrats, tax benefits had to be yielded *to both sides* if the tax legislation was to have a chance of getting through the system of checks and balances. In this institutional context, opposing sides could stymie each other's first preferences—whether tax cuts for the poor or rate cuts for the wealthy—and force them into choosing compromise policies. This general rule has prevailed even when the president and the majority in Congress were of the same party, as was the case in 1949–51, 1953–55, and 1961–69. No one has been able to pass tax legislation without literally buying off opposition from representatives interested in protecting their constituents.

The result of this political stalemate has been that the politics of taxation has degenerated into the micro politics of special interest wrangling. John Witte (1985, 142) describes the Revenue Act of 1951 as follows: "A veritable landslide of special provisions were enacted aiding a wide range of groups.

Foreshadowing a pattern that would emerge in all subsequent revenue bills, tax increases in one form were compensated for by conferring tax benefits in another" (see also Manley 1970, 338).

Even after the Republican president Dwight Eisenhower was elected and his party controlled both the House and the Senate, Republicans were unable to pass broad tax rate cuts as they had promised voters they would. They were instead forced to choose tax cuts by way of exception, special rule, and individual allowance.[31] The Republicans, too, fundamentally accepted the role of the federal government in the modern economy and understood that the modern tax system must reflect this reality. Witte (1985, 149) sums up the politics of taxation in the 1950s as follows:

> The U.S. economy had become much more complex by the 1950s, and the rudimentary laws of the early income tax were no longer sufficient. To match this complexity, the code needed to distinguish between corporations with income earned abroad, partnerships, holding companies, closely held corporations, and a wide variety of tax-exempt organizations. Complex organizations lead to complex sources and flows of income and costs, which in turn lead to demands for different treatment. Although one interpretation of this situation is that each type of group and organization uses arguments about differential status solely to gain exclusive benefits, another is that such laws are simply based on honest efforts to treat different cases fairly relative to others. Either way, the result is bound to be a long and complex tax code.

Tax Expenditures

Sweden, as noted above, had also introduced tax expenditures intended to effect certain social and economic outcomes during this period. There were, however, crucial differences between the kinds of special amendments implemented in the American and Swedish tax systems at this time. The differences were largely a result of the respective processes by which these rules were passed. In Sweden, the tax rules attempted either to regulate the timing of investment decisions or to encourage investment in capital intensive industry and machinery. These general measures were instigated through careful and steady cooperation with industry and labor associations and were explicit attempts to ensure both stable employment and stable profits for large, successful companies. They were not, however, detailed attempts to micromanage the economy via special measures to certain industries or companies.

The American tax rules were quite different. Rather than set general rules regulating the timing or general character of investment in the economy, Congress preferred to write tax laws *benefiting* particular industries and corporations. Often, these tax laws failed even to define how or under what conditions these tax expenditures might be used. Far from being regulations for industry, they were political plums. While tax policy experts around the world were lauding Sweden's efficient use of investment taxes and incentives as tools of economic management, the following comment, published in 1951 in the *National Tax Journal,* summarizes economic analyses of U.S. profits tax policy at the time: "The Excess Profits Tax Act of 1950 is not a very good law. . . . The rate structure reflects too many points of evidence of the haste with which it was drafted, and of the compromises which had to be made if any bill was to be brought out within the time limits" (Keith 1951, 206).[32]

The fact that tax expenditure policy has been used more as a political plum than as an effective instrument of economic management in the United States does not imply (a) that tax measures were not justified as being necessary for economic growth or productivity or (b) that the United States did not try to regulate the economy through tax or fiscal policy. In fact, taxes have been fundamental elements of economic management both at the micro and macro level in the United States; the critical difference between the American and Swedish experience has been that the incentive structure facing tax policy decisionmaking in Congress demands that members be attentive to their constituents' interests. This means that Congress writes tax law that pleases particular constituents even if it has weak general economic policy implications.

Absent the requirement that tax expenditures be justified by compelling economic arguments, the demand for equity became a vital force shaping tax expenditure policy. When one group or interest is offered a tax break, other groups can and do make the claim that it would be unfair if they did not get the same treatment. Stern provides the following example to illustrate the process of tax expenditure policy in the United States: During World War II, special oil depletion allowances were given to encourage oil and gas exploration and development; soon other mining interests demanded similar treatment. Before the war was over, a long list of mining interests and oil product interests had gotten in on the oil and gas depletion allowance bonanza. Even asphalt was given special tax treatment. In 1951, the National Sand and Gravel Association used the tax expenditure for asphalt to propose their own tax break. They argued that "it seems unreasonable discrimination against our industry to continue to be denied the benefit of a taxation policy already extended to other members of the non-metallic minerals family" (Stern 1973, 297). Congress agreed. This brought on cries of unfair from the oyster and clam shell industry, and so they too were given a special depletion allowance. By 1954 the list of material extraction industries receiving special allowances became so long that Congress decided to "clean up" the code and specify what *was not* given special depletion allowances.[33]

Subcommittee Government

The congressional reforms of the late 1940s did reassert Congress's autonomy from the executive branch, but they did not turn Congress into an efficient decision-making institution. Indeed, as Lawrence Dodd and Richard Schott (1979, 92) point out, the reforms of 1946 "contributed to the *isolation* of most members from congressional power. In streamlining the committee system, the 1946 Act left a relatively small number of positions that carried with them real power and status." The revenue committees were the prime examples. Given the importance of revenue to the state, it made good sense to insulate these committees from normal politics. But this organizational solution created its own problems. These committees—conspicuously the Ways and Means Committee under Wilbur Mills—became too powerful. Not only were they largely impervious to the influence, leadership, and authority of the president, they also developed autonomy from (and ultimately power over) Congress itself (Fenno 1966; Manley 1970; Strahan 1986; Rudder 1977).

By the mid-1970s the problems with this organizational structure became obvious. On the one hand, committee chairmen, all too secure in their positions, often used their positions of authority to bottle up legislation that was favored by the majority in Congress and often by the president as well. The revenue committees were notorious sinners in this regard. On the other hand, as the power of the committee chairman grew, the ability of junior members to effectively develop policy-making authority with which to provide benefits to their constituents shrunk. Again, the revenue committees were seen as the greatest problems.[34] The Ways and Means Committee was "a 'bastille' that symbolized the inequities of the old order" (quoted in Strahan 1986, 5).

These strains combined to build momentum for another major reform era in the U.S. Congress. In the 1970s, reforms that reorganized congressional decisionmaking were aimed at Chairman Mills of Ways and Means (Strahan 1986). Three essential changes in congressional rules were directed at his committee. First, all committee markups were henceforth to be held in public, unless a majority of the committee agreed to a closed session. Second, the Democratic Steering and Policy Committee was given authority to individually appoint chairmen to committees, rather than simply follow the seniority rule. Finally, the closed rule was altered so that it would be easier to offer amendments to Ways and Means bills on the floor of the House.

The explicit intent of these measures was both to unseat Wilbur Mills and to democratize the revenue process (Rudder 1977, 118–30). The effect of these rule changes, however, was to break open the tax policy-making system and undermine the already weak forces of restraint. One reason Mills had been accused of being autocratic and unresponsive was precisely that he did not give in to every request from House members for special tax amendments to favored constituents. To be sure, over the years hundreds of special amendments had been introduced, but many more were rejected. This made the inequities of the system even more difficult for junior members to accept. Only those who had Mills's confidence were able to get tax breaks for their supporters. This cronyism was patently unfair.

Unfortunately for the coherence of the American tax code, the legislature's answer to the cronyism of revenue politics was to distribute responsibility for taxation ever more widely. This made an already overly open process even more open and made an already porous system even more loophole-ridden. In the context of the continuing institutional conflict between the legislative and executive branches of government, especially in the Watergate era, Congress had no incentive to yield tax-writing power to the executive branch. Thus, the option of shifting responsibility for tax policy management to the executive, as was done in Sweden in the 1950s and 1960s, was scarcely considered in the United States.

The strategy of centralizing power within Congress in the hands of the congressional leadership—a strategy obviously favored by the leaders themselves—had to be "purchased" from the lower-ranking members. Congressional reforms thus went in opposing directions. On the one hand, the Democratic Party Steering Committee was given new powers, most important, the authority to select and in effect fire committee chairmen. On the other hand, junior members of Congress were given more influence as well. In exchange for their support of the Bolling Committee's attempts to centralize power in Congress and make it a more effective instrument in its dealings with the president, Congress also passed the Sub-Committee Bill of Rights. This set of reforms *de*centralized policy-making authority, dividing it among the hundreds of subcommittees that had proliferated since the reorganization in 1946. The bill allowed each member of Congress to be a subcommittee chairman and gave these chairmen substantive legislative powers. With the enactment of this reform, virtually every member of Congress would have the might to bring home benefits to constituents.

These two conflicting reforms, then, gave even junior members power over policy in Congress (power they could use to logroll even senior members) *and* stripped the Ways and Means Committee of its ability to stand somewhat above the particularistic needs of individual members. The effects of these two reforms on the American tax system were disastrous.

Loophole Madness

By the end of the decade the scrambling for special tax breaks for ever-smaller groups had reached absurd proportions. Thomas Reese (1980, 163) provides an example of the "tax politics as usual" of this era, reciting an exchange between Senator Gaylord Nelson (D. Wisc.) and Finance Chairman Russell Long (D. La.): " 'I understand,' said Nelson, 'that in my absence we passed the tax breaks for railroads, but omitted railroad-overwater ferries—such as the one in Wisconsin.' 'I'll be happy to give you that one without need for further discussion,' replied Long, 'but I expect you in exchange to vote for this next tax credit we're about to discuss.' " [35] Table 5.3 shows the total revenue loss from tax expenditures between 1973 and 1986. Keep in mind that the vast majority of tax expenditures in the American tax code are focused quite narrowly and therefore do not individually cost great sums of money.

There were, of course, many attempts at reform. Tax expenditures were by now a major contributor to the continuing and growing budget deficits, and they also inspired numerous attacks on Congress over its basic ability to govern. But until the mid-1980s, these efforts at reform failed miserably. In 1978, for example, President Jimmy Carter introduced a major tax reform bill based on *Blue Prints for Tax Reform,* the comprehensive review of the system conducted under the Gerald Ford administration. Even with the strong support of the chairman of the Senate Budget Committee, Edmund Muskie, and a media campaign, tax reform was a dead letter. As the bill worked its way from Ways and Means to House floor to the Finance Committee to the Senate floor and finally to the Conference Committee, it "abandon[ed] any pretense of tax reform." Indeed, "the final Conference bill was a complete renunciation of the Carter tax proposals and any notion of tax reform" (Witte 1985, 209, 213).

Faced with a growing fiscal crisis, the new chairman of the Ways and Means Committee, Al Ullman, took a different tack and introduced a proposal for a new VAT. Ullman and Finance Chair Long agreed about the need for revenue and also agreed that, given the deepening fragmentation of authority in Congress, neither income nor profits was likely to generate enough revenues in the foreseeable future.

Table 5.3

Revenue Losses from Tax Expenditures, 1973–86

	1973	1979	1981	1983	1986
Tax expenditure totals ($ millions)	65,370	149,815	228,620	253,500	424,700
Percentage of GNP	4.7	6.4	8.0	8.4	10.0
Percentage of federal outlays	24.3	30.3	34.6	34.6	42.9
Percentage of federal revenues	24.7	32.3	37.9	40.8	55.3
Percentage of income tax receipts	40.7	54.7	65.9	73.5	103.0

Source: Calculated from CBO, *Tax Expenditures: Current Issues and Five-Year Budget Projections for Fiscal Years 1983–1987*, Nov. 1982, table 3; CBO, *The Economic and Budget Outlook: an Update*, Nov. 1986, tables, I-3, II-3, II-8; and Witte 1985, table 13.4

The revenue committee chairmen, moreover, were acutely aware of the need for revenue leadership and of Carter's inability to provide that leadership. "I see my role as altogether different than chairmen used to see theirs," said Ullman in an interview in 1978. "They were worried about image and not losing any bills and not bringing a bill to the floor unless they had all the votes in their pockets. You can't operate that way anymore. I see my role as one of leadership and trying to expand the thinking of Congress in new directions in order to meet the long-term needs of the country" (Strahan 1986, 11).

In October 1979, Ullman introduced the Tax Restructuring Act of 1979, which would institute a 10 percent federal VAT to raise $130 billion a year and cut income and social security taxes by an equal amount. Trying to distinguish the VAT from the increasingly discredited income tax, he introduced his bill by saying, "The VAT in my bill is virtually a tax without loopholes." [36] But the reaction on Capitol Hill quickly grew negative. In a now-familiar litany of complaints against national consumption taxes in the United States, the bill was denounced as too regressive, too complicated, and ultimately too much of a revenue producer. The proposal appeared to have no chance of passing.

Ullman reintroduced the VAT the next year, in 1980, but that bill also went nowhere. It did, however, teach Ullman and his congressional colleagues a lesson about attempting to provide leadership on tax matters. Though Al Ullman was noted as having one of the safest seats in Congress when he took the chairmanship of Ways and Means, he was unseated in his reelection campaign of 1980, and his VAT proposal was a decisive factor in that defeat. Ullman was caught on the wrong side of the Reagan landslide, but the pundits assumed that his position as chairman of Ways and Means would protect him. The predictions were wrong. Ullman stuck his neck out on the tax issue and had his head chopped off. Some years later, a Republican member of the Ways and Means committee confided that he genuinely felt that a VAT is the only possible alternative to solving the United States' fiscal deficit. When asked why he would not say this publicly, he responded, "Are you kidding? Nobody wants to get the Al Ullman syndrome."

The difficulty with the American tax system by the 1970s was not that policymakers were unaware of the problems tax expenditure policies create for the tax system. Rather, the electoral incentive presented to members of Congress encourages them to look to and act on the short-term interests of their constituencies, even when this compromises the longer term interests of the nation (Fiorina 1977; Mayhew 1974). Dodd (1977, 281) describes the dilemma faced by members of Congress:

> Members of Congress thus are not only faced with the daily dilemma of balancing reelection interests with their efforts at upward power and mobility within Congress; their lives are also complicated by a cruel paradox, the ultimate incompatibility of widely dispersed power within Congress, on the one hand, and a strong role for Congress in national decision making, on the other. This inherent tension generates an explosive dynamic within Congress as an organization and between Congress and the executive.

This paradox has made the American tax code by far the most complicated and particularistic in the world. These problems accelerated in the early 1980s, until, in mid-decade, Congress passed the historic tax reform of 1986. This act addressed some of the most egregious abuses built into the federal tax code; but as I shall show in chapter 6, it scarcely made the tax system fair, simple, and efficient, as the reformers had promised it would.

Great Britain

Two competing models have purported to characterize postwar British politics. The first focuses on the consensus and compromise developed in the 1950s and 1960s and argues that during these years Britain built on its "collectivist" traditions (Beer 1969), pursued "Butskellist" policies,[37] and even developed a version of corporatism that, in principle at least, was similar to that developed in Sweden (Middlemas 1979; Panitch 1979). The second model postulates that postwar British politics are distinguished by and best explained by its adversarial traditions and practices (Finer 1975). Each of these apparently contradictory models contributes essential insights. When seen in the context of the threat of class warfare that hung over Britain before World

War II, and when compared to the electoral promises made by each party when it was out of office, postwar British tax and spending policies have been remarkably moderate. The parties, whatever their rhetoric, have in fact agreed on the basic foundations of a modern capitalist welfare state. British parties have been more bark than bite. On the other hand, if one compares British postwar politics and policies to, say, those of the Swedish over the same period, one is struck by the level of acrimony in British political debate and by the incredible *in*stability of British tax and spending policy. In comparison with many other countries during this era, British politics were indeed adversarial.

To resolve the apparent paradox, one must understand the different comparative referents behind the two characterizations. One needs to appreciate both the broader historical context in which British politics are situated as well as the ways in which national political institutions have shaped political choices and public policies. The following discussion draws attention to both comparisons. The British version of the postwar compromise provides sharp illustration of how the shape and form of the basic historical context have been structured by the political institutions through which this compromise must pass.

Institutional Context

Joseph Pechman, senior economist, the Brookings Institution: "Why are your tax bills less complicated than ours? Ours are over a thousand pages long!"
Ian Byatt, deputy chief economic advisor, Her Majesty's Treasury: "We are bullying Parliament." [38]

In Sweden and the United States, national political institutions were adapted and changed during the postwar era, and in both countries these reforms reflected an ongoing struggle between the legislature and the executive. Although the British Parliament too attempted to assert its authority over legislative decisions in the 1970s, its efforts were for the most part unsuccessful. The explanation for the failure of decentralizing institutional reforms in Britain is twofold. First, power in Britain is substantially more centralized than in either Sweden or the United States. The institutional reforms instigated in Sweden and the United States were possible because the vulnerability of the executive gave the legislatures the political strength to assert themselves. The constitutional separation of powers in the United States and the virtually perpetual minority/coalition status of Swedish governments yield

the respective legislatures resources in their relations with their executive administrations. In British party government, the legislature possesses neither
of these institutional resources.

The second reason for the distinctive pattern of institutional reform in Britain is also rooted in its peculiar democratic institutions. Precisely because the
government is so powerful, the objective of reformers—especially during the
economic crises and social/political malaise of the 1970s—was to seize the
reins of government, not to disable the current system.

The very institutions that had facilitated compromise were under attack
in Sweden and in the United States in the 1970s. Britain, however, with its
decisive electoral system, had neither "incorporated" those with the most
power nor insulated them from popular control. Thus the attention of reformers was not on institutional reform, but on winning the next election and *using*
the considerable strength of the government. To be sure, each party when in
opposition declares its intention to decentralize political power and authority
after it wins the next election. While in office, however, these same elites have
few incentives to keep their promises.

Party Government and Tax Policy

The exclusive, centralized, alternating nature of British party government
adversely affected the stability and efficiency of revenue sources during the
postwar period. At the same time, however, the forces of political and economic reality moderated the adversarial nature of British party government.
The basic story line is repeated over and over: New governments enter office
with a massive reform agenda, but they are soon buffeted by economic reality
and ultimately retreat from the full implementation of their agenda. The opposition makes political capital of the fiscal incompetence of the government
and promises to redress the wrongs imposed by the current authorities. When
they gain power, they simply repeat the process. As in Sweden and the United
States, taxation has been used as a major tool of economic management in
postwar Britain, with less than stellar results. At the macro level, deflations
are invariably too small and too late, and inflation is too long and too strong
(Pollard 1983, 393; Hansen 1969). Balance, then, becomes the major pri-
ority of each government after it has been in office a few months—failure
to achieve balance becomes ever-more capital for the opposition. Successive
governments have also used tax policy as an instrument of micro economic
management. Here, too, the record has been mixed. British governments have
not engaged in the tax policy favoritism so often seen in the United States;
they have instead favored broader, more general tax incentives, such as those

found in Sweden. But whereas Swedish tax incentives have been both technically sophisticated and quite stable (at least until the mid-1970s), the British measures have been phenomenally unstable and often—in part because they have been changed so often—technically sloppy.

Finally, Britain has not had the luxury of a quickly expanding economic pie. Anthony Crosland (1974, 26) notes, "Under conditions of slow growth, efforts to achieve transfers inevitably provoke inflation. For since they cannot come from the fruits of rapid growth, they must come from higher taxation of existing incomes. But higher indirect taxes put up prices; higher direct taxes provoke compensating claims for higher money wages and salaries."

Governments of whichever ideological orientation attempt to adjust their fiscal policies to this reality. Labour governments are soon attacked for making another U-turn and for abandoning the redistributive goals with which they were elected. Tory governments are similarly squeezed between these hard facts. Soon after being elected, they are invariably attacked for failing to do what they say only they can do—effectively manage the economy (Gamble and Walkland 1984, 12). And so the Ping-Pong ball of British party government bounces back and forth.

Harvest Time in Britain?

The Labour government of 1945–51 provides an excellent illustration of the workings of British party government on taxation policy. In the election of 1945, Labour won a resounding electoral victory over both the Tories and the Liberal party, capturing 393 of Parliament's 640 seats. This gave them unmistakable political authority to act on both their ideological beliefs and their party platforms. But here was the rub: by the end of their six years in office fundamental conflicts over the very aims of the so-called socialist Labour party had manifested themselves within the party. On the one hand, the party was eager to take on the challenges of the postwar world and work toward the "Socialist Commonwealth of Great Britain" (Beer 1982, 6). On the other hand, the party elite, at least, had become committed to the basic framework of operating within capitalism. The political and economic realities of governing in a capitalist society, they soon came to understand, prevented them from acting on many of the promises and goals both implicit and explicit in the party program.

The Labour manifesto *Let us Face the Future* (1945) committed the new government to lower taxation on the poor, heavy taxes on the rich, and an expansion of social services. The first Labour chancellor of the exchequer, Hugh Dalton, supported this view. "One of our great achievements on the home front during the war, with the aid of a series of war budgets, has been a notable advance towards economic and social equality," he argued in 1945. "Everybody recognized that in war time this was right. If it was right for war time, it is not wrong for peace." The first postwar budget, then, lowered taxes paid by the working classes while maintaining and in some cases raising them for the rich.[39] The opposition was, of course, livid.[40]

The intensity of argument from the opposite side of the House, however, had little influence over the tax policies pursued by the chancellor. But neither Dalton nor his tax policies would last long.[41] In order to maintain full employment, Dalton had also been pursuing a so-called cheap money policy, which contributed to a steepening inflation rate. At the same time, in no small part because of the government's fiscal policies, capital was flowing out of Britain while imported goods were flowing in. The balance of payments crisis soon became acute and the need for deflationary policies obvious. British fiscal policy was about to take its first postwar U-turn.

The problems in the economy brought concerns that if something were not done to reassure both voters and investors, Labour would lose the next election. Rather than continue to extend the tax system's progressivity, as the Left demanded, the government began leaning toward "the Treasury view" in 1947. Treasury officials persistently argued that Dalton's tax cuts were inflationary and that the tax increases on the wealthy undermined investor confidence. As the economy worsened, these views became more credible. In 1947, Dalton was compelled to freeze the promised reductions of the standard and reduced rates of income tax, although some allowances were augmented to help the very poorest.

Having accepted the need for some deflation, the government soon came to accept the idea that their tax measures had been too small. To mollify the Labour Left and the unions, a capital levy on investment income was imposed. If the poor could not be made better off, perhaps the rich could be made worse off.[42]

Though full employment had been maintained, the British economy continued to be in rather poor shape. The government's tax and spending policies had alienated and frightened capitalists, and investment remained far too low. Indeed, it was only direct aid from the United States that averted a full-scale economic crisis (Pollard 1983, 233–45). Thus the Labour government now felt compelled to stimulate investment in Britain. They therefore concluded that they had to change course and attempt to encourage investors, rather than threaten them. Unsurprisingly, tax incentives were seen as the best means to achieve this new goal: industrial investment allowances were expanded from 20 to 40 percent, and investment in scientific research was given a 60 percent write-off. Still, the government believed that more deflation was called for, and another "hold fast" budget was introduced in 1949—meaning that even though corporations were to get a tax break, workers would have to continue to pay high taxes. The long-promised reductions in taxation on the poor would have to wait. Though the government's new attitude pleased the financial community, it infuriated both the Labour Left and the unions. Why should they hold back wages at the same time that their government was handing away tax benefits to employers?

Eventually, the second postwar Labour chancellor, Stafford Cripps, like Dalton before him, could not withstand the increasingly personal attacks leveled against him by members of his own party. He resigned in ill health before the 1950 budget. Hugh Gaitskell, the next chancellor, inherited the party's traditional antagonisms to taxation on the poor, but his dilemma became even more difficult. By 1950, a wage freeze negotiated between the government and the TUC had fallen apart. The result, of course, was that inflation worsened. The government continued to believe that the country could not afford tax cuts, especially now that the brewing cold war required greater defense spending. This position echoed the last prewar chancellor, who had declared that Britain would not be financially unprepared for another war. Thus in a total reversal of Labour party promises, Gaitskell pushed up income taxes for all income groups as well as the purchase tax. Investment allowances were abolished. And finally, profits tax rates, which companies paid on top of the income tax, were raised to 50 percent.

Both sides of the House were up in arms. The increases in profits taxes were criticized by the opposition as "the most evil thing in the Budget,"[43] despite Gaitskell's protestation that he could do nothing else, "in view of the trade union attitude" (Sabine 1966, 218). The Left of the party were even more furious: Harold Wilson, Aneurin Bevan, and others left government in a huff.[44] Thus, with its own Left, the financial community, and the national press livid about the government's loss of socialist principles or, alternatively, its fiscal irresponsibility and with voters upset about the continued high taxes and war rationing, it is surprising that the Tories won the election in 1951 with only a thirteen-seat majority.

The Tories Return

The 1950s can probably best be summarized as a decade of continual movement and little change. The historian B. E. V. Sabine (1966, 230) writes critically of the "lack of fiscal pattern," pointing to "the field of income tax [where] this deficiency was reflected in a policy of spasmodic remission and retrenchment in both allowances and rates." Having retaken the reins of government in 1951, the Tories faced a new kind of dilemma: on the one hand, their party was committed to tax reductions, but on the other hand, they were committed to both balancing the budget and continuing to finance the welfare state. By 1951, moreover, Treasury officials had come to accept their role as macromanagers of the economy (Weir and Skocpol 1985; Weir 1989; Hall 1986). The Treasury had long resisted fiscal interventionism, but wartime experience combined with the continual preaching of Keynes eventually altered their view (Hall 1986, 76). Thus any changes in tax rates, exemptions, or schedules were certain to be opposed by Treasury officials unless they could be worked into their macrofiscal agenda. Treasury officials were, moreover, regaining influence over fiscal policy. During the Dalton years, the political leadership moved in directions opposed by the officials, but the debacle of economic policy in the later half of the Labour government's reign lent credibility to the official position. The power of the Treasury was further enhanced by the inexperience of successive Tory chancellors. As Samuel Brittain (1969, 113) notes, "In the thirteen years 1951–64, there were no less than six Conservative Chancellors. Nearly all the Tory Chancellors who held office until 1962 were in every sense laymen. Not merely were they innocent of economic complexities but they did not even have the practical financial flair that one might reasonably expect from a party with business links."

In short, the new Conservative government did not start from the strongest position in its desire to turn back the fiscal clock. Despite the new chancellor Richard Austen Butler's valiant promise to "reduce government expenditure and make a significant start at reducing taxation" (Sabine 1966, 214), no one reaped an immediate windfall. Tax rates were eventually reduced but the reductions were in fact quite marginal.[45] Indeed, the standard rate was reduced only twice in the thirteen years of Tory incumbency.

It would not be correct, however, to say that the Conservative government did nothing about taxes during its tenure in office. Chancellors and Treasury officials alike were also under continual pressure to use the tax system to promote investment and economic growth. Corporate tax rates were generally reduced, but instability was by far the most outstanding characteristic of this revenue source. Table 5.4 shows the large number of manipulations made in the taxation of corporate income during Tory rule. Between 1951 and 1963 investment and initial allowances were changed eight times. From year to year, they were increased to as much as 30 percent of the cost of investment and dropped to 0 percent. The tax rates affecting corporate income were changed in eleven different budgets in the thirteen years the Tories were in office.

In some ways, then, British fiscal policy followed a pattern somewhat like

Table 5.4

Grants and Allowances for Plant and Machinery and
Industrial Buildings Capital Expenditure by the
Manufacturing Industry, 1945–72, Years of Change

Announce-ment Date	Investment Allowances Buildings	Initial Allowances Building	Investment Allowances Plant & Mach.	Initial Allowances Plant & Mach.	Direct Grants Plant & Mach.
4 Apr. 45	0	10	0	20	
6 Apr. 49	0	20	0	40	
10 Apr. 51	0	0	0	0	
15 Apr. 53	0	10	0	20	
6 Apr. 54	10	0	20	0	
17 Feb. 56	0	10	0	20	
15 Apr. 58	0	12.5	0	25	
17 June 58	0	15	0	30	
7 Apr. 59	10	5	20	10	
11 Nov. 62	15	5	30	10	
17 Jan. 66	0	15	0	0	20
1 Dec. 66*	0	15	0	0	25
1 Jan. 69*	0	15	0	0	25
17 Apr. 70*	0	30	0	0	25
10 Oct. 70	0	30	0	35	0
7 July 71+	0	30	0	55	0
21 March 72	0	40	0	100	0

Source: Hansard Society, *Politics and Industry, 1979.*
*These were temporary grant increases which affected capital expenditures between specified periods of time. After these periods the "normal" grant would become effective
+This measure was to be short term, affecting expenditures made before March 1, 1973. It was superseded, however, by the 1972 Budget Measures.

the Swedish in these years. Rather than introduce thousands of measures for individual constituencies, as Americans had done, the British chose to introduce and manipulate more general tax incentives favoring broad classes of investment. Still, the British experience with these fiscal policy tools was quite different from the Swedish. Though many of the tools were similar, the ways in which they were used differed markedly. First, the proper roll of micromanagement via tax expenditure policy was not accepted by Treasury officials. This presented a serious problem for British chancellors: When they have wanted to develop effective tax expenditures (like the Swedes had) their experts were less than forthcoming. It was widely accepted among political elites around the world that capital allowances were vital tools for the fine-tuning of the economy. But the British failed to develop the technical expertise necessary to design these programs effectively. The result was that the British experience with these measures stood out for its inadequacy, unpreparedness, and poor timing.[46] "A look through the major book on the Chancellor's post-war economic management (Samuel Brittain's *Steering the Economy*) suggests that in retrospect, Chancellors rarely do the right thing, and if they do, it is often for the wrong reasons" (Heclo and Wildavsky 1981, 60).

There was continual agitation about Britain's lackluster economy (Pollard 1983). Politicians and officials alike repeatedly grasped at any tools that were available, even if they did not understand them. But, having no deep understanding of the meaning or significance of these measures for industry, they were just as likely to reverse them "when things get tough"—meaning when the Treasury needed extra revenue.[47]

In sum, though the Tories had entered office dedicated to restructuring the imbalances of the previous Labour government, in their thirteen years in office they were able to do little more than reduce tax rates slightly. Inflation, however, far outweighed these tax reductions, and in the end the Tories had presided over a massive increase in effective tax rates paid by all but the very richest individuals. Of course this had not been their intent.

A Return to Redistribution? Labour in Power Again, 1964–70

Finally, in 1964, the electorate returned the Labour party to 10 Downing Street. Surprisingly, however, "little detailed work seems to have been done within the party on tax policies" (Robinson and Sandford 1983, 59). According to Richard Rose, "In the 5 years prior to the 1964 General Election policy making was more concerned with the politics of opposition than with plans for governing" (cited in Robinson and Sandford 1983, 58). Indeed, the Labour party had shied away from making any specific tax pledges in the run up to the election of 1964 because, it was believed, their tax promises had cost them votes in the 1959 election (Butler and Rose 1960, 61–62). Thus, when the Left entered power after thirteen years of opposition, they were not in the least prepared to improve the tax system they had so bitterly attacked.

With some exceptions, such as Lord Diamond, Dick Taverne, and Harold Lever, the bulk of the party still felt itself committed to the same program for the income tax that they had instituted during the 1945–51 period. What many failed to appreciate was that during these years a sizable portion of Labour's own constituency had become solid income taxpayers. Although this implied that the working class was enjoying a higher standard of living than at any previous point in history, it also meant that the standard revenue yielder for Labour chancellors, the income tax, was losing its political appeal. This put Labour chancellors into a bind from which they have yet to fully unravel themselves. Financial Secretary Joel (now Lord) Barnett (1982, 71) writes, "It is the unwillingness to recognize the major transformation in our tax system which is what I especially have in mind when I use the epithet 'old-fashioned' to describe some current attitudes towards it. Because we tried to maintain and improve public services against a background of low growth, we had to increase levels of direct taxation to the point where further increases did not hit the rich, but rather we hurt workers, not least the quite low paid."

The new government tried to avoid the horns of this dilemma through the introduction of a new capital gains tax, reform of the taxation of corporate income, increases in the surtax income tax rates, and the closing of many tax loopholes.[48] These measures certainly made the British tax system more progressive. Unfortunately, they generated relatively little revenue to the Treasury.

These measures did, however, evoke strong reactions from the British business community (Stewart 1977, 34). Capital flight became a major concern of the government, even more so in the context of the seemingly ever-worsening economic situation. Riding on a thin majority and faced with an intensifyingly hostile political climate, the government decided to return to the polls in 1966 and attempt to renew their mandate. This they did and, indeed, were returned with an increased majority. But even before the election returns had come in, the gravity of Britain's economic situation forced a reevaluation of the fiscal policy goals on the part of Treasury ministers. Redistribution had not been forgotten, but getting the economy back on track was a more pressing need. In the words of Michael Hatfield (1978, 30), "Former ministers were entitled to plead that they had experienced a buffeting from unforeseen economic winds and had been 'blown off course.' . . . But at the same time, it was difficult to detect any coordinated belief in achieving the promises of a radically restructured industry and a mixed economy."

Thus, once again a British Labour government was about to embark on one of their famous U-turns. In the next three years the demands to balance the budget and reassure capital forced the government to moderate capital taxation and prevented them from substantially reducing taxes paid by the less well-off.

There were, however, some crucial tax policy innovations. The most important of these was the infamous selective employment tax (SET). The introduction of the SET illustrates the level of desperation the government faced over taxation policy.[49] Two months before the election in 1966, no one in the cabinet had even heard of a SET. However, Nicholas Kaldor, a Cambridge economist and fiscal policy adviser to the Labour party for a number of years, was soon to convince Chancellor James Callaghan of the virtues of a tax that was paid by employers and differentially benefited manufacturing industries as opposed to service industries. Thus, the SET would not only bring in revenue, but it would be deflationary, could be seen as a tool of "industrial policy," [50] and might help moderate the wage demands of the more militant unionized workers (Kaldor 1980). Grasping the idea wholeheartedly, Callaghan put the SET into his next budget as the latest answer to the latest crisis. The first public announcement of this new tax occurred when the chancellor drew it out of his red briefcase on Budget Day, only three months after it was conceived.[51]

By the end of 1968, the Labour government was besieged by economic and domestic political problems (Hatfield 1978, 30). In May, Gallup polls showed that if the election were held then only 21 percent of the electorate would vote for the Labour party while 45 percent would vote for the Tories. This was the largest preference lead any party had ever scored since Gallup started polling this question in 1947. Though Labour's standing did improve somewhat in the following months, they continued to stay at historically low levels for more than a year. The government's declining popularity did not result from one big mistake. Rather, the government was besieged on all sides: from the Left for not going far enough in its implementation of redistributive measures conforming to its preelection promises;[52] from the Right for going too far and acting on too much of its radical rhetoric; and from the Middle for apparently waffling and in the process driving down the British economy. Devaluations, increases in the Bank of England rate, an incomes policy, purchase tax surcharges, surtax surcharges, rises in excise duties, capital levies and attempts to hold back government spending were all measures designed to patch various holes in the dikes. Each measure tended to anger one group as it appeased another (Pollard 1983, 411–14). The devaluations were attacked as too little too late, SET premiums had to be withdrawn except from development areas, runs on sterling continued, and investment was abysmal. The unions, in turn, were irate about incomes policy and tax hikes and therefore demanded concession after concession, turning the plan into a shambles. And so it went, until the Tories returned as "the Party of Government," determined to repeal many of the reforms of the last six years.

The Tax Policy Yo-Yo

The new Conservative government was determined to make a break with the past. It stood at the vortex of two opposing philosophies: the traditional conservatism of moderation versus the new liberalism. Edward Heath, the new party leader, dropped the commitment to planning and incomes policy in favor of a stronger commitment to market principles. Other than the elimination of some of the regulatory policies of past governments, however, there were few market stimulating measures available—aside from tax cuts. The centerpiece of Heath's new beginning, then, was a reduction in direct taxes on companies and individuals aimed at encouraging savings and private initiative.

The new Tories thus introduced an overwhelming number of changes in the British tax system. The Inland Revenue's year-end report summarized these changes and found no fewer than twenty-eight major revisions in the personal income tax alone.[53] Broad changes were also made in the corporation tax, and the chancellor promised a restructuring of indirect taxes in his next budget. Finally, SET was repealed, and the purchase tax was replaced with a VAT.

The Tories did not last long, however. A major battle between the mighty miners union and the government eventually brought the government down. Voters apparently hoped that a new Labour government would be more effective in dealing with, or at least appeasing, the unions.

6

Rethinking Modern Taxation:
Taxation in a Global Economy

[Tax policy] has traditionally been thought of as an entirely
domestic matter. [But] in an increasingly global world
economy, nations can no longer afford to design their tax
systems without accounting for the effects on international
trade and investment.—Joel Slemrod, "Tax Principles in an
International Economy"

The world economy has undergone astounding changes since the 1970s: it
has, in a word, globalized. Such globalization is bringing about a dramatic
restructuring of tax systems throughout the world. In chapter 3 I noted how
the introduction of mass suffrage provided a political stimulus that led to the
introduction of progressive taxation and the legitimation of the principle of
ability to pay. In this chapter I shall argue that the ongoing changes in the
world economy are having an analogous impact on tax policy in the modern
world—but with a decidedly different effect.

In the 1980s a huge set of remarkably diverse countries have overhauled
their tax systems. In virtually all cases these tax reforms have meant lowering
income and profits tax rates, cutting back tax expenditures, and broadening
the tax base. In each case, these overhauls have been advertised under the
rubric of simplification, efficiency, and fairness. But when one steps back
and examines tax policy development across the globe in the 1980s, one
sees an unmistakably common trend: *Tax reform* has now come to mean the
redistributing of existing tax burdens *downward*.

To be sure, the institutional structures found in each country shape the way
in which these countries deal with the changing international context in which
they make tax policy. Indeed, this chapter will specifically examine the particular patterns followed in the United States, Sweden, and Britain. But once
again it will be demonstrated that national political institutions operate within
an international context that can shape and influence the ways in which these
institutions structure domestic politics.

Rethinking Tax Policy

The globalization of the world economy provided a powerful set of incentives for reforming the tax systems of Sweden, Great Britain, and the United States, but the nature of these reforms was greatly affected by what was being reformed. We saw in the last chapter that in the postwar era political and administrative elites seemed ineluctably drawn toward manipulating their tax systems to promote favored social and economic outcomes. All three tax systems had, by the mid-1970s, become major instruments of social and economic policy at the macro and micro levels alike. In some cases the use and abuse of tax instruments to achieve social and economic ends reached ludicrous proportions. The United States had gone furthest down this path, but all three countries had created so many tax incentives that most academic economists and many policymakers as well became extremely critical of the practice.[1]

Precisely because of the overuse and abuse of these policy instruments, it became more and more difficult to defend this type of government intervention in the economy and society. It became increasingly easy to attack these tax expenditure systems on the grounds that they allowed wealthy taxpayers to avoid paying their fair share of taxes. Michael Harrington captured much public sentiment when he suggested that a "tax system is a welfare system for the rich."[2]

In many ways it can be argued that the tax systems that had developed by the end of the 1970s were simply examples of what was wrong with modern government. It seemed that the more governments tried to do, the more they failed. Few would argue against a tax system that was fair and also promoted economic growth. But the more these governments tried to manipulate their tax codes, the less fair and more inefficient they became. Nowhere was this problem more acute or more obvious than in the United States.

Times were ripe for some kind of tax reform. But why did tax reform take the direction it did in the 1980s? One might hope that in these three *democratic* countries reforms would have been demanded by a public so frustrated with its tax system that it insisted on this kind of radical reform. Unfortunately, however, this answer misses the mark. Although it was true that the public in all three countries was skeptical and distrustful of their tax system—and while it continued to be true that no one likes to pay taxes—I have found no evidence suggesting that the majority of citizens wanted the kind of reforms that were implemented. The public resented their tax systems but generally on the grounds that they were not progressive enough. Survey after survey indicated that strong majorities believed that corporations and the wealthy

Table 6.1

U.S. Attitudes toward Taxation

Amount of Taxes Paid by Various Types of People Is?	Low-Income Families	Middle-Income Families	High-Income Families
Pay Too Much	53	71	8
Pay Too Little	4	2	75
About Right	31	22	10
Don't Know/No Answer	12	5	7

Source: Roper Organization, "The American Public and the Federal Income Tax," H + R Block Inc., 1986, 20.

paid too little in taxes, while the middle and lower classes paid too much.[3] Table 6.1 demonstrates American attitudes toward the distribution of taxes in the mid-1980s; attitudinal surveys in Britain and Sweden during the same period demonstrate nearly identical results.[4]

Why did tax reform in these democratic nations get defined as policies that patently flew in the face of the voting majority's policy preference? When most people felt that what was wrong with their systems was that the wealthy and the corporations paid too little in taxes, why did policymakers cut tax rates on the wealthy and on corporations? The answer suggested in this chapter is quite simple: By the 1980s, the argument for social justice was overwhelmed by the argument for economic growth. Growth, moreover, was increasingly an issue of international competitiveness. In chapter 2 I suggested that tax policymakers in all capitalist democracies have been faced with two conflicting beliefs: on the one hand, the majority of citizens want taxes on the wealthy and on corporations to be heavy; on the other hand, economic growth depends on the "superfluity" of the rich (Keynes 1936, 372). In the late twentieth century the pace of economic and technological change has accelerated, and these changes have forced tax policymakers to rethink tax policy. It is widely understood that a successful capitalist economy depends not only on a successful capitalist class, but also on that class's willingness to use and invest their money in the domestic economy.

The Changing World Economy

The most salient features of the changing world economy impinging on tax policy are the increasing mobility of capital and the growing flexibility of production technologies. There is no question that capital has become substantially more mobile over the past several years. It is difficult to measure exactly the extent or scope of these changes, but all observers are certain that the changes have been dramatic. Some indication of the degree of the changes can be found in the following statistics: (a) between 1975 and 1985 the annual turnover of the top eleven international stock exchanges grew by more than 600 percent from $236 billion to $1,578.9 billion;[5] (b) between 1984 and 1989 alone the sales of the top twenty nonoil multinational corporations grew from $486.4 billion to $966.7 billion; (c) finally, the number of international transfers of capital from one banking institution to another has exploded over the past decade: whereas in 1978 there were 24 million international capital transfers from bank to bank, by 1985 there were 680 million such transfers— a growth of 2,800 percent (OECD 1987, 165).

This mobility is, moreover, affected by national tax systems. In a recent monograph entitled *Economies in Transition,* the OECD suggested that the rapid growth of international trade and the expansion of transnational corpo- rations are bringing about the "progressive globalization of financial markets" (OECD 1989b, 84). They go on to argue that globalization is encouraging companies to allocate debt and investment strategies according to varying national tax policies:

[Tax policies] affect rates of return and hence portfolio choice, without necessarily increasing saving. . . . International disparities in tax treat- ment impinge on cross-border portfolio movements. For example, the differential treatment of interest payments provides an incentive to shift profits and debts, with possibly important implications for individual countries' revenue receipts. The booking of debt by multinational cor- porations was an important consideration in the recent tax reform in Canada and is of particular relevance for EC countries, in view of the 1992 objective of internal market unification. Tax considerations have been a major factor behind the growth of the Eurobond and Eurocur- rency markets. (OECD 1989b, 105)

Changes in production technology, communication, and transportation costs are also affecting domestic policymakers in that they are making it easier for firms to locate their operations in different parts of the world. This allows companies to take advantage of domestic policies such as tax policy in ways unimaginable only a few years ago. As the international business guru Michael Porter notes in his book *The Competitive Advantage of Nations,* "One of the potent benefits of a global firm is the ability to spread different activities among nations to reflect different preferred locations" (Porter 1990, 57).

The evidence also suggests that companies are in fact paying closer at- tention to tax policy when conducting international business. In a study of

Table 6.2

"Critical Factors" in Foreign Investment Decisions

1. Projected market growth	61%
2. Host government tax policies	60%
3. Host pricing controls	58%
4. Foreign exchange rates and controls on transfers	58%
5. Competition	56%
6. U.S. Tax policy	53%

Source: Cynthia Day Wallace 1990, 167–68.

295 American multinational corporations, Wallace (1990, 167–68) discovered that both American and foreign tax policies were critical factors in these companies' investment decisions (table 6.2).

In sum, growing dissatisfaction with national tax systems on the part of the public and elites and changes in the world economy reshaped the context in which tax policymakers designed domestic tax policy in the 1980s. This altered context helps explain the rising momentum toward tax reform in the United States, Britain, Sweden, and a myriad other countries. In every single case these reforms have had a common set of policy goals: (a) to lower marginal income and corporate tax rates; (b) to reduce the number of tax subsidies offered to particular interests; and (c) to make taxation more efficient so that budgets could be brought back into balance. It is no surprise, however, that the extent to which these nations have achieved such goals has varied dramatically.

The United States

> The collection of all those interests in this country represents what the
> political system is—and the political system creates the tax system.
> And that's why the tax system is sorta' like an inner tube that has been
> patched about 150 times.—U.S. Representative Byron Dorgan, 1986

Although the Tax Reform Act of 1986 is the most widely remembered tax reform of the decade, it was only one of a series of reforms passed in the 1980s. Taken together, these "reforms" have had quite contradictory effects and have produced remarkably complex outcomes. For example, they reduced income tax rates for all income classes and took millions of poor off the income tax roles, but have at the same time made the tax system less progressive overall. Tax reforms introduced early in the decade lowered effective corporate tax burdens by introducing massive tax expenditures on the grounds that such a move would stimulate economic growth, while tax reforms introduced later in the decade increased corporate tax burdens by cutting back many of these same tax expenditures on the grounds that they were bad for the economy. Moreover, every tax reform has been presented as a simplification of the tax system, but each has in fact complicated the tax system. Finally, policymakers have promised to eliminate the federal deficit, but the tax reforms they have introduced have instead inflated it by trillions of dollars.

These outcomes have not, to say the least, conformed to the aims of the major tax policy reformers of this decade. To explain such outcomes one must understand the ways in which economic incentives presented by the changing world economy conflicted with political incentives presented by America's unique institutional structures. The tax policies that evolved were neither the product of any group or interest nor a coherent response to the new demands facing the nation in a changing world economy.

The Economic Recovery Tax Act of 1981

[The late 1970s] marked the beginning of a major shift in tax politics on the Ways and Means Committee, as a new economic policy agenda began to appear. A sluggish economy, persistent inflation, and a growing middle-class "tax revolt" all contributed to the rise of the new economic agenda. Traditional liberal concerns with distributional equity began to be eclipsed by a new emphasis on reducing tax burdens on middle-income taxpayers and encouraging economic growth.
—Randall Strahan, "Agenda Change and Committee Politics"

By the end of 1980, everyone recognized that the American economy was in crisis. Investment and productivity were too low, inflation and unemployment were too high, and America was losing out to her major allies in both traditional industries and future technologies (OTA 1981). The country was, moreover, suffering from a malaise. In the lingering wake of the Vietnam and Watergate debacles, the country was ripe for dramatic changes.

When Ronald Reagan was swept into office in a landslide victory over the incumbent president Jimmy Carter, it was widely expected that he would push for major cuts in personal income taxes. He had, after all, announced on the Capitol steps on June 25, 1980, that the enactment of an across-the-board tax cut would be his first order of business once elected. Thus, as dramatic as his first major piece of domestic legislation was—the Economic Recovery Tax Act (ERTA), a proposed massive 30-percent cut in personal income tax rates—no one was surprised at the direction his administration had taken.

The original ERTA proposal (1981) was intended to be the first part of a broad economic package that included both tax and spending cuts. The logic of this proposal was quite straightforward and remarkably similar to Andrew Mellon's tax cuts in the 1920s: put more money into people's pockets and they will spend more. Reagan's economists believed this would act as a huge supply side stimulus to the economy, producing more wealth in the economy and, ultimately, more revenues to the state. The act, then, was part of an economic strategy based on a new (or at least revisited) economic paradigm which directly challenged the Keynesian paradigm that had dominated American budgetary policy for the past forty years.

Almost no one, however, expected the proposal to make it through the House of Representatives, which was still solidly controlled by the Democratic party. Reagan's tax cut proposal was clearly regressive, and the Democrats were sure to kill it even before it reached the floor. In March 1981 the chairman of the House Ways and Means Committee bluntly declared the plan "dead on arrival" (Witte 1985, 222). We now know, of course, that the proposal did not die. But what did happen to the plan tells much about how the continuing decentralization of power within Congress shaped the political strategies of both its members and the presidency.

"Our enemy is time," David Stockman, director of the Office of Management and Budget, wrote in a memo to presidential confidants Ed Meese and James Baker. Believing that they had fewer than forty days in which to put together a comprehensive package of tax and spending cuts, Stockman and a small group of advisers embarked on a blitzkrieg strategy, bombarding the Congress with a huge array of proposals designed to make it politically difficult for anyone to oppose the tax giveaway (Stockman 1986, 44). Realizing that they had to fight the House leadership, administration officials made individual tax deals with both Democratic and Republican representatives. At the same time, they launched a massive public relations campaign designed to put pressure on Democrats. Thus, rather than calculating or planning a major tax reform, the administration felt compelled to push a tax cut at any cost. When future problems became evident, they convinced themselves that they could worry about them later. When financial projections did not support their claims, they changed the numbers. When goals conflicted with one another, they ignored the conflict. No one, least of all Stockman, believed that this was a good way to make budget policy—especially radical budget policy— but the realities of the system of checks and balances left the administration no other choices. If the administration did not sweeten the tax package with special favors to individual members and move very quickly at that, they had almost no chance of implementing the Reagan Revolution.

Thirty, twenty, even ten years before, Democratic party elites had the power to stop presidential tax policy initiatives seemingly at will. Chairman Mills, in particular, used this power to both shape tax policy and to dominate congressional policy outcomes generally. But with the congressional reforms of the 1970s, power over tax policy had been "democratized." This diffusion of power offered the administration the opportunity to cut deals with individual members of Congress (both Democrats and Republicans) and eventually break the lock that the revenue committee chairmen had traditionally held over the tax policy process. In so doing, the administration blew the doors open to a mass feeding frenzy. Congressmen introduced every imaginable tax incentive for their constituents and for the economy. If tax breaks would bring about economic renewal and please potent interest groups, members of Congress could not resist handing out lots of them.

No doubt many groups, interests, and industries genuinely believed that if they could just get a tax cut, they would really help stimulate the economy. Others simply argued, "If they get a cut, why not us too?" But whatever the justifications, the ERTA ended up as a frenzied craze of tax giveaways, with members of Congress attempting in essence to outbid each other in who could bring the most lucrative tax breaks back home to their constituents. "The hogs were really feeding. It was gross," said one Senate staffer in an interview with this author. "The greed level, the level of opportunism, was just out of control" (Greider 1981, 5). The result was a tax bill which John Witte (1985, 235) has described as "historically in a category by itself. . . . However," Witte adds, "it should be remembered that this bill was unique only because it was extreme, not because it established new trends in tax legislation." Thus, a program that one might argue had started as an economically coherent policy ended up being little more than an incoherent tax giveaway. Congress not only passed an average 25-percent tax cut to all income tax payers, but also handed out literally hundreds of special tax amendments to constituents.[6] No one went away empty-handed. Before they had finished, $750 billion dollars of tax revenue was set to be given away over the next five years.

Reforming the Tax Reform: The Tax Equity and Fiscal Responsibility Act

Getting Congress to go along with huge tax cuts proved easier for the administration than getting it to approve massive reductions in public spending. This basic fact, along with President Reagan's commitment to greater defense spending, annihilated any chances that the government could achieve its first major economic commitment—to balance the budget. Indeed, the U.S. budget deficit skyrocketed from $40.2 billion in 1979 to $207 billion in 1983.

Congressional elites launched several efforts to clean up the tax code and remove some of the most glaring tax loopholes introduced in the past decade, but they met with modest success at best. Republican Senator Robert Dole, chairman of the Finance Committee, attempted to reassert the revenue committee's traditional role as the gatekeeper of the tax system. Despite lukewarm support from the administration, Congress was able to pass the Tax Equity and Fiscal Responsibility Act in 1982 and another loophole-closing measure in 1984.[7] Together these bills took back nearly $98 billion of the revenues passed out by ERTA. Still, as Birnbaum and Murray (1987, 32–33) note, these bills were largely "collection[s] of odds and ends . . . [that] demonstrated the impressive power of the interests who backed certain breaks." Once again, the result was not determined by a coherent strategy weighing one alternative against another—but rather by a political calculus in which determining winners and losers is not decided on the merits of their cases, but on the depth of their wallets. Indeed, it could well be argued that the only reason anyone lost in 1982 and 1984 was that in the frenzy of 1981, even relatively impotent groups got in on the tax bonanza.

The Tax Reform for Fairness, Simplicity, and Economic Growth

Tax fairness is a great idea. It makes for a great speech. But after the speech the deficit is still there.—Senator Christopher Dodd, 1985

To many the success of "tax reform" in the United States, and of the Tax Reform Act of 1986 in particular, was as surprising as it was monumental. As late as 1985 virtually no one believed that the United States was capable of reforming its tax code. In his study *The Politics and Development of the Federal Income Tax* John Witte (1985, 380) *correctly* noted, "There is nothing, absolutely nothing, in the history or politics of the income tax that indicates that any of these schemes have the slightest hope of being enacted in the forms proposed." The American tax system was one of the most complicated and inefficient tax systems in the world. Nearly everyone agreed, moreover, that it was the American political system that had created this mess. Absent institutional changes, it was indeed difficult to imagine how or why American tax policymakers would behave any differently than they had in the past.

As individual members of Congress had gained more influence and power over tax policy outcomes in the 1970s and 1980s, they concomitantly developed a major new resource to fund their reelection campaigns. The cost of campaigning had surged over the past decade, and these expenses were being financed by special interest groups and their political action committees (PACs). Members of the revenue committees were, for obvious reasons, the darlings of the PACs' lobbyists, commonly known as the Gucci Boys. Members of the House Ways and Means Committee collected $8 million in 1985 alone, three times the amount collected by this committee in the last nonelection year, 1983. Members of the Senate Finance Committee received $6.7 million in campaign contributions from special interest PACs alone in 1985 and banked a total of $11.8 million in this one year (Birnbaum and Murray 1987, 180). During the deliberations on the Tax Reform Act of 1986, "so much money was floating around Washington, that even lawmakers themselves began to look askance. Rostenkowski, whose own panhandling missions to Los Angeles, New York, and St. Louis brought him more than $500,000 during the tax-reform years, told the *Wall Street Journal* that he was 'nauseated' at the influence that campaign money seemed to have on some of his own Ways and Means members" (Birnbaum and Murray 1987, 181).

By 1985 it was almost universally recognized that the American tax system was a mess. Henry Aaron and Harvey Galper (1986, 1) described it as follows: "The U.S. tax system has become a swamp of unfairness, complexity, and inefficiency. The accumulation of credits, deductions, and exclusions designed to help particular groups or advance special purposes conflict with one another, are poorly designed, and represent no consistent policy." The tax system not only was incoherent and frustrating to taxpayers, but was perceived as producing a host of economic problems. A critical problem was, as James Hines (1988, 34) notes, that "there is a widely held view that the U.S. tax system encourages American companies to invest excessively abroad, thereby depriving this country of capital, jobs and productivity growth." In spite of these glaring problems, practically no one took President Reagan seriously when he requested that the Treasury Department look into reforming the tax system. Divided government would certainly kill anything but cosmetic tax reform.

Of course, the historic Tax Reform Act of 1986 did eventually wind its way through the congressional labyrinth and, despite some initial doubts, was signed by the president. There are a number of excellent accounts of the fascinating history and politics of this act. Each tells a story of a policy process that was out of control, in which no one could have possibly predicted the outcome.[8] Indeed, everyone was not just surprised, but stunned, that a package did finally get through.[9]

Participants, analysts, and pundits alike were amazed because the act did

Table 6.3

Effective Tax Rates for State, Local, and Federal Taxes in
the United States, by Population, 1966–88

Population Percentile	1966	1970	1975	1980	1985	1988
Top 5%	32.77	33.0	28.4	28.9	26.0	27.8
Top 1%	39.6	39.0	29.0	28.4	25.3	26.8
All Deciles	25.2	26.1	25.0	25.3	24.5	25.4

Source: Joseph Pechman, "The Future of the Income Tax," *American Economic Review* 80, no. 1 (March 1990): 4.

what no one thought the American political system could do: take away tax benefits from some powerful political interests. As this book and many others have demonstrated, the fragmentation of authority in American politics makes it highly difficult for political elites to impose costs on influential constituents. Absent a national crisis it is almost impossible for these elites to overcome the many veto points built into the system, even when there is broad political agreement over policy goals.

It is, of course, not difficult to explain Congress's willingness to cut individual income taxes in 1986. This kind of so-called reform has been passed almost gleefully many times before in American history. It was instead Congress's eventual willingness to pay for the individual income tax cuts by increasing someone else's tax burden that is more difficult to explain. This is especially confusing given the argument that it was concerns with international competitiveness that motivated the reforms in the first place. Still, we find that the final bill signed by the president financed the massive individual income tax cuts by raising corporate taxes by nearly $120 billion dollars over the next five years. These tax changes continued a trend in tax policy that had been developing for many years (table 6.3).

Had the business community been united in its opposition to the tax bill, it could have vetoed this bill at any number of stages. But American business interests were far from united. Even though the final bill would boost corporate taxes, large sections of American business actively supported the plan. Who were these corporate supporters? Generally the business sectors that actively supported the reform included high-tech industries, service industries, and certain multinationals. A cut in corporate tax rates would benefit these companies more than the removal of some tax expenditures. Extant tax expenditures tended to favor firms with substantial property holdings, firms heavily involved in manufacturing, as well as older companies. Unsurprisingly, the real estate, retail trade, construction, and most traditional rust-belt

Table 6.4

Import Content of "Supplies" of
Finished Manufactures, 1971 and 1985

Country	1971	1985
United States	9	24
United Kingdom	12	29
Sweden	37	45
Germany	16	26
Japan	4	6

Source: OECD, *Structural Adjustment and Economic Performance*, 1987

industries generally opposed the reform. In short, as the world economy has internationalized, the tax policy preferences of America's corporate sector have diverged.

Over the past decades American business interests—which had long been the least internationalized among its competitors—had in fact become much more deeply involved in the international economy. Not only did trade contribute to enlarging the share of the American economy in the 1980s, but a growing number of American firms were also coming to rely on foreign production and products. The result was that tax incentives found in the U.S. tax code were becoming less significant and less attractive. Tax incentives tend to have "lock-in" effects. The emerging mobile corporation does not want to be locked in.

In short, by the mid-1980s, American corporate interests had become more diversified than ever before in American history. As table 6.4 indicates, even companies that produce finished manufactured goods for the domestic market are integrated more and more tightly in an international market. Thus, even companies and industries that one might expect to be purely domestic may have cross-cutting pressures. Moreover, as table 6.5 indicates, U.S. capital had moved abroad in substantial ways.

Tax Reform Outcomes

What exactly was accomplished in this historic decade? First, Congress did what no one believed it could do; it imposed some losses on some mighty political interests. But the Tax Reform Act did not do what its original authors promised it would do. When President Reagan introduced the proposal, he declared that it would simplify the tax system, make it more fair, and contribute to economic growth. The reality was somewhat different.

Table 6.5
U.S. and Foreign Assets
(U.S.$ billions), 1979–86

	U.S. assets abroad	Foreign assets in U.S.
1979	511	416
1980	607	501
1981	720	579
1982	825	688
1983	874	784
1984	896	893
1985	949	1061
1986	1068	1332

Source: Pirages, 1989:209.

Regardless of the economic logic behind the Treasury Department's original proposals, Congress's desire to once again bring home tax cuts to constituents overrode virtually all other policy desires. These rate reductions came at a real cost. First, *rather than simplify the tax code, the 1986 act took an already incredibly complex tax code and made it even more complicated.* In their desire to ensure some degree of distributional equity (given the hefty rate cuts) Democrats in Congress insisted on a number of accounting changes and requirements for "minimum taxes" which have very substantially increased the complexity of the code. And as Birnbaum and Murray show in fascinating detail, in order to get the final act passed through Congress, reformers were forced to give away a huge number of tax breaks to an incredible array of political interests. Even though a number of loopholes were cut in this tax act, numerous others were either introduced or expanded.[10]

Second, the deep cuts in personal income tax rates were expensive. A revenue-generating tax reform was politically out of the question—no matter how obvious the need to balance the budget—owing in large measure to Ronald Reagan's firm commitment to veto any tax bill that raised the overall tax burden. Still, if Congress was going to be able to give their middle-class constituents tax cuts, new revenues would have to be found. These personal tax cuts were largely financed through hikes in taxes on the corporate sector. To be sure, neither congressional reformers nor the administration constructed or calculated a coherent economic logic that could then be used to decide which types of tax expenditures should be cut back and which should remain or be expanded. As all of the blow-by-blow political histories of this reform demonstrate, those who "took a hit" and those who were spared were defined by a political calculus, not an economic one. In the end, the economic logic of this tax reform was specious at best. It was precisely for this reason that Congressman John Danforth of the Senate Finance Committee, one of the original supporters of the idea of tax reform, argued stridently against the bill during the final debate: "We in Congress have become—myself included—intoxicated by low rates. We were willing to dump more and more taxes on our [domestic] industrial sector, on the research and development sector, on education in order to placate this god we had formed of low rates. . . . So, Mr. President, over and over we have failed to take into account economic reality and we have, in effect, doctored numbers in order to create the illusion of revenue neutrality when this bill is not going to be neutral at all." [11]

Thus, despite the fact that a major incentive for the tax reform was continuing economic performance of the American economy, in the end, the tax reform increased the tax burden borne by capital and in the view of many has damaged the competitive position of American corporations.

In sum, the American tax policy process did prove capable of passing major tax reform acts in the 1980s, notwithstanding its institutional fragmentation. But institutional fragmentation shaped these reforms in perverse ways. In Jeffrey Birnbaum's words, "Tax reform passed not because anyone really wanted it. Indeed, it was the bill that nobody wanted. It succeeded because so few people were willing to kill it once it got rolling. Put another way, no one wanted the dog to die on his doorstep." [12] The fragmentation built into committee government profoundly shaped both the political strategies of the actors involved and, ultimately, the policy outcome as well. The domestic institutional context thus has critically defined this country's response to the changes in the international context. It is far from clear that the response has been what any one would predict or advocate. Indeed, perhaps Richard Doernberg (1988, 965) is accurate when he describes the outcomes as follows: "One might describe the 1986 Act as rearranging the deck chairs on the Titanic—surely a bustle of activity but with little, if any, meaningful improvement."

The United Kingdom

Whatever else might be said about changes to the tax system in the 1970s and 1980s, most observers of the British fiscal system would agree that there have been a great many of them. . . . But to the extent that progress in achieving these new objectives has been made in Britain—and some has been made—it has been the result of reductions in the rates of tax rather than improvements in the structure. . . . In the main, these cuts in rates were little more than political gestures and never touched more than a small minority of the population. . . . Where structural changes have been needed, the record has been disappointing. . . . A style of government— characteristic of Britain in the 1980s—that is at once secretive and decisive may be effective if you have solutions, but is self-defeating if you are still in search of them.—Andrew Dilnot and J. A. Kay, "Tax Reform in the United Kingdom"

Three successive electoral victories led by Margaret Thatcher gave the Tories large majorities in Parliament for more than a decade, allowing them to pass a succession of tax reforms that were impressive by any measure. They served principally to redistribute the British tax burden downward. By the end of her reign as prime minister in 1991, Thatcher's governments had (a) reformed the personal income tax by drastically cutting marginal income tax rates—from top rates of 98 percent to 40 percent and bottom rates of 33 percent to 25 percent—and eliminating the "reduced rate" of tax paid by the poor; (b) reformed the corporation tax by reducing tax expenditures and cutting corporate tax rates from 53 to 35 percent; (c) reformed the capital transfer tax by both cutting rates and opening new loopholes; (d) reformed the capital gains tax by partially indexing it to inflation; and (e) reformed consumption taxes by raising excise taxes, broadening the VAT base, and increasing the VAT rate from a split 8–12.5 percent to a flat 15 percent. Finally, in one of her most impressive legislative feats, Thatcher rebuffed many of her most trusted advisers, ignored public opinion, and reformed the system of local government finance by abolishing local property taxes (rates) and replacing them with the massively unpopular and highly regressive head tax called a Community Charge. If British governments are good at bullying Parliament, Margaret Thatcher was perhaps Britain's toughest bully.

Of course, Margaret Thatcher's legislative and political success was in part due to her remarkable personal talents. One would, however, be seriously mistaken to assume that the Thatcher Revolution was merely the result of her individual traits. Her government was indeed successful in pushing through massive tax policy agenda unthinkable in almost any other country. But the government's legislative success was a product of the deep social and economic malaise that had beset Britain by the mid-1970s and was made possible by the county's uniquely centralized institutional structure.

Of the three countries examined here, Britain was in the worst economic position by the end of the 1970s. Certainly, Britain had been suffering from long-term relative decline throughout much of the twentieth century, but in the 1970s Britain's economic and political problems seemed to intensify. Economic growth stagnated, real incomes fell, union strife brought down first a Conservative and then a Labour government. Public spending skyrocketed, as did the budget deficit.

These problems contributed to a crisis of confidence on the part of both British and foreign capitalists. Net fixed capital investment as a percent of GNP declined by more than one-third between 1969–71 and 1978–80. While direct foreign investment in Britain rose from $631 per year in 1967–69 to $1,353 in 1976, the outflow of direct investment in the same period went from $1,027 to $3,379 (Pollard 1983, tables 7:39, 7:15). In sum, when a new Conservative government was put into office at the end of this depressing decade, it was desperately looking for new solutions to Britain's woes (Krieger 1986).

The Tax Policy Agenda

Margaret Thatcher was somewhat of an expert on taxation by the time she reached 10 Downing Street and believed that a major source of Britain's economic stagnation was its inefficient and nominally progressive tax system. Thatcher was convinced that the extraordinarily high rates of tax found in Britain contributed mightily to her countrymen's apparent unwillingness to invest in their economy. But even though taxation played a key role in Thatcher's overall political economic strategy, it was only part of her government's economic agenda. Her first commitment was to reining in inflation (MacInnes 1987), and for Thatcher this meant balancing the budget. Alas, as anyone but a voodoo economist knows, you cannot cut taxes and balance the budget at the same time.

In the American case, the conflict between these two objectives was ignored. Phony numbers, magic asterisks, and accounting gimmicks were used to allow this conflict to be brushed under the rug. This was possible, and indeed politically rational, because when the deficit increased, the administration could blame the Congress and Congress could blame the administration. Given British party government, however, Thatcher did not have this option. Irresponsible tax cuts could be a win-win solution for politicians in the United States, even if they were a lose-lose solution for the economy in the United States. But in Britain the political calculation had to be different. If the government massively increased the deficit, everyone would know where the responsibility lay. The kind of sweeping tax cut at any cost that took place in the United States, while certainly politically possible in Britain, given the legislative strength of the government, was never a serious option. Sweeping tax cuts would have economic costs, and given the centralization of power in the British system, the government would sooner or later have to pay those costs in votes.

Faced with these political realities, Thatcher and her various chancellors of the exchequer plotted a head-on attack on the distribution of the tax burden. If the overall burden could not be reduced, at least the rich, whose increased superfluity would, in their view, have the greatest effect on the overall health of the economy, should be relieved of much of their crushing tax burden.

No one was surprised, of course, when the new government's first budget in 1979 announced deep cuts in taxes paid by the wealthy and steep rises in taxes paid mostly by the poor.[13] Of course, howls of indignation were heard from the opposition parties—as they were following all subsequent budget presentations—but these cries, in the view of the government, were simply background noise. The government had the votes to sustain its new tax policy objectives in Parliament.

Subsequent budgets continued the downward distribution of the tax burden in Britain. The budget for 1980, for example, continued income tax cuts but, more important, introduced major changes in capital taxation: the capital transfer tax, the British form of death duties, was reformed in ways that have substantially reduced the tax's effectiveness as a redistributive tool. In this case, the government apparently decided that it was politically more palatable to reform the tax into oblivion rather than baldly admit that they wanted to abolish the tax (Sandford 1983). Capital gains taxes were indexed (and thus cut) in 1982. In the budgets for 1982 and 1983 the government continued marginal rate cuts. In addition, the investment income surcharge was abolished in 1983.

In 1984 the government returned to tax reform and introduced sweeping changes in the system of corporate taxation (see discussion below). In this year the chancellor, Nigel Lawson, also broadened the VAT base, halved the stamp tax, and abolished the social security tax (called National Insurance) surcharge paid by employers. The budgets of 1985 and 1986 were somewhat less dramatic than those that were about to follow.[14] The 1987 and 1988 tax reforms were indeed monumental. In these years income tax rates were cut radically, personal allowances were increased, capital gains taxation was liberalized, as were inheritance and death taxes, the National Insurance system was reformed, limits on Personal Equity Plans were raised, and, finally, the stamp tax was once again scaled back.[15] The reforms of 1988 were unusually impressive in their unabashed effort to cut the taxes paid by the wealthy in Britain. This had always been a goal of the Tories, but it was never so cogently expressed as in 1988. This budget was bluntly headlined by the *Financial Times* with the following two captions: "Dramatic Gains for the Rich" and "An End to Old-Fashioned Egalitarianism."[16] After the tax breaks of 1988, economic troubles once again returned to Britain, and the government felt

Figure 6.1 Average Tax Rates, Great Britain,
1979 and 1988, All Taxes and Cash Benefits

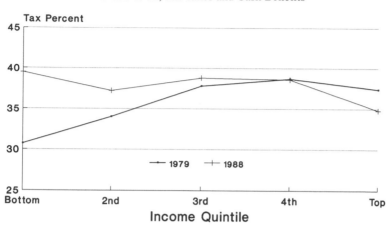

Source: Central Statistics Office, *The Effect of Taxes and Benefits on Household Income* (London: Her Majesty's Stationery Office, 1989).

that it could no longer substantially cut taxes. They did feel, however, that the system of local government finance could be reformed, and it was to these changes that most people's attention was now directed. I shall discuss this last set of reforms below. Figure 6.1 summarizes the distributional effects of these reforms (see also figures compiled by John Hills [1987]).

In sum, if one focuses on the distribution of the tax burden within society, the Tories have been effective at attaining their tax policy goals in the 1980s: personal income tax rates have been radically reduced, especially for the rich, consumption taxes have risen, and capital taxation has been liberalized. In short, the tax burden has been largely shifted downward. But the Tories have been dedicated to more than simply redistributing the tax burden. They have also attempted to make their tax system more economically efficient and to use tax limitation to hold back government spending. On these fronts they have been less successful. The following brief examination of the politics of corporation tax reform as well as of the infamous poll tax reveals some of the limitations on the powers of the government in the British system of party government.

Corporation Tax Reform

One of the most unexpected changes in the tax system pursued during the Thatcher years was the corporate profits tax reform of 1984. This reform was surprising because it ultimately augmented the overall tax burden borne by British corporations. Given that it was a Tory government that passed this reform and given my argument that the underlying logic motivating tax reform in the eighties was the desire to enhance economic competitiveness, a discussion of this tax change not only is appropriate, but also offers an excellent example of how the system of party government lends itself to a very different political logic from that of American committee government, even when the ideology and policy goals of the executives in these two systems are fundamentally identical.

By the time Margaret Thatcher entered office, the British corporation tax had been reformed multiple times since its introduction in 1965. It was widely recognized that these changes had inconsistent effects, at best. The economists M. P. Devereux and C. P. Mayer (1984, 5) of the Institute for Fiscal Studies describe the system as follows:

> The problem with these adjustments is not that they were inappropriate; it is that they were incoherent. In fact all of them . . . were made, not as the result of any sustained analysis of the underlying weaknesses of the company tax system, but as rapid responses to what had suddenly emerged as urgent problems. . . . The result was a series of ad hoc modifications to the tax structure which, taken as a whole, made little sense. By 1983 corporation tax was evidently not a tax on company profits, but it was very difficult to discern what it was actually a tax on; it raised little revenue, but in the process occupied substantial amounts of time and energy and created extensive distortions to business behavior.

The problem with corporate taxes in Britain, from the government's point of view, was not that companies paid too much in taxes.[17] Rather, the Tories believed that the tax system led corporations to make economic choices that were not necessarily driven by market principles and that consequently were not economically efficient. For example, the extant tax system encouraged British companies to invest locally in plant and equipment, and the system decisively favored the manufacturing industry over financial institutions. These distortions in the market, according to the government, undermined Britain's international competitiveness. "The evidence suggests," the new chancellor Nigel Lawson declared in his budget speech announcing the reform in 1984, "that businesses have invested substantially in assets yielding a lower rate of return than the investments made by our principal competitors" (House of Commons Debates, March 13, 1984, vol. 56, col. 296). The Corporate Tax Reform of 1984 was meant to address these ills.

The reform contained many components: corporate tax rates were reduced

Figure 6.2 Taxes on Corporate Income as a Percentage of Total
Taxation, United States, Sweden, and Great Britain, 1955–90

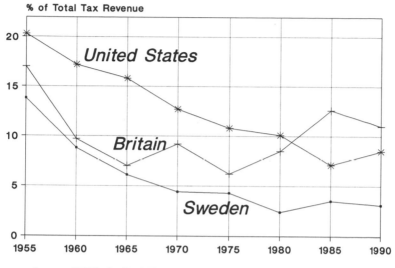

Sources: OECD, *Studies in Taxation: Long-Term Revenue Trends 1955–80*
(Paris, OECD); OECD, *Revenue Statistics, 1965–1991* (Paris: OECD, 1992).

from 52 percent to 35 percent for large companies and from 42 percent to 25
percent for smaller companies; major investment incentives and stock relief
deductions were removed or reduced; corporate capital gains were indexed;
the National Insurance surcharge was abolished; stamp duties on stock and
bond transfers were halved; and finally the investment income surcharge was
eliminated. Taken together this was a remarkable list of tax policy changes
designed to provide a new basis for investment and corporate decisions by
radically altering the tax distortions then found in the economy. It was also,
according to the chancellor, going to *lower* the overall tax burden borne by
British companies: "During the transitional period as a whole, these measures
should have a broadly neutral effect on the financial position of companies.
But when the changes have fully worked through, companies will enjoy very
substantial reductions in the tax that they pay" (House of Commons Debates,
March 13, 1984, vol. 56, col. 297). As figure 6.2 indicates, however, this
promise was not exactly realized.

The key to what appears to be a miscalculation on the part of the government almost certainly lies in the near-vacuum in which this tax reform
was conceived.[18] Like most others in Britain, it was secretly drawn up by a
small group of Treasury officials in consultation with the chancellor of the

exchequer. Amazingly, despite the magnitude of the reform, no one outside
the government and the very elite levels of the Treasury knew that the chancellor was even contemplating major reforms of company taxation until they
were announced, "fiscal fait accompli," in the budget speech on March 13
(Gammie 1984, 92). Even Peter Cropper, then head of the Conservative Party
Research Department, a tax economist and later adviser to the chancellor,
admitted that he did not know that corporate tax reform was on the government's agenda until he heard the chancellor's speech on Budget Day.[19] Indeed,
even though this was Conservative party government, which gets much of its
financial support from British industry, there was no consultation between the
government and the private sector (to say nothing of the opposition parties)
over this reform. In sum, at least in part because of the astonishing distance
between those who wrote the new law and those who were affected by it, the
government seems to have miscalculated its effects. Once the changes in the
law had been announced, however, the government was unlikely to review its
policy, especially as new crises inevitably take the agenda. Instead, officials
defended their plan as being more economically efficient and neutral, which
it certainly is, and downplayed the fact that it has increased the tax burden
borne by some of their most ardent supporters.[20]

The lack of consultation in the case of this corporate tax reform is by
no means exceptional. Malcolme Gammie (1988), in his exhaustive review,
tells us, "In consultative terms, the capital taxes and corporate taxes reviews
should overall be rated a failure." Even in the deliberations over international
elements of the tax system—an extremely complex arena of taxation—the
Treasury failed to consult relevant affected interests. John Wilkins of the CBI
echoes Gammie's thesis: "Back in the 1950s it was obvious that there could
be no consultation over Budget matters at all. . . . [In the seventies, however,]
the idea that consultation could improve policy had become more accepted.
But in the last four or five years, consultation has been a matter of lip service. . . . On some very big matters there has been no consultation at all."[21]
Indeed, there seems to be a sense within the Treasury that the more momentous the reform the *less* they should consult with outside groups and interests.
"If you consult," a senior economist at the Treasury told me, "you'll be
told all the things that are wrong with your idea." Speaking of the corporate
tax reform of 1984, Robert Weeden, the Inland Revenue's senior tax policy
economist, echoed the Treasury official's sentiment: "Yes, that was a case
where there was no consultation. But had there been consultation, it would
never have gotten through."[22] "Of course there are advantages to consultation," the Treasury official admitted, "but there are tremendous disadvantages

as well." When one thinks back to the tax reforms attempted in the United States during this same era, it is difficult to argue this point.

The Poll Tax

Certainly the most famous, if not infamous, tax reform introduced during the Thatcher years was the community charge, or, as it is more commonly known, the Poll Tax. This tax reform both illustrates the striking powers held by the government in British parliamentary democracy and demonstrates the potential boundaries of that power.

Reforming the rates system had long been a general goal of the Conservative party. In their election manifesto of 1974, for example, they proposed abolishing the rates and replacing them with taxes "more broadly based and related to people's ability to pay" (quoted in Pierson 1989, 15). Property taxes, after all, fell most heavily on the Conservatives' core constituency, property owners. The central motivation for the reform under the Thatcher regime seems instead to have been the desire to control the spending of local government authorities. Thatcher believed that spending by local governments (at least those controlled by the Labour party) was out of control. The argument was that because the majority of local constituency voters did not own property and were thus not directly taxed by the rates there was a systemic bias in favor of higher spending. Property owners, in contrast, were politically isolated in many communities but were forced to foot the bill for local government finance (Ridge and Smith 1990, 39–40).

To correct these ills, the government, in its Green Paper *Paying for Local Government*, published in January 1986, proposed a massive revision of local government finance.[23] The Green Paper spelled out a plan to abolish property taxes for both businesses and individuals and replace them with a flat head tax on all adults over the age of eighteen. The actual distribution of new tax burdens was not explained in the government's proposal, and almost no one believed the government's assertion that the community charge would be no less regressive than the rate system it replaced (*HMSO 9714*, 24). It was widely agreed, instead, that the tax would not only place a much higher burden on the poor while cutting the tax burden of the rich, but also dramatically redistribute the tax burden among communities (Smith and Squire 1986; Ridge and Smith 1990; Muellbauer 1987).[24]

The vagueness of the original proposal diffused public criticism at least until after the national election in 1987 (Morrissey et al. 1990).[25] However, it was not long before the general public came to understand the implication of this new tax reform. When they did, they were decidedly hostile. By the end of 1987, 65 percent of the public opposed the poll tax and only 23 percent favored the measure. Undaunted, Thatcher and her environment minister, Nicholas Ridley, decided to push forward with the bill. Despite the outcry of opposition from both inside and outside her party, Thatcher was determined. Even her own cabinet was opposed to the new tax reform (*London Times*, May 9, 1988), fearing that it was so unpopular that it could cost the party votes in the next election.[26] To some small extent Thatcher bent to the wishes of her colleagues: while she would not agree to abandoning her plan, she did agree to look into the possibility of making it somewhat less regressive than the original flat-rate head tax. She also agreed to delay its introduction in England until the early 1990s.[27] Still, Thatcher did go ahead with the reform. Though the government did make some concessions, it was able to pass the plan over vocal objections of not only all opposition politicians, but her own party's preferences as well.[28] It appeared that the government had once again prevailed.

As is well known now, the decision to stick with the poll tax was a huge political miscalculation. The tax became a central example of the spirit of the Thatcher government and a major embarrassment to Tory politicians. At first, attempts were made to lessen the political damage after riots had broken out over the issue, but the tax had done serious political damage to the party as a whole. At this point the Tories are attempting to figure out how to abandon the poll tax without looking too foolish. It has become clear, at any rate, that the tax will not collect the revenues necessary to supplant the rates unless the charge is put to politically unacceptable levels. Tax evasion and noncompliance have been extremely high, and the tax has also become an administrative quagmire. In the end it is far from certain that the tax, even if it were retained in some form, which is unlikely, will have the desired political effects: i.e., the Labor party local governments would be fiscally starved and thus run out of office.

In the end, of course, Margaret Thatcher took the blame for the poll tax, and this, along with her unpopular stand on the European Community, led to her being removed from 10 Downing Street by her own party. Having taken this step, the Tories are still today (1993) attempting to dig themselves out of the political mess created by the poll tax. Even in Britain there are limits on how far the government can go.

Sweden

The trend towards more radical reform began in the early 1980s, with the fundamental overhaul of the British and the American tax structures. It has gained further momentum since the 1986 Tax Reform Act in the United States, partly because of evidence that high rates of tax in one country can lead to an exodus of labour and capital to another. . . . Although there are widely differing degrees of change and implementation, the freer movement of labour and capital between OECD economies has meant that reforms have been to an important degree international.—OECD 1989, 169

The 1980s witnessed sweeping tax reforms in Sweden as well. By the end of the decade, both personal and corporate income taxes had been simplified, had their tax base broadened and their tax rates slashed.[29] Many tax incentives were removed or scaled back, and both consumption and social security taxes had been increased. In short, Swedish tax policy during this decade was in perfect keeping with the worldwide tax reform movement: capital was given more freedom and the tax burden was redistributed downward.

The process by which Sweden achieved these tax policy ends was, however, uniquely Swedish. The constitutional reforms of the last decade had, as we saw in the last chapter, materially changed the strategic context for major policy actors—the halcyon days of the great corporatist compromise were waning. But many of the institutions and patterns of behavior developed in the fifties and sixties remained. Thus, in the end, the politics of tax reform in Sweden in the 1980s represented a fascinating mix of old-fashioned compromising, plodding, technocratic reformism and the newly politicized, confrontational, and often fickle high politics of a new era

The Middle Way at the Crossroads

By the 1980s it appeared that something had gone very wrong with the Swedish model (Heclo and Madsen 1987; Pontusson 1991; Weaver 1987). First, the constitutional changes of the 1970s made Swedish political parties more responsive to the Swedish citizenry. Slowly at first, but more so over time, partisan elites, finding their short-term electoral interests improved by wrecking political deals rather than constructing them, developed new, more confrontational political stances. Second, economic change brought with it new political demands on the part of both labor and capital. These changes, in turn, forced the Social Democrats to rethink their traditional relationships with these groups. The success of the Swedish model depended upon the willingness of key economic interests to cooperate with the government in establishing and implementing common economic ends.[30] By the early 1980s, however, both the SAF and the LO had become considerably less cooperative (Rothstein 1986).

In the last chapter I argued that institutional changes brought about by the new politics in Sweden had begun to create fissures in the logic of the corporatist compromise. The election of 1976 demonstrated that no one could continue to depend on the fact that the Social Democrats would hold the reins of government virtually in perpetuity. This basic electoral fact soon changed the strategic choices and the policy preferences of almost all relevant political actors. For example, the LO elite had repeatedly been willing to yield short-term sacrifices for the economic good of the nation (or for the political good of their patrons, the SAP). In the new institutional climate of Swedish politics, however, it made much less sense to sacrifice or compromise. By the late 1970s, no one could guarantee that sacrifices would be compensated for later.[31]

Economic changes both in the world economy generally and within Sweden itself critically redefined the economic and political interests of the central participants in Sweden. Though corporate interests had done very well within the traditional Swedish model, they were quite constrained by it (Rothstein 1990). By the mid-1980s the balance between the advantages gained and the costs yielded was being seriously challenged. Key elements of the historical compromise—for example, the very strict international exchange controls, a prohibition against serious foreign investment, the national wage bargaining system, and the corporate tax/incentive system—were being reconsidered. Though the tax system assured that successful companies would have low tax bills, it also locked profits into investment in Sweden. In 1988, Finance Minister Kjell-Olof Feldt explained the traditional approach in this way: "It was basically the idea to use the tax system for holding profits inside companies and thereby more or less force them to invest instead of distributing the money among the shareholders. Again, the idea was to lock profits up in our corporations."[32] As the world economy globalized, Swedish capital began to demand greater flexibility. The problem was less that Swedish capital resources were insufficient than that in order to maintain their competitiveness, they too needed greater access to the lower rates available on the international financial market as well as access to the international labor market.

Changes in the Swedish economy also forced the SAP to rethink its traditional political/economic strategy. The very success of Swedish tax policy in the postwar years had led to massive concentration of both economic and political power. In the changed political and economic climate of the 1980s, it was far from obvious that this concentration was desirable. For example, Feldt argued in 1988 that "of all investments made, 75 percent are made by the twenty-five largest companies, which have about 80 percent of our exports, and this degree of concentration means that enormous amounts of profits are in these twenty-five, or let's say fifty corporations. . . . What we have is a financial concentration—more of a financial problem—built up around a big pile of cash. I must say, our beliefs are that it is not good even for our party to have the mastodons growing much more." [33]

Finally, the politics of Swedish labor unions were changing in the late 1970s and 1980s. It was becoming evident not only that the historical compromise was less and less viable because of the changing strategic interests of Swedish capital, but also that the political unity within the labor movement was also becoming more and more difficult to maintain. This new political dynamic had two sources: first, as has often been noted, the very success and growth of the Swedish welfare state undermined the unity of the labor unions (see Swenson 1989, 1991). In the 1970s and 1980s white-collar unions, generally represented by the Tjänstemännens Centralorganisation (TCO) grew much more rapidly than the traditional blue-collar unions generally represented by the LO. Over time, these unions came to see their interests differently from those of the traditional blue-collar unions. Central LO unions had long since agreed to the basic principle that their wage policy should facilitate Sweden's comparative advantage in export-oriented industries—even when this sometimes meant constraining wages (Hadenius 1966; Swenson 1989). White-collar unions, however, did not necessarily share this basic economic premise (Rothstein 1989). For them, the economic logic of holding down their wages in order to make Swedish exports more competitive simply did not make sense. Given the sheer size of the public sector, this attitude presented obvious problems for whomever was in government and also for LO elites: how could they tell their members that they should hold back wages when white-collar workers would not hold back theirs (Swenson 1990)? If these unions, then, were going to continue to make the kinds of sacrifices they had made in the past, they wanted to be able to show their membership that the government was answering with corresponding benefits for their constituents. However, as we shall see below, the government's reform agenda, and tax reform in particular, seemed to demonstrate just the opposite.

Rethinking Swedish Taxation

The very high level of progressive taxation just doesn't work.
—Swedish Minister of Finance Kjell-Olof Feldt, 1978

In chapters 4 and 5 I showed how postwar economic growth turned the progressive taxes introduced during World War II into enormously lucrative revenue machines. They were so lucrative that tax policymakers could offer special tax expenditures *and* increase tax revenues. Economic growth caused even moderate wage earners to creep up into higher marginal tax brackets. Faced with this fiscal reality, state officials had the following options: (a) cutting tax rates across the board, (b) offering selective tax cuts in an attempt to pay off special constituents, or (c) holding tight and watching state revenues grow. The three countries studied here chose some mix of these options; but each country combined their options in different ways. On balance, U.S. tax policymakers preferred option *b*, the British seemed to prefer a combination of *a* and *b*, while the Swedish chose option *c* for taxes on individuals and *b* for taxes on capital.

While perhaps fiscally rational, the Swedish approach did have its political costs. Whereas it was true that the top marginal income tax rates found in Sweden in the late 1970s (80 percent) were lower than those in the United Kingdom at the time (98 percent), it was more significant that the average tax rate paid by normal working Swedes was higher by a good degree than that in any other country in the world. By the mid-1970s, Swedes were internationally famous as the most heavily taxed people in the world (table 6.6). And, as the bourgeois parties were constantly pointing out, there was no mistaking which party was responsible for this inglorious reputation.

In addition to fearing public backlash against high taxes, Swedish tax policy elites became convinced that the tax system was producing a variety of negative social and economic consequences. In arguments quite similar to those made in Britain and the United States, a growing number of respected economists argued that high rates reduced the incentive to work, save, and invest and also that tax incentives were either ineffective or simply wrongheaded.[34] High taxes were said to create a host of social ills as well. The economist Gunnar Myrdal argued, for example, that whereas Swedes were world renowned for their honesty, the tax system was creating "a nation of cheaters" (Myrdal 1978, 500). High tax rates were also making wage negotiations much more difficult (cf. LO Tidnignen, 6/17/88; Ståhl 1983). Finally, because interest payments were deductible from income taxes, there was a strong incentive for individuals to "tax finance" consumption by borrowing

Table 6.6

Personal Income Tax Paid by the
Average Production Worker, U.S.,
U.K., and Sweden, 1984 and 1987
(excluding the effects of
nonstandard tax reliefs)

	Single People		Two-child Families	
	1984	1987	1984	1987
Sweden	36.1	36.6	34.2	35.0
U.K.	22.4	20.3	18.1	16.6
U.S.	22.9	20.0	15.2	13.3

Source: OECD, *The Tax/Benefit Position of Production Workers, 1984–1987*, 1988, table 1, p. 50.

to pay for consumer goods rather than saving for them. By 1980, private individual savings in Sweden had fallen to 0.0 percent.[35]

In sum, there were lots of good reasons to cut taxes in Sweden. That did not mean, however, that cutting taxes would be easy. Swedish voters, like all voters, enjoy the public spending that taxes finance.

Bourgeois Government at Last, 1976–82

One of my great disappointments with the bourgeois government
[1976–82], is that they did not manage to reform the tax system for us.
—Kjell-Olof Feldt, interview with author, 1988

When the bourgeois coalition finally assumed power in 1976, cutting taxes was very high on their agenda. But this was a coalition government, and though they all agreed on the need to cut taxes, they patently did not agree on the questions of who should get the most tax relief and how tax cuts should be financed. To oversimplify a bit: the Center party, formerly the Farmers party, wanted consumption taxes cut. The Liberal party wanted middle-class and salaried employees' taxes cut. The Moderate party wanted to cut taxes paid by high-income earners.

The late 1970s in Sweden were also tough economic times. The realities of a changing international economy and very high wages in Sweden meant that several key industries were in crisis. In an earlier era, tax cuts could perhaps have been financed through economic growth, but this option was not available in the late 1970s. Instead, because each party in the coalition had its own constituency to protect from economic decline, public subsidies were broadened rather than trimmed back.

The bourgeois block had offered itself as an alternative to the continued growth of government and what they perceived as fiscal irresponsibility. Unfortunately for them, they were not able to deliver on their promises. Five years, two elections, and four governments after the first bourgeois victory, taxes for most groups were marginally cut. Income taxes were indexed, and a number of tax loopholes were opened. At the same time, public spending rose, and for the first time in recent Swedish history, the government began handing out generous direct public subsidies to failing Swedish corporations. The net result was neither economic renewal nor a shrinking of the state's role in society. Instead, the economy continued to decline, and the budget deficit skyrocketed to 13 percent of GNP by 1982–83 (Weaver 1987, 312). This was not a record that the bourgeois parties could be proud of.

The Wonderful Night

The persistent indecisiveness and instability of these bourgeois governments, combined with intensified discontent with the system of taxation, provided a strategic opening that the (now opposition) Social Democrats used to split the bourgeois block and bring down the government. In a clever set of maneuvers, subsequently called the Wonderful Night, the Social Democrats offered to cooperate in a tax policy deal that would reduce marginal rates, above all for the middle and working classes, in exchange for limitations on the deductibility of interest payments. The Social Democrats were thus able to use the policy differences between the governing parties to drive a wedge between them and shake the foundations of this tottering government. In the end, the conservative Moderate party, which also wanted rate reductions but staunchly opposed limitations on interest deductions, walked out of the government.[36] The political confusion over this reform and the consequent fall of the government were central components of the Social Democratic party's electoral victory the following year (Hadenius 1981).

In the final analysis, the bourgeois coalition was indeed a failure. As any student of continental European politics understands, proportional representation often makes for weak and unstable governments. Moreover, having been left out of the inner sanctums of political power for so long, these three parties were ill-prepared for the tasks at hand (Bergström 1987). One must also remember that this coalition government came to office at a difficult juncture economically and politically in Swedish history. The Social Democrats had headed a number of coalition governments in the forty-four years before 1976, but in every case the constitution essentially protected the SAP by in effect guaranteeing their dominance over the Upper Chamber even in the event of temporary electoral losses. As a consequence, all parties understood that short-term party political strategies would not directly translate into short-term electoral success. In the late 1970s, however, these constitutional buffers were gone. Now temporal popular opinion could have a much more direct impact on the political fortunes of each party. In short, the incentive to wheel, deal, and cater to the masses had been enhanced in the past decade. The first bourgeois government in nearly half a century had the misfortune of coming to office just as the realities of the new incentive structure were taking hold in Swedish politics.

The Party of Government Returns to Govern

The debate about tax policy in Sweden took a new direction in the beginning of the 1980s. More emphasis than before was placed on efficiency and incentives and less on the goal of an equitable distribution of income. —Jan Södersten

When the Social Democrats returned to office in 1982 they were faced with huge budget and trade deficits, a restive labor movement, and a public weary of indecisive government. Within the government there was a growing insecurity over the appropriate direction for a socialist government in the 1980s and beyond. The LO and many of the Left in the party felt that the time for the final transition to socialism was at hand, but others, notably those in the Ministry of Finance, believed that Sweden should turn in a more market-oriented direction. Though the reformists had no intention of rolling back the welfare state or radically cutting back Sweden's famous safety net, they did feel that policies that would further reward individual initiative and effort were required. Reforming the tax system was to be the core of this new economic strategy (Pontusson 1990).

On a more general level, the reformists believed not only that the tax system needed reform, but that the Socialists' basic attitude and approach to capitalism needed rethinking. In an explicitly provocative article, "What Shall We Do with Capitalism?" Feldt wrote,

What conclusions should we draw, then? The first is to stop bad mouthing the market economy (defined as decentralized economic decision-making, free competition in open markets and free choice of consumption). On the global level, we know, the market economy in this form has won a total victory over its only known alternative, central economic planning.

Our party program states that a market economy can only yield acceptable results under certain conditions. It should be described the other way around—only under certain conditions and in certain markets is economic planning better than market solutions.[37]

To say the least, these views were not widely accepted by either the Social Democratic Left or by the LO executive. On the contrary, it was often argued that Feldt had abandoned his socialist credentials and instead adopted bourgeois politics. Still, the Ministry of Finance would not be detoured.

Tax Reform Swedish Style

Traditionally, the minister of finance in Sweden is, after the party leader, by far the most influential cabinet minister.[38] Kjell-Olof Feldt was no exception. Under Feldt's direction, the Socialists systematically marched toward reforming and redirecting Swedish taxes in an attempt to bring them into closer alignment with other tax systems in the world. In his view this meant doing three things: cutting marginal tax rates, removing unnecessary tax loopholes, and simplifying the tax system. Simultaneously, he sought to bring the budget back into fiscal balance.

To bring both party and country around to their way of thinking, Ministry of Finance officials and Feldt personally spoke at every opportunity about the need for tax reform. They also published numerous articles decrying the current system (Eklund 1984, 70–71). Feldt even allowed two reporters to engage him in a series of interviews and then publish them as a book.[39] Feldt also closely consulted with both academic and interest organization experts on tax matters. They too published widely, arguing for tax reform.[40] Finally, Feldt commissioned a series of official research studies on tax reform, each of which was to examine problems in the extant system and propose reforms.[41] The objective of the last three of these studies—by far the most important— was to make proposals for an overhaul of the entire tax system.

In traditional Swedish fashion, each official commission (known by the acronym SOU) issued reports recommending in detail what Feldt had been recommending in general. The government then wrote versions of these recommendations into legislation. The tax reform of 1990, commonly referred to as Århundrets Skattereform (The tax reform of the century), was by far the most sweeping and far-reaching. However, just as in Britain and the United States, there were a series of smaller reforms that in some fundamental way set the stage for the final tax reform of the decade.[42]

Among the preparatory tax changes legislated between 1982 and 1989 were (a) a series of measures that broadened the income and consumption tax bases; (b) a hike in consumption and social security taxes; (c) initiation of a temporary withholding tax on corporate profits; (d) simplification of the income tax code; (d) a so-called mandatory savings system that increased withholding taxes in order to reduce inflationary pressures; (e) introduction of a "one-time tax" on inflationary wealth gains of the insurance industry; and (f) reform and an increase of wealth and death taxes. By the end of the decade not only had the budget been brought back into balance, a stunning feat given the 13 percent of GNP deficits in 1982, but also the income tax system had been simplified to the point where now only a fraction of taxpayers would have to fill out a year-end tax return.[43] As impressive as this list is, however, these changes were only a precursor to the major tax overhaul pushed by the government at the end of the decade.

The Tax Reform of the Century

The world's tax systems are changing quickly. This is particularly true in the area of corporate taxation. The openness of the Swedish economy and its dependence on growth of international markets for capital, labor, goods and services makes it natural that the tax reform process takes notice of these international changes. The Swedish corporate tax system needs to be designed so that it contributes to the effective use of resources and to that portion of the Swedish economy that operates in the international marketplace.—Swedish Royal Commission on Corporate Tax Reform, SOU 1989, 34, p. 179

The government's problem, of course, was not how to get commissions and tax experts to recommend the proposals it desired, but rather how to get these proposals through the Riksdag. Though the dominant party by far, the Socialists controlled only 166 of the 349 seats in the Riksdag in 1982–85. Therefore, to pass a reform of the magnitude desired by the government, it would need the explicit support of at least one other party. Because the major impetus behind the restructuring was the Ministry's belief that marginal income tax rates needed to be reduced, the sometimes coalition partners, the Communists, were not an option. The bourgeois parties, on the other side, were all generally in favor of reduced income and corporate tax rates, but of course each had its own interpretation of who should benefit most and, more important, how the rate reductions should be financed. Equally important, the opposition parties were still smarting from the political wounds inflicted during the Wonderful Night. They were therefore not disposed to cooperate with the SAP—even when they shared many of the tax reform goals of the government.

The Social Democratic government was in quite a different structural position than either their British or American counterparts. On the one hand, the SAP did not have the votes to ram whatever bill it chose through the Parliament, as Thatcher had been able to do. On the other hand, they were not forced, as the Reagan administration was, to simply throw their preferred package to the wolves (Congress) and hope that what came out would be acceptable. Instead, the Swedish government would have to cut an explicit deal with at least one opposition party if it hoped to implement its general strategy.

At last, in June 1989 the long-awaited reform proposals of the three commissions were issued. Almost immediately it appeared that the tax reforms were dead in the water. Minister Feldt had, at some political cost, staked his position on their success.[44] And the bourgeois block was anxious to stick together in order to both extract further concessions on the spending side of the budget and bring about a governmental crisis. Why, after all, not use tax reform against the Socialists in 1989 just as they had used tax reform against the bourgeois parties in 1981? None of the parties, moreover, was happy with all of the reform package as proposed by the three commissions.[45] Tax reform's problems were exacerbated by the outspoken opposition voiced by the Communist party and growing uneasiness within the SAP. Finally, the LO pressured the government intensely to change the tax proposals by raising the top tax brackets and minimizing the increases in consumption taxes.[46] The reform package was unraveling.

What the government did next brilliantly illustrates how the structural position of the still-dominant SAP within parliamentary democracy had changed in the past two decades. On October 3, 1989, the Social Democratic prime minister, Ingvar Carlson, announced that rather than postpone the reform package for further debate in the 1990 session of the Riksdag (such a delay would have constituted normal politics in an earlier era) the government now intended to push forward with its package and implement the first stage of the tax reform in 1990!

The proposal shocked and amazed most Swedes, but in retrospect it can be seen as a deft political parry and riposte that forced the hand of opponents on both the Left and the Right. Immediately upon announcing its intentions, the government called the leaders of all major parties as well as the representatives of the major interest groups to a summit meeting at the king's traditional summer home in Haga. On October 27, after short but intense negotiations during which the Communists and the conservative Moderate party left in a huff, the Liberal party chairman, Bengt Westerberg, shook hands with Finance Minister Feldt, sealing a deal for a radical overhaul of the Swedish tax system.[47]

The details of the negotiations are not publicly known, but the facts of the case speak to some rather obvious conclusions: first, the SAP as well as the opposition elite all agreed that the proposals of the tax reform commissions constituted a marked improvement over the current tax code. Second, the Liberals also saw that the government was under intense pressure to make the tax system more progressive and thereby undermine key features of the reform package.[48] "If you want to have tax reform," the government appeared to say to the Liberals, "then we've got to cut a deal now." The government's plan would create a simpler, more efficient system than the old one and would eliminate the national income tax for the vast majority of Swedish taxpayers, bringing their top marginal tax rate down to only 30 percent. It would also greatly simplify the corporate tax system, cut tax rates dramatically, and remove a wide variety of tax expenditures. Finally, it would finance these reforms by boosting the more economically neutral VAT.

Still, even though the major business federations were pressing hard in favor of the reform, not one of the bourgeois parties was eager to break ranks and help out the Socialists. Finally, however, the Liberals went the last mile. The Liberal party had, after all, been actively advocating precisely this type of reform in recent years. Westerberg played hardball and was able to extract some critical concessions from Feldt in the final moments of their negotiations.[49] But all in all, the package, which redirected close to Skr 60 billion from income taxes to consumption taxes, was broadly what the finance minister had argued for the past five years.

The LO and the Left of the SAP were furious (V. Bergström 1989). But the reality is that the LO has no vote in the Riksdag, and even the Left of the SAP has to vote the party line, unless they would prefer to see a bourgeois government in power. In short, as had happened many times before in Swedish political history, the Left was outmaneuvered by a Social Democratic party elite who, in attempting to translate their broad policy agendas into practical reality, were forced to compromise with the political Right. It is ironic that, as the *LO Tidningen* put it, "the bitter truth is that the government in fact gave advantages to social groups who have never considered voting socialist and never will vote socialist." [50]

Postscript

As of spring 1993, the Swedish government was again in turmoil. A bourgeois coalition government was once again at the helm. But it is far from certain that they will be able to govern any more coherently or decisively than they did the last time they were in office. In fact, the evidence suggests that they will have even greater problems, despite their wider experience. Not only have they returned to office with the Swedish economy once again in crisis,[51] but also the election of 1991 brought in a new political party, New Democracy, which potentially holds the balance of power for the bourgeois block. Because New Democracy is both more populist and more rightist than any traditional party, the bourgeois parties have refused to allow it into the government, but without them they must rule as a minority coalition government.

The uncertainty of Swedish politics today goes even deeper than the instability of another bourgeois government. A resurgence of popular support for the SAP would hardly bring back the traditional Swedish model. First, institutional reforms introduced in the 1970s undermine the incentives for either party or interest group elites to engage in conciliatory or compromising political strategies, for which the Swedish model has become so famous. Instead, there are now strong incentives for them to engage in even more confrontational public attacks. Now that all governments are electorally vulnerable, it can pay both interest groups and opposition parties to block legislation in the Riksdag, rather than seek out points of agreement and compromise.

Second, the economic realities of global capitalist economy make the Middle Way an untenable option. If Sweden is going to compete in the flexible world market for capital, labor, and services it will be forced to adopt public policies more in line with those of the rest of the world. As we have seen, for most of the 1980s, the SAP realized this and pursued policies that patently favored capital. The most recent tax reform was but one example. The decision to join the European Community is another. Unsurprisingly, local unions and workers at the shop-floor level have become embittered and hostile toward these market reforms. Their response has been to become more strident in their wage demands and, when this showed small signs of success, to strike.

Prime Minister Ingvar Carlson's "crisis package," introduced in February 1990, would have frozen prices, wages, and dividends, but it only demonstrated the weakness and desperation of the Social Democrats as they attempted to deal with these new economic realities. The government's proposal to impose a ban on strikes, with legal penalties of up to Skr 5,000 (approximately $800) for those who broke this law, was even more significant.[52] No other act could have demonstrated more emphatically the extent to which Social Democratic hegemony has declined. Without this hegemony, the Middle Way is clearly a Dead End.

In their survey of major changes in macroeconomic policies in the late 1970s and early 1980s, *Why Economic Policies Change Course,* the OECD's first conclusion was as follows:

> One clear lesson is the importance for countries of paying due attention to developments and policies abroad. The majority of situations considered were, or would if left untended have become, unsustainable in their own domestic terms—although it is hardly possible in today's world to visualize any national situation in purely closed-economy context. But many of the cases considered . . . bear eloquent witness to the realities of interdependence: what is sustainable can depend upon what is happening abroad. This conclusion should not be thought of merely as expressing the constraints on national performance; it can in principle be built on to devise internationally co-operative sets of policies for a better (and sustainable) global outcome. (OECD 1988b, 11)

The present chapter bears witness to this general hypothesis. The changing international context in which domestic policymakers make tax policy has critically redefined perceptions about what kinds of tax policies are in the national interest. Tax policies changed course in the 1980s not because new or revolutionary ideas had suddenly entered public debate. Indeed, there is nothing in the arguments of the tax reformers in the 1980s that had not already been equally well articulated by conservatives for most of the past century. Nor is it the case that the voting public suddenly changed their attitudes toward the aims of progressive taxation.

What has changed, over the past decade or so, is the ability of each country to define its own tax policy course. The fear that tax policies of the past decades have undermined each country's economic strength has led to dramatic, worldwide changes. Perhaps it is too early to tell whether these changes will lead to a new tragedy of the commons, in which each country's attempt to attract and retain highly skilled labor and capital ultimately undermines their individual abilities to finance the infrastructure upon which a successful economy and society depends. Focusing on the United States, the purported leader of tax reform around the world, one would certainly be lead to this conclusion. But as we have seen in the preceding pages, the institutions through which each country will introduce these reforms will critically shape their outcomes. It does seem, however, that the tax policy agenda has grown beyond the boundaries of the nation-state. It remains to be seen whether new institutions can or will be created to deal with this new context.

7

Taxes, Democracy, and the Welfare State

A state's means of raising and deploying financial resources
tell us more than could any other single factor about its existing
(and immediately potential) capacities to create or strengthen
state organizations, to employ personnel, to coopt political
support, to subsidize economic enterprises, and to fund social
programs.—Theda Skocpol, "Bringing the State Back In"

The size of the welfare state varies dramatically from one country to another—
and so does the size of the tax burden. Though I have never seen it explicitly argued, I think that most political scientists believe that differences in
tax burdens are explained by differences in spending desires. In short, the
United States taxes its citizens less than Sweden because Americans do not
like government spending as much as Swedes. I suggest that the causal arrow
in fact points the other way. Both Swedes and Americans like public spending and hate taxes. The key difference in the size of the U.S. and Swedish
welfare states has less to do with dissimilarities in public attitudes toward public spending and more to do with tax policy choices made for those citizens
by political elites. Tax policy choices, in short, not only make the modern
welfare state possible, but have helped create quite different welfare states.

Taxes and Citizens

In an influential article entitled "Why the Government is Too Small in a
Democracy" (1960) Anthony Downs presented what I believe is one of the
central dilemmas faced in modern democracy: Voters are largely uninformed
but rationally self-interested. First, because benefits are often diffuse, citizens
are insensitive to or unaware of a large share of the benefits they receive.
Because taxes are direct, citizens are painfully aware of the costs of government. Because they are rational, they will oppose paying for benefits that they
do not perceive. Given the complexity of modern government and the scope
and reach of activities that the government involves itself in, it is difficult for
citizens to accurately evaluate costs versus benefits: citizens feel the costs of
government in the form of taxes directly, while such benefits as clean air,
good roads, an educated workforce, national defense, and the reduction of
poverty are felt much less precisely or are assumed.

Second, because public transactions are different from private transactions, peoples' attitudes toward the two vary. Private transactions are done on a quid pro quo basis: one pays a specific amount for a specific good or service. With most taxes, however, the payment is for services or goods that we do not directly receive. This leaves the impression that taxes are confiscatory and not a payment. Finally, different people are willing to pay for different public programs. The result is that taxpayers often correctly believe that their taxes pay for something that they do not like. For the political Left, taxes pay for too many bombers. For the political Right, taxes pay for too many welfare cheats. People deeply resent the "waste" of their hard-earned money but feel that they have little control over how this money is spent. The result? Citizens feel that their tax dollars are being wasted on policies they do not like. In sum, every government is in a political bind. Governments, all governments, must walk a fine line between these conflictual pressures.

Taxation differs from other policy issues because virtually all voting citizens confront its effects with each paycheck. Even ardently antipolitical citizens—those who don't read the newspapers, don't watch TV news, don't vote, and refuse to discuss politics at any time—pay taxes. It might therefore be reasonable to assume that taxation is a unique policy in that citizens know more or understand more about taxes than they do about other issues. After all, we can see on each paycheck how much the government takes from us, and we can see how they take it. This assumption, however, is wrong. Citizens are generally ill-informed about the structure, effects, and design of their country's tax system; they are even remarkably ignorant of the taxes that they themselves pay. Ask yourself what percentage of your income you pay in income, social security, property, and consumption taxes. If you are even close in your estimates, you are the exception (Lewis 1982, 1978; Roper Organization 1977; Hansen 1983).

In all three countries examined here, study after study demonstrates that citizens believe the government should do more about social and economic problems, that is, increase spending—but at the same time, they feel that taxes are too high.[1] Public opinion polls show highly inconsistent attitudes toward taxes and spending.[2] Alan Lewis (1982, 49) puts it this way:

> For most people fiscal policy is not an important issue, and respondents look for guidance to the interviewer's questions as to what their answers ought to be. Few of us have the tenacity to admit our ignorance in public, especially about things which we feel we ought to know. . . . Inconsistencies may not be apparent to the non-attentive public, which sees no inconsistency between favoring increases in public expenditure on the one hand and reductions in taxes in the other. There is no conflict

to be resolved; the two things may never have been considered together before the interviewer asked about them.

If citizens are poorly informed about taxes—even their own taxes—how can they be expected to provide guidance to political leaders? The answer, I submit, is that citizens provide little guidance indeed. Citizens instead act as constraints on the state. This point has several broad implications for the politics of revenue and, ultimately, for the size of the welfare state.

Because of the disjuncture between taxing and spending desires on the part of average citizens, political elites are faced with opposing incentives. If political elites are able to override initial public resistance to taxes—that is, do what voters don't want—they will have much greater scope for expanding welfare state programs—that is, doing what voters do want. Thus, perhaps unsurprisingly given these conflicting incentives, political elites in all democracies have responded similarly. They have ratcheted up both tax rates and tax bases during times of crisis, relied on economic growth and inflation to push up revenues, and attempted to hide tax hikes via indirect, or hidden, taxes.

The specific tax policies chosen from within this menu, however, have differed from democracy to democracy. These choices, though, which when made can often appear quite small or incremental, can have enormous revenue implications over time. This is because not all taxes are equally hated by citizens. Indeed, citizens' resistance to taxes depends more on the type of taxes they pay than on the total burden of those taxes on the economy (ACIR 1985; Coughlin 1980; Hadenius 1985; Hibbs and Madsen 1981; Wilensky 1979). Faced with the inconsistency of public attitudes toward taxing and spending, those governments that are best able to create more efficient or less visible tax structures are in the best position to expand the realm of public activity. In short, because spending is constrained by the need for revenues, the structure and design of a nation's tax system critically determines the level of public spending.

Institutional Structure and Tax Policy Choices

If the structure of the tax system is decisive in determining the total tax burden, what determines that structure? This book has shown that the structure of a nation's tax system is a consequence neither of vast and immutable differences in public values nor even of coherent differences in the elite's attitudes toward the proper size and functions of the welfare state. Rather, tax policy choices are most directly the result of differences in the structure and design of each nation's political decision-making institutions. Decision-making processes help define both the roles and perspectives of bureaucrats, politicians, and interests in every polity.

E. E. Schattschneider's insight that organization is the mobilization of bias, then, is even broader than he suggested it to be. Organizational structure influences not only the distribution of taxing and spending priorities in a polity, but also the very size of the welfare state. America is a social welfare laggard, in sum, not simply because of the prominence of individualistic values, but rather because of the tax policy biases inherent in the fragmentation of its political institutions.

Bluntly stated, the argument here is that Sweden spends more on public programs than the United States because the Swedish state collects more tax revenue. Swedish authorities are able to collect more revenue than Americans because the Social Democrats in Sweden have been able to build a tax system that is very broadly based and efficient. Not a lack of will but the fragmentation of political authority in America has stifled both presidential and congressional reformers in their efforts to broaden the tax base and introduce consumption taxes.

This book has clearly shown that throughout the twentieth century Democrats and Progressives in the United States have imposed steeper and more progressive taxes than have Social Democrats in Sweden. This has probably not been because Americans are more ideologically committed to income and wealth redistribution than Swedes. Rather, Socialists in Sweden have been institutionally stifled and have had to compromise, yielding their demands for confiscatory taxes in favor of broader-based taxes with lower marginal tax rates on the very wealthy. This was not part of a preconceived strategy on the part of the Socialists, but rather the product of institutionally shaped compromises.

Americans have had to compromise too, but in the American institutional context the compromises have required that reformers yield a huge number of tax breaks designed for particular constituencies. The result is a tax system that on its face is quite progressive, but that is "riddled with loopholes" (Wilbur Mills). No one intentionally designed the American tax system to be the way it is, and few approve of its design.

Of course the single biggest difference between the American and European tax systems is the fact that the United States does not have a national consumption tax. Indeed, if the United States collected the same average amount of consumption taxes as the average European OECD nation (12.7 percent rather than 4.9 percent), it would collect 37.8 percent of GDP in taxes. In short, if the United States had such a tax, we probably would not consider America a social welfare state laggard (Wilensky 1976; Steinmo 1993).[3]

As we have seen, national consumption taxes have been proposed many

Table 7.1

Swedish Attitudes toward the Growth
of Public Programs, 1960–79

	1960	1964	1968	1970	1973	1976	1979
Agree	60%	66%	46%	62%	65%	65%	71%
Disagree	40	34	54	39	35	35	29

Source: Korpi 1983, 209.

times in the United States. But each time such proposals are aired they are defeated in committee. There is no evidence that the committee defeats these proposals because the American public resisted the idea more than the Swedish public. No one, anywhere, likes the idea of new taxes. These proposals were defeated because the fragmentation of the American decision-making structure provides numerous veto points (Immergut 1992) for those who oppose new legislation to defeat it—even when a popular president offers the proposal.

In 1968, when taxation was less than 35 percent of GNP in Sweden, 70 percent of Swedes felt that marginal taxes were "far too high" and 63 percent felt that "taxes must be reduced at all costs." Even the statement "taking into account the *benefits* which the state gives the citizens, the taxes are not too high" received a 54 percent negative response. In the twenty years since these polls were taken, however, the tax burden has grown massively to over 56 percent of GNP.[4]

These figures may even understate the degree of public resistance to tax increases in Sweden. After all, 1968 was a high point of social activism in Sweden and elsewhere. Table 7.1 shows the responses to the following statement, which was asked in each election year: "Social reforms have gone so far in this country that in the future the government ought to reduce rather than increase allowances and assistance to citizens."

The massive growth of the Swedish state is *not* the result of power-hungry bureaucrats trying to expand their domain of influence irrespective of the interests of the citizen. It is a response to the ever-present desire of the citizenry for more and better public programs, on the one hand, and Sweden's governing elites' ability to override short-term resistance to tax increases, on the other. Moreover, Swedes, like all other publics, strongly support the particular programs financed by the welfare state (for example, health, social security, education, housing, food subsidies, child subsidies) and generally want to see these programs expanded.

When Downs assumed that government in a democracy would be too small, he assumed a constitutional format that would emphasize citizens' short-term preferences over their long-term interest. He assumed a particular institutional bias. Different institutions yield different biases. One wonders whether Downs would have written his famous article if he had been a Swede.

Tax Preferences and Rational Actors

I am not arguing here that Swedish, British, or American voters are stupid. I am instead arguing that they want many things, and often what they want in one area conflicts with what they want in another. Perhaps it is not rational to want broadening of public programs concomitant with cuts in the size of the state—but it is certainly human.

People do not have a single definable and stable hierarchy of preferences that can or should be used to decide between competing policy choices (North 1990). What we want can depend upon how it is presented to us and the general context in which the choice is offered (Beer et al. 1987; Kahneman, Slovic, and Tversky 1982). This is equally true of political elites and political scientists as it is of average citizens. I, personally, want to spend more time with my children *and* I want to finish this book. These are, it appears, incompatible goals. But I have not and probably cannot rank these goals and stick to that preference ordering. I compromise and I frequently change my preference ranking, depending on the context of the choice and how I feel. How I feel also generally depends on a variety of contextual factors over which as a rule I have little or no control: how well my writing has been going, how close I am to tenure, other demands placed on me by my students, wife, or colleagues. I also very often follow the patterns that I have most recently followed and avoid making new choices at each possible decision point (DiMaggio and Powell 1991; Alford 1991). Yet these contextual factors will often, in the end, define my choices.

Citizens and state officials alike are faced with similar dilemmas. This is why political institutions are so vital in shaping policy outcomes. If citizens' opinions were unambiguous, then the mechanisms by which these opinions are translated into public policy should (in a democracy) have relatively little independent effect on the policy outcomes. But when the public's guidance is unclear or subject to varying interpretations, then it is reasonable to expect that the mechanism for that interpretation can have significant effects.

Political institutions are the context in which we make political choices, yet voters and policymakers alike generally have little control over that basic context. An example will help illustrate: No one who has studied American politics closely is unaware of the frustration of elected officials with respect to the power of special interest groups. Most politicians would agree that the influence of special interest groups in America often undermines their desire to make good public policy. But the rub is that these same officials have a competing preference—they want to get reelected (Mayhew 1974; Fiorina 1977). Getting elected requires the support of the special interest groups.

Most elected officials have not abandoned their desire to make good public policy; they merely feel compelled sometimes to prioritize the competing preference. Much as in the personal case I noted above, the decision of which preference to prioritize is commonly beyond the immediate control of the actor. With respect to tax policy, there is no question that U.S. legislators are deeply frustrated with the U.S. tax code they write. In 1985 President Reagan's Treasury Department proposed a comprehensive reform of the system (Treasury I) that promised to cure many of the system's greatest ills. The proposal failed. But it did not fail because a majority of legislators thought it a bad law; it failed because a majority of legislators recognized that their support for the proposal would conflict with their desire to get elected.[5] Representative Robert Matsui captured the complexities involved in the vote: "This is not a clear-cut issue like apartheid. There were so many shades of gray: What are we doing to housing, to student loans, to the future ability of government to raise revenue? . . . The easiest vote would have been to vote no and have the bill pass, or to vote yes and have the bill die" (Russakoff 1986, 1).

In the abstract, I believe that both citizens and elites in Sweden, Britain, and the United States would make highly similar decisions if offered similar choices.[6] I have conducted several dozen interviews in each of these countries that appear to confirm this hypothesis. When asked, "If you could be guaranteed that increased government spending would be efficiently and effectively used to address society's problems, would you agree to an increase in your taxes?" the vast majority of people I interviewed, even the Americans, answered, "Yes!" The respondents, especially the Americans, quickly add, however, that they do not believe that revenue from higher taxes would be used efficiently or effectively and therefore they would not approve tax increases if they were given the choice.[7]

I also asked both liberal Democrats and labor union officials in the United States specifically if they would approve of the introduction of a VAT in view of the fact that substantial rises in income tax revenues appear extremely unlikely and that other countries, notably Sweden, have used these taxes to generate huge sums of revenue for public programs much like those liberals in America would like to see. The response has been unanimously, "No." In each case the respondent explained that given the way in which politics worked in the United States, they would not trust the system to use the increased tax borne by the poor to pay for programs that benefited the poor. "This is not Sweden," one Senate staff member observed. "How can we be sure that that extra money won't just be used to cut the taxes of the rich even more, or to buy more B-1 bombers?" The answer, of course, is that given the fragmentation of authority in the United States, no one can be sure.

The key issue here is that in the real world of politics neither citizens nor political elites are offered simple, obvious theoretical choices like the ones suggested above; and the real choices in one country are not likely to be offered in the same way that they are in another country. Instead, choices are offered differently because the institutions through which they are offered differ. Americans do not elect politicians who cater to special interests because they prefer this type of politician to a programmatic party any more than American politicians cater to special interests because they like such behavior. Rather, the political fragmentation built into the system via checks and balances and American federalism neuters political parties while it strengthens special interest groups.

Similarly, British voters do not elect politicians who will ignore the will and interests of the opposition because they prefer this type of politics. Instead, once in power British governments simply do not have the institutional incentives to compromise and dilute their agenda in the way that American and Swedish politicians must routinely dilute theirs. Analogously, British governments do not believe that the highly unstable and constantly changing tax system they have created over the years is good. But once elected, the preference for stability in the system generally takes a back seat to their desire to shape the system according to their electoral promises and ideological agenda. Finally, Swedish citizens in the fifties and sixties did not elect minority governments to the Riksdag because they consciously and collectively decided that they wanted to force the kind of compromising political style developed in this nation. Neither did they change these institutions in the 1970s because they collectively agreed that it would be good to move away from the "politics of compromise" (Rustow, 1955).

Institutional Dynamism

This last point reminds us that while the institutional context can shape political decisions, decisionmakers can also sometimes change the institutions. This book has tried to show the dynamic interaction among political institutions, the broader socioeconomic context in which these institutions operate, public policy, and, ultimately, attitudes. By *dynamic interaction* I mean to explicitly emphasize change. Too often social scientists, wishing to emphasize the primacy of their favored variable, deemphasize the interrelation between their variable and those of others. Ideas, institutions, interests, or the state too easily become *the* variable of concern.

Perhaps it is necessary to take a proprietary interest in certain variables simply to clarify our points and drive home our arguments. This tendency, however, has its costs. If, for example, America's individualistic values and political culture explain the weakness of certain welfare state programs, how and why has the United States developed one of the most generous social security systems in the world? Similarly, if the fragmentation of political institutions explains why the United States has not introduced broad-based consumption taxes, why did it not prevent the introduction of broad-based income taxes?

The answer to these questions is that neither institutions nor values nor economic interests for that matter by themselves provide adequate explanations for significant political outcomes over time; and that these variables interact with one another and, in so doing, change with time. The examining of the dynamic interaction among these variables provides the best hope for posing satisfactory explanations of the complex realities of political, economic, and social history.

On Theory and Method

The view of comparative political analysis presented here implicitly confronts some of the basic methodological and epistemological assumptions held by many political scientists. I would like to make this disagreement explicit. To some, the very purpose of social science is the uncovering of universal laws governing social and political behavior. Przeworski and Teune (1970, 4), for example, assert in their highly regarded volume *The Logic of Comparative Social Inquiry*, "The pivotal assumption of this analysis is that social science research, including comparative inquiry, should and can lead to general statements about social phenomena. This assumption implies that human behavior can be explained in terms of general laws established by observation." This view of political inquiry assumes and indeed searches for a set of neo-Newtonian laws that can be used to explain political outcomes over time and across space.

What if the major variables shaping political behavior and outcomes are in fact dynamically interactive, as I argue in this book? What universal laws can we establish? We can study history and construct explanations for how and where our variables played their roles in shaping political outcomes. This book has offered such an analysis. But can we draw from this analysis a fixed set of universal laws with which we can explain all political outcomes and, even more, predict future ones? I do not think so.

Human beings are both the agents and objects of social, political, and economic change. Therefore, both the rules and purpose of social scientific inquiry must differ from those of the natural sciences. Chemicals and atoms cannot consciously change the environmental context in which they exist. They cannot consciously change themselves. Humans can. Understanding the ways in which human beings shape their environment—and thereby their attitudes, values, and interests—is the central purpose of comparative political inquiry.

Political Institutions in Historical Context

This book thus attempts to weave an explanation for the politics of revenue that is sensitive to the interrelation between economic interests, public ideas, and political institutions. The focus on common paths and divergent patterns is a heuristic tool through which this story has been told. Through this telling, I have shown how Britain, Sweden, and the United States each constructed and reconstructed their decision-making structures in response to the changing economic and political contexts. Differing institutional structures have enormous implications not just for the character of each nation's revenue system, but also for the construction of political/economic interests and, ultimately, public attitudes as well. Differing interests and attitudes have, in turn, helped shape the reconstruction of political institutions in these countries as they have moved through the twentieth century.

We have seen, for example, that each of the three countries examined in this book rather drastically reformed its political/institutional structure as it attempted to cope with the new challenges and demands evoked by modernization and industrialization in the early twentieth century. In each case, the decision-making institutions they built were products of the institutional and political configurations extant in the country, interacting with a loosely similar set of demands or imperatives.

The massive economic transformation these countries underwent at roughly the turn of the century brought with it a new set of political ideas and laid the foundations for the development of both the modern welfare state and the modern tax system upon which it is financed. In all three countries there were challenges to the institutional authority of the dominant political/economic elite, on the one hand, and substantive policy demands for greater social and economic equality, on the other. The ways in which the institutions and the political/economic elite that controlled them responded to the new political context varied in each country. The political solutions struck in each nation, in turn, are critical for explaining the different policy paths these nations took as they moved into the twentieth century.

In Britain and Sweden, strong programmatic political parties became instruments through which middle- and working-class interests attempted to seize power from the entrenched elite. In both of these countries, progressive reformers had powerful incentives to organize and strengthen mass political parties in their attempts to democratize and gain control of their political systems. In the United States, in contrast, a highly decentralized federal democracy, the right to vote had been extended to most white males long since. Mass parties were thus well established, but for those who wished to push a national political agenda they were weak instruments. Progressive reformers in the United States, then, had no incentive to strengthen political parties and instead worked to undermine these obstacles to democratic accountability.

Britain and Sweden naturally responded differently to the challenges presented them in the early decades of the twentieth century. But faced with the growing complexities of governing in the modern era, both countries instituted reforms that effectively unified the executive and legislative functions of government. Strong parties became strong governments. This was, of course, most clear in Britain, where the House of Commons became "little more than an electoral college for the Prime Minister."[8] In Sweden, the traditional elite was able to hold on to power somewhat longer, and they extracted a set of institutional compromises designed to prevent the rise of majoritarian governments of any political color. These different choices were not made because Swedes like to compromise and the British do not. They were instead strategic calculations made by those in power over how to protect their political and economic interests. No one could have predicted the long-term consequences of these institutional choices.

The separation of powers dictated by the American Constitution inhibited this outcome by protecting the legislature from the predatory interests of the executive. The U.S. Constitution was very consciously designed in the late eighteenth century to divide the legislative and executive functions, pit these institutions against one another, and give each institutional prerogatives and powers enabling them to protect their separate realms of authority. But by the early twentieth century the task of governing a much larger and more complex nation required that these institutions adapt. The institutional solution in the United States was not to centralize political authority in the executive but to set up an elaborate committee system and divide political authority for discrete policy decisions to subunits of the congressional whole.

The centralization of executive and legislative functions in parliamentary regimes resulted in both the decline of legislative power and the legitimation of centralized authority under new and different forms of democratic institutions. In the United States, in contrast, committee government allowed Congress to become expert on the intricacies of modern policy making so that it was able to assert its authority vis-à-vis the presidency. This system also gave individual members of Congress autonomous bases of legislative power so that they have become less dependent upon their own leadership in the legislative branch. This unique outcome facilitated the continued dominance of the legislature over the legislative process, further ensconcing the legitimacy of individual representation of local and regional interests in national politics.

The same political/economic impulses driving institutional reform at the turn of the century evoked new demands for tax reform. As with institutional reform, neither those who proposed nor those who opposed these new taxes fully appreciated the revolutionary implications of their tax innovations. Instead, each decision to introduce or reform new taxes was made in order to adapt the current system to a new fiscal or political context. But each of these policy decisions in turn shaped and redefined the fiscal and political context in which future choices would be made. To paraphrase Hugh Heclo (1974), "new policies create new politics." In the case of taxation, however, new policies can have a multiplier effect. New tax policies not only establish the basis for a new and altered politics of taxation, but also make possible a new politics of spending.

These new taxes did not remain small for long. The changing economic and political context in these democratizing nations effectively ruled out significant boosts in tariffs or excises to finance the Great War. State officials quickly learned, moreover, that modern taxes were uncommonly buoyant sources of revenue and that they could be collected much more efficiently and effectively than traditional taxes. With these new taxes governments could now fight a new kind of war. "Total war" was not only horrible, it was expensive. Once the war was over, though, tax levels did not ease back to prewar levels. Experience with these new sources of revenue forced a rethinking of both mass and elite attitudes about taxation.

The Second World War had remarkably similar effects, but now the fiscal climate had dramatically changed. Richer societies with new taxes meant much richer states. These richer states were able to finance new technologies for even more horrible war. And now average citizens were part of the political system and could therefore be relied upon not only to man the battlefield, but also to finance the war effort. In most countries national sales taxes were introduced and personal income taxes became mass taxes. In addition—so that income tax revenues could be brought in more quickly and efficiently— the Pay-As-You-Earn system was introduced. State revenues exploded. Once again, society got used to the new levels of taxing. The new mass taxes continued to grow, even though politicians passed out tax breaks to those influential enough to demand them.

As government revenues grew, so did government's responsibilities. And as governments began to take on these responsibilities, both mass and elite attitudes toward the proper role of the state in society and economy began to shift as well. The same democratic institutions that made possible the expansion of taxes brought government into the management of both the society and the economy. In the society, governments became responsible for the public welfare. Slowly, but surely, governments became no-fault insurance agencies. Though small at first, these dedicated insurance taxes and the social security programs they financed eventually became core elements of the modern welfare state. They are, moreover, now intrinsically embedded in our societies and cultures, and no individual or group would seriously propose taking them away.

State officials too learned that these huge, efficient taxes gave governments the possibility to manage the economy. At both the macro and micro levels, they quickly found that taxes could be expanded or contracted to regulate the pulse of the capitalist economy. Keynes personally played a role in this development in the United States and the United Kingdom, but these ideas were imaginable only because of the new kinds of taxes that the world wars had brought.

These new ideas were predicated on the policy innovations that preceded them. Once again, institutions, interests, and ideas are neither fixed nor do they develop in vacuums. These taxes were developed in order to finance wars, but once they existed it became possible to think of new ways in which the state could be involved in the economy and society. These new ideas could only then be translated into new institutions. The development of these institutional mechanisms for state intervention in turn reshaped the political matrix of interests in each polity. In short, new tools reformulated old interests and made possible new ideas.

The different institutional structures built in these democracies, however, shaped the ways in which these new ideas were translated into specific policy instruments. The division of institutional responsibility inherent in American committee government both weakened political leadership and created "a lack of fiscal coordination" (Dodd 1977, 278). Frustrated with institutional obstacles to using these tools for broad or encompassing solutions to policy problems, tax policymakers in the United States increasingly chose to use these new instruments in favor of more narrowly defined constituency interests. The cracks in the door eventually became a flood of special interests seeking equal treatment before the tax code.

The institutional context in Britain and Sweden similarly shaped both the conceptual and policy horizons. In Britain the growth of single-member districts led to powerful majoritarian governments. Strong majoritarian governments can be certain that their legislative agenda will be passed by its legislature. Thus, there has been little incentive to compromise and cooperate with the political opposition or with hostile interest groups. And, indeed, there has been little incentive to develop institutional mechanisms to facilitate such compromise. A committee system like that developed in the United States in order to find arenas of compromise and conciliation is quite unnecessary because the legislature has little to no real policy-making power. Indeed, as Nelson Polsby (1968, 153) notes,

> In the United Kingdom . . . purely legislative committees are regarded as a threat to the cohesion of the national political parties because they would give the parliamentary parties special instruments with which they could develop independent policy judgements and expertise and exercise oversight over an executive which is, after all, not formally constituted as an entity separate from Parliament. Thus committees can be construed as fundamentally inimical to unified Cabinet government.

The tax policies constructed in this institutional context did not cater to special interests in anything like the way that had become common in America. This is not to say, however, that the British tax system developed more coherently or rationally than the American. Instead, as each new British government took the reins of power they faced strong incentives to act on the promises they had made when in opposition. At the same time each new government not only lacked institutional experience, but was insulated from the policy commitments made by those who had built the then-extant tax structure. The result, as we have seen, has been the dramatic see-sawing of tax policy and the fiscal incoherence these changes have wrought.

In Sweden, the conservative bureaucratic elite's desire to protect their interests at the turn of the century led them to demand a form of checks and balances quite different from that found in the United States. In this case, rather than institutionally separating the executive and legislature, the "conservative garanti" was a move to the proportional representation electoral system, on the one hand, and the continuance of the legislative authority of the conservative Upper Chamber, on the other. But these designed inefficiencies in Sweden, much as in the United States, were an obstacle to effective government. As the task of governing became more complicated, institutional solutions had to be found. Perhaps purely legislative committees were an option in Sweden, but owing to a unique confluence of historical factors—

the fact that PR often led to stalemated partisan squabbling, the tradition of strong and efficient bureaucratic mechanisms, and the existence of potent, centralized institutions representing both labor and capital in the Swedish economy—a more efficient solution to the governing dilemma evolved.

Rather than redesigning the system and pushing power back into the legislature, the Social Democrats built and strengthened extraparliamentary decision-making institutions. Rather than develop a legislative committee system, as the Americans had done, the Swedes developed neocorporatist decision-making institutions that incorporated strong economic interests, often to the exclusion of legislative representatives. The accident of Sweden's relatively late industrial development contributed to the centralization of labor market organizations (Ingham 1974), but its effect was to lend the government powerful tools with which to manage the national political economy—tools simply unavailable to governments in the more decentralized American and British economies.

In Sweden, these unique institutional structures aided the reconstruction of political/economic interests quite different from those found in either Britain or the United States. Representative authority was granted to key interest organizations. At the same time, corporatist decision-making institutions lent power to the more technocratic experts in both the interest organizations and the Social Democratic party. In short, by midcentury the structure of economic interest organizations in Sweden made it possible to think about new kinds of decision making-institutions. The establishment of these institutions, in turn, shaped the character and development of these economic interests. Both British and American governments attempted to establish neocorporatist institutions somewhat like the Swedish. But in each case these institutions failed, in large part because of the fragmentation of economic interest in these political economies.

In Sweden, as we have seen, these peculiar decision-making institutions made possible the construction of a markedly efficient and revenue-rich tax system, a tax system that centralized Sweden's capital base into its largest and most efficient corporations while at the same time providing the revenue for the world's most expansive welfare system. This substantive experience built a continued faith in the legitimacy of the state's role in society.

Looking Forward

As these countries have moved through the later decades of the twentieth century, political institutions, economic interests, and public ideas have not remained static. Changes in the economic context of domestic tax policy making, on the one hand, and the apparent omnipresence of the interventionist welfare state, on the other, have evoked a response of growing frustration by both the elite and the public. Once again, the economic and political context of modern politics is reshaping interests, attitudes, and political institutions. The responses of each nation to these broadly common forces will once again be shaped by ideas, institutions, and interests peculiar to each of these democratic states.

That the redistributive efforts of democratic states will be turned back seems a most likely outcome. At the same time, each of these nations will almost certainly turn down this broad path in different ways and to different extents. The largely successful history of the Swedish experience will inform even Conservative policymakers as they construct new tax policies and new political institutions. The new Conservative government has to deal not only with the perpetual problem of finding compromise within a coalition government, but also with the political reality that most Swedish voters have come to accept, generally approve of, and become quite comfortable in the welfare state constructed by the Social Democrats over the past sixty years.

As I noted in chapter 5, however, the basic institutional foundation upon which the historic compromise was constructed has already been changed. It seems unlikely therefore that the kind of corporatist solutions to policy problems for which the Swedes have become famous can be reconstructed. Sweden today is left with a very heavy tax burden, extremely mobile capital interests, and influential, increasingly assertive labor unions without the institutions that can forge compromise. Small wonder that observers are seeing more confrontation and less compromise (Pontusson 1991; Rothstein 1991). The once-admired political culture of compromise populated by the deferential "old Sven" is being replaced by a more individualist culture populated by the "ugly Swede" (Heclo and Madsen 1987).

British governments would appear to have the greatest scope for adjusting to the new international economic imperatives and reallocating tax burdens within society. The system of "alternating party political tyrannies" (*Economist*, November 22, 1975) gives the current government the power to continue the redistribution begun by Thatcher. This system allows for far greater autonomy and ability to change policy directions than any of the other democracies studied in this book. Recent experience reminds us that there are no truly autonomous democratic states. Though they were able to prevail in the most recent national election (1992), the massive public backlash against the poll tax suggests that there may be real limits to how far this new redistribution can be taken. The current government, at any rate, promises to revise the hated poll tax in favor of a somewhat less regressive measure. Once again, the government is making its choices in private, with little direct political consultation and no attempt to compromise with the opposition. In short, one cannot know the most likely outcome of even this one specific measure— much less of the system as a whole.[9] We can say, at any rate, that the British tax system is certain to be in continued flux.

Finally, the American response to the changing international context is problematic at best. The increasing fragmentation of political authority in this country has further delegitimized that authority in profound and troubling ways. Precisely because political authority has lost legitimacy there appears to be little hope for specific policies that could, for example, balance the budget. At the same time, the decline of legitimacy suggests that the kinds of institutional reforms most likely in this polity will be ones that further decentralize authority. Rather than centralize political power, as has been done in every other political democracy, the demands for reform are focused on a greater fragmentation of that authority in the name of making the system more democratic. These institutional reforms (term limits, referendums and initiatives, taxing and spending limitations), if successful, will indeed make political elites less autonomous. This, however, will make it more difficult for these elites to make tough policy choices and help reverse the nation's slow but steady economic decline.

As the public debt increases—it had risen to more than $3 trillion by the end of 1992—all major political aspirants are forced to promise more spending *and* tax cuts for average voters. This, of course, is what citizens want. America may have indeed become the most democratic political system in the modern world. This may be its undoing.

Notes

Chapter 1
Introduction

1. A few books that explore the politics of taxation in a single country have been published in recent years. The best are Hansen 1983; Murray and Birnbaum 1986; Conlan, Wrightson, and Beam 1990; Martin 1991; Hadenius 1981; Robinson and Sandford 1983; Rose and Karran 1986; Witte 1985; and White and Wildavsky 1991. In the past several decades only three books have made a serious attempt to explain the politics and development of taxation from a comparative perspective. See Levi 1988; Peters 1992; Weber and Wildavsky 1986.
2. Unfortunately, the data from which this figure was constructed are not available for more recent years. There is no reason to expect that the differences between these tax systems are substantially different today than they were a decade ago, but, as I shall show in chapter 6, all three systems have become substantially less progressive over recent years.
3. Pluralists, of course, suggested this explanation several decades ago, but it is continually being revived in new versions. For a corporatist version, see Korpi 1983; Castles 1982. See also Wilson 1983.
4. Anthony King has presented the clearest articulation of the values (or in his words, "ideas") thesis. See his three-part article in *The British Journal of Political Science* (1974).
5. State-centered theory, most often used to explain differences in political development among developing countries (see Evans et al. 1985), has also been used to explain policy variation in democracies (see Weir and Skocpol, 1985).
6. See also Steinmo, Thelen, and Longstreth 1992.
7. Indeed, American voters have put majorities of Democrats in *two* Houses in twenty-two of the last twenty-six elections.
8. The relatively long tenure of the Conservatives since 1979 has effected this pattern. But as the recent flip-flopping over the poll tax demonstrates, these tendencies play a powerful role in shaping British tax policy—even when there is no change in government. See chapter 6 below.
9. This problem was considered quite serious by many during the nonsocialist government tenure of 1976–81. See Bergstrom 1987.
10. Aristotle, Montesquieu, and James Madison were most definitely institutionalists. See Steinmo, Thelen, and Longstreth 1992.
11. Conference entitled "The New Institutionalism," Jan. 12–14, 1990, University of Colorado.

Chapter 2
Common Paths, Divergent Patterns

1. Margaret Levi (1988) provides a much more nuanced and appealing argument, using similar logic to build a theory of political development. Her theory of "Predatory Rule" does not argue that rulers are acting against the interests of their constituents. Moreover, her theory does not imply that state actors are able to raise revenue exactly as they wish. Instead, she recognizes that there are substantial constraints on rulers.

2. If a 100-percent tax on all incomes over $100,000 were imposed, the government would raise only $368.5 billion, or 43.1 percent of total government receipts. IRS Publication 1304 (Rev. 8–90) "Individual Income Tax Returns 1987, Table 1.1 Selected Income and Tax Items, By Size of Adjusted Gross Income," p. 20.

3. The use principle drove tax policy for centuries before the ability to pay principle became dominant. According to the use principle, those who benefited from state spending should pay taxes in relation to their use of state services. Thus, it would seem perfectly reasonable that in a social welfare state the poor should bear the heaviest burden.

4. In 1989, personal income taxes alone accounted for an average of 29.4 percent of total tax revenues in the OECD. Social security taxes contributed an average of 23.2 percent and general consumption contributed 17.2 percent.

5. Indeed, one of the most significant changes in the tax policy environment in the 1970s and 1980s was the introduction of indexing. Under these new rules—imposed in a large number of OECD nations, including all three studied here—income tax brackets were indexed to inflation, thus eliminating (or slowing) the automatic revenue growth generated by bracket creep. This apparently "technical" rule change has had enormous implications for the growth of state revenues in the 1980s and 1990s. See chapter 5.

6. Social Security taxes are technically flat rate "insurance" charges in virtually all countries.

7. Estimates of effective tax burdens are difficult to come by in the best of circumstances. Historical estimates are both scarce and somewhat unreliable. The best figures I have been able to find indicate that with all taxes combined in Britain in 1903/4, those earning less than fifty pounds a year paid 9.5 percent of their income in taxes and those earning over fifty thousand pounds a year were estimated to have paid 8.0 percent. This study indicated that by 1918/19, taxes on the poorest individuals had increased to 11 percent. They increased to 58 percent on the wealthiest individuals. See Report of Committee on National Dept. and Taxation, 1927, 95–96.

8. We should recognize that the newfound ability of nation-states to raise unimagined revenues for defense in itself affected the character of this new kind of war.

9. Morgenthau, *Pathfinder,* March 14, 1942, 4. Of course the Swedes were able to remain noncombatants, but defense expenditures skyrocketed in this country as well.

10. In fig. 2.7 we see that income tax revenues as a percentage of GNP dropped in Britain. This is largely explained by the introduction and expansion of numerous allowances and by the raising of tax thresholds in the immediate postwar period.

11. We take it as self-evident, for example, that a single yuppie who lives on a thirty-thousand-dollar-a-year trust fund and rents a condo in Aspen should probably pay more taxes than a single parent who, on the same income, supports four children and has a house mortgage.

12. In 1989, seven countries collected more in corporate profits taxes (as a percentage of tax take or GNP) than the United States. Only Britain collected more revenue via property taxes (U.K. = 12.6 percent; U.S. = 10.3 percent). Since these data were reported, however, the United Kingdom has abolished its property tax system.

13. The Swedish minister of finance (1932–47) Ernst Wigforss was fond of telling his political adversaries that his death tax proposals were not nearly as radical as those proposed by the American president Franklin Roosevelt.

14. Very few tax capital gains at the same rate as earned income. In Britain there are separate thresholds for capital gains as well as adjustments for inflation that can substantially lower the effective rate of tax.

15. This is an enormously complicated and controversial arena of tax law. For general introductions, see Musgrave and Musgrave 1980; M. King 1977; Lodin et al. 1978.

16. Break (1985) argues that nearly 50 percent of what the Joint Economic Committee calls a tax expenditure may not be a tax expenditure at all. For discussions of this concept, see Surrey 1970, 1973; Bittker 1969; McDaniel and Surrey 1985; Steinmo 1986b.

17. See, for example, P. Fisher (1981, 769), who writes the following: "The preferential treatment of long-term capital gains under the individual income tax . . . should be seen for what it is: A tax concession to the rich and a stimulus to unproductive speculation in financial and real assets." See also any of the several publications put out by the Citizens for Tax Justice.

18. Charles Daley (moderator), "Tax Cuts and Tax Reform: The Quest for Equity," a round table held on February 27, 1978, sponsored by the American Enterprise Institute.

19. All three of these countries have attempted, with varying degrees of success, to tighten up on these rules in recent years. See chapter 6.

20. To say that the United States has no VAT does not imply that there are no consumption taxes there. In fact, there are hundreds. Most states and a large percentage of local governments have some form of general sales tax (two-thirds of which exempt food or basic necessities), and all states impose specific excises on such goods and services as motor fuel, alcoholic beverages, tobacco, car licenses, etc. In addition, in 1986 the federal government had specific excises on seventy-two items, ranging from inner tubes to deep-seabed minerals. As complex and wide ranging as these various forms of consumption tax may be, they collect nowhere near the revenue of the VATs in Europe. Of all OECD countries only Japan collected as little or less revenue as a percent of GNP in general consumption taxes as the United States in 1989. Japan has now introduced a national VAT, however, and it is likely that in the 1990s the United States will be at the bottom of the list. Only Turkey collects less in taxes on specific goods and services (OECD 1991).

21. See, for example, Stephens 1979; Milner 1989; TCO 1982.

22. Of all OECD countries, only Denmark, Norway, and Sweden had no reduced rates

for basic necessities in 1990. Denmark, Germany, Ireland, Luxembourg, Norway, Sweden, and currently Britain have no special high VAT rates on luxury goods.

23. The Swedish social security tax is less regressive than the British and American, however. While both the British and American versions have a ceiling on their social security tax, the Swedes tax all earned income at the same rate. Capital income is exempt from the Swedish social security tax.

24. The main explanation for this curious outcome is that there are a large number of credits and deductions available for capital investment that can be written off against other income sources.

25. Recent reforms of the Swedish tax system have altered this picture somewhat. See chapter 6.

26. Service and financial companies, on the other hand, pay heavier rates of tax in Sweden. This is the inverse of the pattern in the United States, where service and financial companies traditionally pay a lower effective tax rate than manufacturing concerns (see Surrey 1973).

27. Normann and Södersten (1978, 184) have shown, for example, that for fifty-one industrial companies examined between 1963 and 1968 effective tax rates and inventory size were negatively correlated. Moreover, expansion rates were positively correlated to both profitability and inventory size and inversely correlated to the effective tax rate. Finally, and most surprisingly, profit rates and effective tax rates were inversely correlated.

28. Investment allowances are somewhat analogous to accelerated depreciation schedules; initial allowances are a type of investment tax credit. Different rates apply to machinery vs. buildings.

29. The student of American tax policy history may be unimpressed. In the United States there may be over thirty specific changes in a single year in tax provisions affecting various types of investments in different industries, different products, or different companies. The difference, however, is that these changes in the British system were quite general and often affected all industry, not just particular firms or types of industries as is common in the United States. There were also specific changes made during these years in favor of particular industries in the United Kingdom. But these were in fact fewer in number than the general changes listed above.

30. This curious outcome was the result of the unplanned interaction of the social security taxes, means-tested public benefits, and income taxes. Controversy over the so-called implicit tax rate evoked changes in the later 1980s. Now this tax rate is somewhat less than 100 percent.

31. On consumption taxation, see Morrissey and Steinmo (1987); on death taxes, see Sanford (1983); on capital gains, see Robinson and Sandford (1983) or Kay and King (1983, 1987).

Chapter 3
The Emergence of Modern Taxation

1. B. E. V. Sabine (1966, 25) argues in his exhaustive study *A History of Income Tax,* "It is clear that the imposition by Pitt of income tax in 1799 was not by any means a complete break with the theory and practice of the past, but rather a gradual development in both aspects." He also quotes Kennedy, who argues, "The essential difference between the direct taxes of this period and the income tax of the nineteenth century is not one of intention but of execution" (W. Kennedy, *English Taxation 1640–1799* [London School of Economics, 1896]).

2. This explicit choice was clear with the passage of the Reform Bill of 1884, which extended the franchise from 6.4 percent to 12.1 percent of the male population. Britain long had had a few single-member districts represented in Parliament, but up to this point they were a relatively small portion of total districts. Even after the reform of 1884, several districts were still multimember. Several interests (Oxford and Cambridge, for example) continued to have explicit representation well into the twentieth century. For a detailed discussion of the history of electoral laws in Britain, see Carstairs 1980, 189–200.

3. The tax imposed rates of up to 10 percent on incomes of more than two hundred pounds per year.

4. The new income tax changed Pitt's general assessment to a system of in effect five different income taxes on different types of income: income from land and buildings, agriculture, public securities, profits from business, and salaries or wages. This system remains in effect today. For a general discussion of the politics and significance of this tax, see Levi 1988, 122–23.

5. Income taxes were self-reported, and only if the Inland Revenue suspected fraud did they investigate individual taxpayers.

6. In 1894 Benjamin Disraeli increased the standard exemption to £150 a year and pushed through a moderate form of progressivity by giving those with incomes between £150 and £400 a tax reduction. In 1894 new deductions were introduced for child support to compensate for the growing rates of tax.

7. Unearned income is income from capital.

8. Britain's equivalent of the American Internal Revenue Service (IRS).

9. The commission suggested that if the government were to move in this direction it would be best to institute a "super tax" on incomes above a certain level.

10. In its first year the pension scheme was financed out of current general revenues. Asquith remarked that the scheme was "the garnered result of the prudent finance" of his years as chancellor. Few doubted, however, that more resources were soon to be needed.

11. It was reported that with the exception of Churchill and Asquith the entire cabinet was opposed to Lloyd George's budget. Neither the cabinet nor the Parliament, however, was able to influence the substance of the proposals. The weight of these three

individuals and particularly the autonomy allowed the chancellor in Britain carried the day.

12. The income tax system was also made more progressive, and tax exemptions for children were introduced.

13. Apparently the government did not have time to consider these details during the consideration of this proposal. But even after these taxes were introduced the government continued to ignore demands for special compensation and/or deductions from the business community for several years after the tax was introduced. Demands for depreciation allowances, for example, "received a curt, 'The answer is in the negative.' " See Sabine 1966, 150.

14. Changing philosophy toward the use and purpose of taxation can also be seen in reforms of death duties. In 1894 Sir William Harcourt (Liberal) reformed the death duties and made them progressive, rising from 1 percent on estates over £150 to 8 percent on estates over £1 million. By the last prewar budget, these rates had been increased to 20 percent. Indeed, death duties contributed an average of 16 percent of central government revenues from taxation between 1908 and 1915. See Sandford 1971a, 68.

15. Official Report, House of Commons Debates, Series V, volume 4, April 23, 1909, col. 507.

16. See Frazer 1973, 144. Snowden called for the abolition of indirect taxes altogether and their replacement with increases in income, capital, and death taxes.

17. Quoted in Frazer 1973, 146. The question of whether Lloyd George meant to invoke the constitutional crisis with his People's Budget is one which historians have long debated. None have been able to answer the question definitively.

18. Part 1 of the plan (health insurance) stipulated that all wage earners were to pay 4d weekly, while their employer was to pay 3d and the national government would contribute 2d to an accumulating fund to finance benefits. In exchange for this, workers would receive 10s per week if taken ill and free medical care from a doctor selected by the local Insurance Commission. Part 2 (unemployment insurance) defined a ratio of one benefit week for each five weeks' contributions. The program was compulsory for a specific set of industries that were subject to great employment fluctuations. Employees and employers alike paid 2.5d a week for the insurance; the state subsidy was 1.66d per week. Benefits were set at 7s a week for up to fifteen weeks.

19. Though the budget was not quite balanced in 1913/14 taxes of £163 million nearly covered the expenses of £197 million. Figures from Coffield 1970, 165.

20. Owing to the very limited size of the franchise and the existence of single-member constituencies, representatives to both houses of the Swedish Riksdag developed quite close relationships with their local constituencies, but at the same time tended to be the dominant men of their district. Political parties, then, were more like loose affiliations of like-minded men rather than the strong political associations that developed as the franchise was broadened. A *Dagens Nyheter* article commented in 1902, for example, "our Riksdagmen are—and are all too readily considered to be—something like political saints, something like mediators between the desires of the people and

the powerful government, but are much less accessible than are the Catholic saints."
Dagens Nyheter, August 23, 1902, quoted in Carlsson 1987, 201.

21. At the turn of the century, indirect taxes—mostly customs, tax on alcoholic drinks, and sugar taxes—contributed between 80 and 90 percent of the national government's receipts. Rodriguez 1980, 46.

22. Knut Wicksell wrote in "The Right to Vote and Taxation" that universal suffrage would solve the problem of the unfair tax burden borne by the working-class family because of the heavy reliance on indirect taxes at the turn of the century (from Rodriguez 1980, 66). Today, Wicksell is thought of as one of the originators of rational choice theory for his writings on the subject of taxation and the franchise.

23. Quoted in Rodriguez 1980, 71. The progressive income tax rose to a maximum of 4 percent of income and generated only 4 percent of total government revenue by 1904.

24. For new income tax rates, see Bevillningsutskottets Betänkande no. 25, 1909. Income and wealth tax revenues rose from Skr 18.4 million in 1910 to Skr 255 million in 1916. Wealth tax was integrated into the income tax. The top tax bracket with income and wealth combined was 5 percent. The corporate income tax system was imposed at progressive rates, computing profits as a relation among stocks, income, and a special "reserve fund" that helped protect the most profitable enterprises from paying taxes. See Eberstein 1937; Rodriquez 1980, 70–77.

25. Though nominally head of a Conservative party government, Lindman, the prime minister from 1906 to 1911, was considered to be a civil servant by his parliamentary colleagues. See Verney 1957, 159. Heclo identifies Lindeman as an "industrialist." Heclo 1974, 190. His government, moreover, in fact contained both Liberals and Conservatives, much to the dismay of the leadership of the Liberal party.

26. By 1918 this tax alone brought in Skr 303 million and was the single largest source of revenue for the government.

27. The marginal rate of 18.5 includes the local income tax (which averaged 6.5 percent in 1918), the national income tax (top marginal rate of 5 percent), and the defense levy (7 percent). The top death/gift tax rate was only 3.8 percent for bequests to the immediate family, and 18 percent for distant relatives. *Svensk Forfattningssamling,* 1914 Nr. 381:1169–71.

28. In fact there were still minor barriers to truly universal manhood suffrage relating to age, military service, etc.; most of these were abolished in the early 1920s. See Stjernquist 1987, 221.

29. I ignore here the issue of whether the Constitution actually gives the Supreme Court veto authority. The point is that by 1800 (*Maybury vs. Madison*) the issue was settled.

30. See also Federalists 31, 32, and 33.

31. For a general discussion of the politics of this era, see Burnham 1970. Ronald King 1983 discusses the economic background and populist revolt that specifically lead to the demand for the income tax. See also Stephen Skowronek 1982 for a discussion of political and administrative changes in this era.

32. The income tax was not the most prominent issue before the nation at the time; it

was one of a series of issues that pitted the wealthy (especially those in the northeast) against farmers and working people (especially those in the south and west). The demand for progressive taxation was also a major rallying cry for Social Democratic activists in Sweden and Labour Party candidates in Britain. In both cases the demand the new principle of just taxation was intimately intertwined with the demand for the right to vote.

33. Senator David Hill, quoted in Eisenstein 1961, 18.

34. Senator David Hill anxiously explained that the bill was devised by "the professors with their books, the socialists with their schemes . . . and the anarchists with their bombs . . . in the midst of their armed camps between the Danube and the Rhine." Quoted in Eisenstein 1961, 18.

35. In a first-past-the-post electoral system, a candidate needs simply to win more votes than the other candidates in any particular district in order to be declared the winner; a majority is unnecessary.

36. The Democrats won 236 seats (versus 87 for the Republicans) in 1892. Cleveland won the presidency in 1892 with 46.0 percent of the votes cast. He won 62.4 percent of the electoral votes, however. In 1890, the Democrats won 50.3 percent of the popular vote but received only 45.9 percent of House seats.

   Moreover, despite the fact that the Democratic Party candidate for President in 1888, Grover Cleveland, had actually won more popular votes than his Republican rival Benjamin Harrison (5.54 million versus 5.45 million) the electoral college sent Harrison to the White House.

37. Between the Reconstruction and the 1890s there had been a relatively even balance in Congress, with the Democrats largely sweeping the South but more or less splitting the North and East. In 1896 this changed. The populist policies of the 1984–86 Congress (especially its tax policies) frightened middle-class interests in the rest of the country and pushed them decisively into the Republican party camp. The Democrats were routed, losing the presidency, 121 seats in the House, and control of the Senate.

38. The United States had a temporary income tax during the Civil War; see Hansen 1983, 79–81.

39. Significantly, in both Sweden and Britain the unjust distribution of taxes proved to be a major rallying cry used by political reformers to mobilize support for their cause.

40. The move to the Australian ballot was intended to purify elections of corruption and intimidation by stripping the parties of a major organizational function—the printing and distributing of ballots to be cast in the election. This reform was associated with ballot forms that made straight party line voting much more complicated and confusing.

41. Taft's administration also conceded to the demand to tax corporations directly in an attempt to take the wind out of the sails of the personal income tax. The corporate income tax was passed in 1909. For an excellent discussion of the summary of the politics surrounding these reforms, see Hansen 1983, 81–84.

42. Revenues from income and profits taxes grew from $124 million in 1915 to $3,945 million in 1920 (Ratner 1967). These years also saw the introduction of the first tax on

inheritances in the United States and steep increases in corporate profits taxes. Mining companies that employed child labor were also subjected to new taxes. In addition, a $1 tax per $1,000 of capital stock was levied against capitalists in these extraordinary years. Finally, special luxury taxes were introduced on a number of specific commodities.

43. For example, as the 1917 tax bill was being considered, charitable organizations put on a full court press for tax deductions for charitable contributions. The nation's colleges and universities joined the battle. The tax committees resisted these interest group pressures on the grounds that the benefits for these tax breaks would go to the same wealthy individuals these taxes were attempting to squeeze. But, in what became a familiar story in the politics of taxation the United States, even the powerful Finance Committee, could not fight these "worthy causes" once amendments had been put forward in their behalf on the floor of the Senate. In the end, even the chairman of the Senate Finance Committee voted for another major loophole in the code.

44. The new loopholes included special deductions for corporate dividends, for dependents, one year loss and carry back for business, more advantageous tax accounting principles for industry, oil depletion allowances, special tax reductions for the mining and timber industries, and tax reductions for soldiers returning from the war.

Chapter 4
The Historic Compromise

1. Though the principle of parliamentary democracy was gradually being accepted in Sweden, the king still was responsible for selecting a government. Formally, government ministers, Statsråd, were ministers of the king. The king could, technically at least, select a government consisting purely of civil servants, ignoring the Parliament altogether. By 1917, however, the king was in effect bound to select a government from the dominant parties in the Riksdag. It was not until the constitutional reform of 1973 that the government was made formally responsible to the Parliament rather than the king. Still, civil servants can be appointed cabinet ministers, even if they do not hold a seat in the Riksdag.

2. Early in the decade the party's policy positions generally and tax policy positions specifically were quite radical. For example, Ernst Wigforss, the SAP's leading economic thinker and spokesman, advocated what he called a "social policy tax principle," which flatly rejected bourgeois arguments suggesting that high wealth and income taxes were harmful to the economy. He argued instead that these taxes did not go far enough. Furthermore, he argued that capital flight and the threat of poor economic growth were unimportant obstacles when compared with the need for a more equitable and just society. See Rodriguez 1980, 88.

3. For discussions of the various type of parliamentary representation systems, see Carstairs 1980. For a discussion of the Swedish system, see Von Sydow, 1989.

4. The Social Democrats only moderately inflated government expenditures between 1932 and 1938. Taxation, for example, rose no more than from 11.8 percent of GNP

in 1932 to 12.1 percent of GNP in 1937. Perhaps more interesting, public expenditures rose from Skr 1,528 million in 1932 to only Skr 1,744 in 1936. By 1940, however, war preparation rocketed total expenditures to Skr 4,311 million. Figures from Forsman 1980.

5. Ohlin, however, later became the highly popular leader of the Liberal party and brought the party its greatest electoral successes in the 1940s. Myrdal also later became the minister of trade because of Wigforss's confidence in his technical abilities, though Myrdal had not declared his allegiance to the Social Democratic party.

6. The Stockholm school continued to have influence for the next several decades. For example, in 1936 a commission entitled *The Total Tax Burden in Sweden and Foreign Lands* (SOU 1936, 18) argued strenuously against increasing taxes too heavily in Sweden, on the grounds that high tax rates would drive away capitalists and their investment kronor.

7. Wigforss also pointed out that Swedish death taxes were "extraordinarily mild" in comparative perspective. Even very large inheritances (to direct descendants) were taxed at no more than 10 percent. English death duties at the time went up to 40 percent. Wigforss 1980, 128.

8. A special wealth tax was imposed on the very wealthy, with rates going up to 5 percent of net assessed wealth holdings. This wealth tax was different from the imputed income from wealth tax of 1910 in that it was a direct levy and its rates were unrelated to the taxpayer's income tax rates. Income taxes were not raised until 1938. The maximum combined income and wealth tax rate thus rose from 26.7 percent to only 42.2 percent by 1939. Genberg 1942, 23–24.

9. See also Casparsson 1966, 80. Indeed, in 1936 a labor law was passed to penalize labor market organizations for not participating in a conflict mediation process established under two 1928 labor laws.

10. The five most significant innovations in corporate profits taxation were (1) profits taxation was made proportional rather than progressive, and the new rate was established at 30 percent; (2) companies were free to depreciate machines and buildings according to any schedule they preferred, including 100 percent first-year write-off, if they so chose; (3) employers could set aside tax-free pension reserve funds at any amount they chose, and these funds could later be taken back into the working capital of the corporation, though they would then be taxed; (4) companies could write off the full costs of inventory against profits (*varulagernedskrivning*); (5) the Investment Reserve Fund was established, though it did not come into full operation until the 1950s. For a discussion of these corporate tax expenditures, see Steinmo 1986. Also see Norr et al. 1959; Rodriguez 1980; Lindbeck 1975, and Bergström 1982.

11. We do not know the exact debate because of the informal and secretive nature of this process.

12. The *Rationalization Commission,* 1936–39 (*rationalizering utredning*) was the last of the many influential ad hoc commissions of the twenties and thirties that helped turn Social Democratic and LO elites alike in this direction. This commission, which was chaired by an apolitical civil servant and had two labor union representatives as well

as two prominent industrialists on its board, unanimously rejected the notion that individual firms should bear the costs of adapting to technological change (paying unemployment benefits). While the commission's report conceded that the state had a right to regulate the economy, it argued that selective interventionist measures should be avoided because the political dynamics of such a process would inevitably hinder the structural rationalization of the Swedish economy (Pontusson 1986, chap. 3, pp. 15–18). The fear of politics is precisely why general tax incentive policies were favored over selective interventionist policies as means to bring about the desired rationalization.

13. As far back as 1926, the chairman of the LO had argued in a statement to the LO congress that real wages "can only be gradually increased to the extent improved production methods and economic organization create conditions for this to occur." Quoted in Hadenius 1966, 37.

14. Wealth taxes were increased to 0–6 percent and gift and inheritance taxes went up to 50 percent in 1938. The inheritance tax, however, still seemed too low to many, especially given Wigforss's belief, stated in 1928, that the main source of inequality in society was inheritance. Wigforss 1980, 122.

15. For an excellent discussion of the Ghent system in Sweden and the politics behind it, see Bo Rothstein, "Labor Market Institutions and Working Class Strength" in Steinmo, Thelen, and Longstreth 1992. Rothstein convincingly shows both that the Ghent system in force in Sweden is a central explanation for the high rates of unionization found in Sweden and that the unions and Social Democrats built this system precisely to strengthen unions.

16. The Republicans were undoubtedly helped by the extension of the franchise to women as well. Though there is no direct evidence that the women voted disproportionately for Republicans, the GOP was considered more friendly to women's issues (and to prohibition as well). The suffrage movement, moreover, publicly campaigned against the party in power, the Democrats and Wilson in particular, for not having extended the right to vote earlier. The most radically feminist wing of the movement, the National Women's party, endorsed Hoover's bid for the presidency in 1928.

17. Andrew Mellon wrote a book on taxation policy, *Taxation, The People's Business,* which first introduced what is now called supply side tax policy. Mellon eloquently argued that reducing the marginal taxes of the rich would spur investment, increase economic growth, and thus increase tax revenues to the Federal Treasury. See Mellon 1924, 17. Mellon, moreover, was noted to be a particularly powerful Treasury Secretary whose term lasted from 1920 to 1932. It was often said at the time that "Three Presidents served under Secretary Mellon." Harding was perhaps the most deferential to his Treasury secretary, out of his lack of interest, or mental capacity, to grasp the complexities of taxation. He once confided to a friend, "I can't make a damn thing out of this tax problem. I listen to one side and they seem right, and then—God!—I talk to the other side and they seem just as right." Quoted in Waltman 1985, 83.

18. Claude Kitchin (Dem., N.C.), the party leader and chair of Ways and Means in 1916, told his colleagues when considering the steep increases in surtax rates in the

war years: "You can tell your people that practically all of this will go north of the Mason-Dixon line." See Witte 1985, 79–86.

19. The Revenue Act of 1921 did, however, abolish the wartime excess profits tax.

20. Two of the most successful proposals were Ogden Mills's so-called Spendings Tax (Mills later became Treasury secretary under Hoover) and Senator Reed Smoot's proposal for a manufacturers' sales tax. While the first of these was buried in the Ways and Means Committee, the latter was defeated on the Senate floor by forty-three to twenty-five in the late summer of 1921, when seventeen Republicans defected from their party and voted with the Democrats against the measure. *New York Times,* November, 4, 1921.

21. Waltman 1985, 88. The amendments covered a wide array of interests, and the final legislation provided special measures for interests as diverse as oil and gas and "the American Legion or the women's auxiliary units thereof." Waltman 1985, 94.

22. In 1919 public spending was still more than double public revenues, with ordinary receipts at $5.4 billion and spending at $18.8 billion. By 1920, however, public spending was cut to $6.9 billion and the budget was balanced.

23. For more detailed discussions of this era, see Ratner 1942, 400–33; Blakey and Blakey 1940.

24. Proposals for Manufacturers' Sales Taxes went the furthest. On March 5, 1932, a nonpartisan proposal for a 2.5-percent tax was defeated on the House floor by 223 to 153 votes. Two months later a similar bill proposed by Senator David Walsh was defeated on the Senate floor by a similar margin.

25. Interestingly, Budget Director Lewis W. Douglas originally asked Congress to pass both increases in income and corporate profits taxes *and* a national manufacturers' sales tax. The Congress essentially ignored the request for a sales tax because of public indignation over the disclosure that J. P. Morgan and his associates had paid no taxes in 1932. To impose a regressive sales tax was more than even traditional budget balance advocates were willing to do, even if it was an administration proposal.

26. For closer discussions of these budgets and the politics surrounding them, see Ratner 1942, 463–72.

27. The business community also felt that Roosevelt could be trusted more than many prominent members of Congress. "Conservative acceptance of Roosevelt's program was fortified by awareness of greater dangers on the horizon. The Democratic victory in the 1934 elections had confirmed a political dominance which might have seemed accidental and temporary when first acquired in the darkness of 1932. What the Democrats would now do with that power was uncertain. One possibility was 'greenbackism' as represented by Congressman Patman's popular and populist proposal for a veterans' bonus to be paid in paper money. Another was Huey Long's share-the-wealth tax ideas which also had considerable support in Congress. By contrast, the President's conventional, if large, program and his call for a period of 'good feeling' were a great relief." Stein 1969, 77.

28. For discussions of the New Deal and the politics behind it, see Greenstone 1969. See also Skocpol and Amenta 1986; Weir et al. 1988; and Heclo 1974.

29. Much like his tax policy proposals of the era, even his spending plans were often modified *before* they were introduced. For example, instead of pushing a fully national and comprehensive system, the final Social Security plan pushed by the administration both exempted a broad range of politically powerful groups (such as federal workers) and was also much smaller in terms of coverage than many social reformers—even those inside the administration—believed necessary. See Derthick 1979; Heclo 1974.

30. The Social Security Payroll tax levied a 2-percent charge on income (to be split by the employer and the employee) on income up to $3,000. This explicitly regressive tax was to increase to 6 percent by 1949 and was expected to create a very large reserve fund. See Derthick 1979, 228–51.

31. This package of measures included (a) the introduction of an inheritance tax to go along with the existing estate tax; (b) a graduated corporate profits tax; (c) a tax on intercorporate dividends; and (d) an increase in income surtax rates on individuals with incomes over $1 million. See Witte 1985, 100.

32. The decision to finance the program regressively was not without its critics. Several proposals to restructure the program, both in terms of coverage and financing, were made in following years. None of the proposals to partially finance the program from general revenues, as was done in Sweden and Britain, however, were successful. See Committee on Long Range Work and Relief Policies, *Security, Work and Relief Policies* (Washington, D.C.: Government Printing Office, 1942), 515–28. See also Light 1985; Derthick 1979.

33. Robert Doughton of North Carolina headed Ways and Means while Senator Byron "Pat" Harrison of Mississippi chaired the Finance Committee. William Bankhead of Alabama was the majority leader of the House at the time, while Joseph Robinson of Arkansas lead the Senate. See Patterson 1967.

34. This change came about so late that the original proposal sent over to the Congress did not have the financing scheme attached, as it was still being worked out by the executive branch. See Derthick 1979, 229.

35. In 1935, for example, Roosevelt announced what would be the most controversial tax policy proposal of his administration. Continuing his attack against the economic royalists, he proposed an undistributed profits tax. This tax, if passed, would replace existing corporate taxes with a single progressive tax on profits not paid out in dividends to stockholders. This rather complicated tax was hotly contested by business interests, who managed to convince Congress to substantially modify the tax. Still, this tax was considered a victory for the administration. It would, however, be one of the last, at least as far as tax policy was concerned.

36. Though the top marginal tax rate was increased from 63 percent to 79 percent in 1935, the income at which the top rate took effect was increased from $1 million to $5 million.

37. For example, the undistributed profits tax was cut back in 1938 and eliminated in 1939. Roosevelt was "greatly disappointed by Congress's action" and allowed these measures to become law without his signature. Ratner 1942, 479.

38. For an excellent study of American and British propaganda efforts to sell wartime taxes, see Jones 1990.

39. Personal exemptions were cut in half to $500 in 1942; the tax rate paid in the bottom bracket was increased from 4 percent (1939) to 19 percent in 1942 and to 23 percent in 1944.

40. More people were also taxed at the higher rates. Whereas the top tax bracket only impacted income over $5 million in 1941, by 1942 the top bracket struck incomes of $200,000 or more.

41. In 1942, despite the massive increases in income and profits taxes already legislated, the budget deficit skyrocketed to 13 percent of GNP; it rose to 29 percent of GNP by 1943. Exactly like their European counterparts, American officials argued that national consumption taxes were appropriate because they also served the purpose of helping manage the macro economy. Thus the administration claimed that, in addition to the need for new revenues, consumption taxes would help cool inflation. See "Morgenthau's Statement," *New York Times*, September 4, 1942, 16.

42. Of the eighteen candidates fielded as Coalition Labour, ten were elected to Parliament.

43. Together the three coalition parties won 47.6 percent of the electoral vote and took 478 of the Parliament's 707 seats. Though the Coalition Liberals received only 1.45 million votes to the Liberal's 1.3 million, the Coalition Liberals took 133 parliamentary seats while the Liberals took only 28.

44. There is a huge literature on the politics and ideas of traditional versus Keynesian attitudes in the United Kingdom. For some of the best of these discussions, see Clarke 1988; Stevenson and Cook 1979; Weir 1989; Weir and Skocpol 1985; Middleton 1985.

45. Silverman 1982, 80. See also Board of Inland Revenue and Board of Customs and Excise, "Industry and the Weight of Taxation," January 11, 1922, PRO T171/203.

46. In the election of 1922 the Liberal party was split between the National Liberals, who took 11.6 percent of the vote and won 62 mandates, and the Liberals, who took 17.5 percent of the vote and won 54 mandates. In the election of 1923 the Liberal party won 29.6 percent of the vote and took 159 seats in Parliament. Figures from Butler and Freeman 1969, 142.

47. The Conservatives were still the most popular party among the electorate, with 38.2 percent of the vote. But once again, owing to the unique British electoral process, the Tories ended up with 260 seats against Labour's 288. Of course it was the Liberals who had the greatest claim to having been unfairly discriminated against in this system. Though they increased their share of the vote to 23.4 percent, they won only 59 seats in Parliament (9.5 percent of the total).

48. Interestingly, this budget also yielded increased wear and tear and obsolescence allowances to industry. We do not know if these measures were specific concessions to industrialists for their support of the national government, but the comparison to the 1938 reforms in Sweden is provocative.

49. Quoted in Sabine 1970, 98. A graduated National Defense Contribution on increased wartime corporate profits was proposed in 1937, but due to a storm of protest from industry it was replaced by a flat rate (5 percent) duty on all profits of companies. Income taxes for all taxpayers were increased in the 1939 budget (the maximum marginal rate was on investment income, set at 17 shillings to the pound). Additionally,

personal allowances were lowered, bringing substantially more income earnings into the tax net.

50. Some form of weekly assessment was clearly in the cards because of the government's need to bring revenues up immediately. Though an American-style pay-as-you-go self-assessment system was considered, it was rejected on the grounds that the British working classes were not considered competent to compute their own tax burden. The Internal Revenue simply did not believe reports that the American system had functioned quite nicely. R. Willis 1985, interview with author.

Chapter 5
Postwar Tax Policy

1. Books of this era are worth examining both for their substantive analyses of how the Swedish system had developed and how it functioned and for an interesting view of Anglo-American attitudes about the genius of the Swedish model. See, for example, Childs 1974; Rustow 1955; Hancock 1972.

2. Interestingly, despite the fact that the SAP popular vote dropped from 50.3 percent in the last Kommunal elections in 1942 (and from 53.8 percent in the national elections of 1940), their share of Upper Chamber deputies increased. Largely because it was the small Communist party that gained in this election, the indirect PR system for Upper Chamber members of Parliament strongly favored the largest Left party. Thus, the SAP increased its representation in the Upper Chamber from 75 to 83. The Communists moved from just one Upper Chamber member to two.

3. Elvander seems to believe that "party-tactical reasoning" was decisive in Wigforss's choice of tax policies. Elvander 1972, 31. See Tilton 1979 for a discussion of Wigforss's ideological development and influence over Swedish political economy.

4. An ad hoc commission on direct taxation was established in 1945, and in an unusual step Wigforss openly stacked the commission with SAP members and decided to personally chair its deliberations. There were four other SAP members, one communist and one member from each opposition party.

5. The most important of these included child support allowances, national health insurance (to become effective in the mid-1950s), housing subsidy programs, town planning, and agriculture reform.

6. In 1942 Sweden passed a tax amendment which declared that no matter what an individual's income, he or she could not be forced to pay higher than 80 percent of income in all taxes combined (e.g., state and local income taxes, wealth taxes and special war levies).

7. In Sweden, though, the inheritance and estate taxes worked simultaneously; thus net wealth at death was subject to the progressive 5-percent to 50-percent tax and then the inheritance was subject to the existing 2-percent to 35-percent marginal tax rates. Calculating the complex interaction of these two taxes is very difficult. This is especially true because the rates of effective inheritance tax vary in Sweden according to the relationship between the deceased and the inheritor. For direct descendants the top

marginal inheritance tax rate was only 20 percent according to the 1941 legislation. See Svensk lagstiftning 1941, nr. 416, paragraph 28. For a historical discussion of Swedish inheritance taxation, see Eberstein 1937, 375–91.

The top marginal rate of federal estate tax in the United States at the time was 77 percent. In the United States, state governments impose inheritance taxes, and these taxes paid could be taken as a credit against the federal estate tax up to a maximum credit of 16 percent. See Pechman 1983a, 234–355

8. Rothstein 1988, 237. Rothstein argues in this very interesting article that participation on government boards over the years eventually coopted the representatives from business interests. Indeed, his paper demonstrates that by the 1980s, business representatives who sat in many policy/administrative agencies fought against the Social Democrats and demanded increased spending for "their" agencies even while the SAP tried to cut them back.

9. Norr et al. 1959. For a discussion of the various instruments and how they affect economic management from the government's point of view, see Sträng 1956a.

10. The investment reserve allowed companies to set aside a share of their profits during boom years that could then be brought back into the corporation during years of lower profits, ironing out fluctuations in the business cycle and lowering effective tax rates at the same time. See Steinmo 1986b; Taylor 1982; Lindbeck 1975. The investment tax was designed to discourage investment when the Ministry of Finance and its advisers felt that the economy was overheating. While not loved by business interests, the 10-percent levy on new investment was accepted as necessary. Amazingly, these taxes evoked almost no public controversy. Indeed, Nils Elvander (1972) does not even mention these taxes in his detailed study of the politics of taxation in Sweden from 1945 to 1970.

11. One might have expected the supplementary insurance funds (ATP) social insurance fund issue to have been a major exception to the depoliticization rule as well. This social security fund was perhaps the single most divisive issue in Sweden in the 1950s. Interestingly, however, the question of how to finance these funds was not a major source of controversy at the time. When the government did finally introduce its program the question of how the funds were to be paid for was scarcely discussed in the Parliament. Apparently this issue had been agreed upon already in extraparliamentary negotiations among the government, the LO, and the SAF.

12. The central actor at this early stage was Gösta Rehn. He began pushing for the reintroduction of the sales tax at almost the same moment that his employers, the LO, finally won this tax's repeal.

13. As recently as 1956, however, Sträng had written that a central objective for Social Democratic tax policy (along with managing the economy) was to *lower* the taxes paid by those of lesser means. In a monograph published in 1956 entitled *Stable Economic Policy and Just Taxation,* he noted that the burden of indirect taxes was a major problem and though the 1956 budget reduced direct income taxes, he strongly suggested that it would be his intention to work on cutting the more "troublesome" indirect taxes in the future. Sträng 1956b, 8–11. Interview with author 1984.

14. Sven-Erik Larsson, editor of the *Uppsala Nya Tidningen*, was reported as saying flatly, "We in the Liberal Party will never agree to a sales tax. With such a tax you would be able to introduce so many and such extensive reforms that you would be able to remain in power for an indefinite length of time!" Quoted in Stjernquist 1987, 277.

15. There were two elections in 1958. In the July election, the Communist party received only 3.4 percent of the popular vote. In the September election, they scored 4 percent.

16. The electoral system worked as follows: the Upper Chamber operated on the St. Lague electoral system from 1954. One-eighth of the representatives were selected each year by different *Communal styrelse* (regional governments). Upper Chamber members were appointed for eight-year terms.

17. Consider the political implications of a situation in which the United States president could guarantee that all of his policy proposals would be supported by the Senate. Of course, this would imply a transformation of presidential/Senate relations, but it would also have a tremendous impact on the president's relation with the House.

18. The new electoral system that went into effect in 1970 divided the nation into twenty-eight electoral districts, each electing members to the Riksdag according to a strict proportional representation principle. Of the new Riksdag's 350 seats, 40 were held in reserve to be used as adjustment seats for parties that had the largest number of excess votes after the 310 constituency seats were distributed. The total number of seats was reduced to 349 after the electoral deadlock that occurred in 1973, when the bourgeois and socialist blocks each received 175 votes. To guard against the splintering of the new system into small factional parties, all parties had to receive a minimum 4 percent of the national vote or 12 percent of a constituency vote to get any representation in the Riksdag. Finally, to further enhance the direct impact of the national vote, local and city councils were to be elected at the same time and for the same electoral period (three years) as members of the Riksdag.

19. Interview with author, January 8, 1991.

20. The king appointed the government. Thus, with one party in a virtually perpetual majority in one house, there was no chance that the other parties could form a coalition that would work. The SAP was the only party, and could be the only party for many years in the future, that would be able to form a government. Everyone understood this well.

21. In 1974–76, there was an equal split between the Socialist block and the bourgeois block in the Riksdag (150–150). This period was called the lottery Parliament, but the SAP stayed in government. There was also a one-hundred-day period in 1936 during which the Farmers party tried to form a government.

22. Many interesting anecdotes illustrate the problems of the new government. For example, more than one new minister had to ask where his new offices were because he had never even been to the ministry. A minister who had a penchant for showing up at work early was said to have been denied access to the ministerial offices by the doorman, who had never seen him before (Bergstöm, *Rivstart*).

23. The much more fundamental causes of Sweden's economic performance at the time had to do with its international position in industries that suffered long-term sectoral

decline in these years. Still, the bourgeois governments were far from blameless. Owing to the dire economic position of many Swedish firms, the bourgeois governments of 1976–81 felt compelled to nationalize more companies than the Social Democrats had done in the previous forty-four years. The net effect was that the public debt grew astronomically.

24. Hadenius 1981 gives a detailed analysis of the failure of the bourgeois governments to enact the general reductions they all favored.

25. The total tax burden increased from 48.5 percent in 1976 to 49.9 percent in 1980. For a broad evaluation of Sweden's economic performance in the late 1970s through 1980s, see Bosworth and Rivlin, 1987.

26. As in Sweden, the U.S. administration established a number of wartime commissions and committees bringing together politicians and interest group elites in an effort to facilitate the successful prosecution of the war. But in the American case, these commissions tended to be viewed as temporary instruments needed to coordinate business government activities and state, local, and federal activities during the wartime crisis. The level of acrimony between the administration and both Congress and the business community had been too high for a permanent solution to be struck at this point. "Roosevelt relied heavily on businessmen to staff these emergency agencies, partly because the United States lacked sufficient administrative capacities and partly because he wished to avoid recreating the political divisions of the late 1930s." Amenta and Skocpol 1988, 111–12.

27. Reforms in the immediate postwar era included (a) a reduction in the number of committees from forty-eight to nineteen; (b) the creation of a sort of super Joint Budget Committee—unfortunately, electoral considerations came into play, and this committee was expanded to include nearly one-fourth of all House members; (c) systematic development of an expanded congressional staff; (d) Congress worked for the passage of the 22nd Amendment, limiting the president to two terms.

28. The Ways and Means Committee was given particularly important measures to protect its autonomy and power: not only were subcommittees abolished, but the committee was also allowed to operate under a closed rule, meaning that both noncommittee congressmen and interest group representatives could be expelled from the room if the chairman felt that the matters at hand could best be handled in private.

   The Senate, a smaller and more collegial body, operated more on the basis of norms of conduct and professionalism, and thus did not impose strict rules protecting the Finance Committee's autonomy like those found in the House. The result was that the Ways and Means committee took on even greater significance, while the Senate generally developed the reputation as the haven for special interest group influence.

29. The original proposal made by Harold Knutson, chair of the House Ways and Means Committee, offered a 20-percent across-the-board income tax cut. The final bill, which passed over the president's veto, cut marginal tax rates (especially for the wealthy), raised the basic exemption from $500 to $600, and introduced new tax exemptions for the blind and for the aged.

30. Holmans, *United States Fiscal Policy,* 66–67, quoted in Stein 1969.

31. Democrats were far from innocent of this behavior, and in many ways were able to have it both ways. They could, on the one hand, decry the Republicans for their attempts to gouge the working people and offer huge tax breaks to the "fat cats," while, on the other hand, supporting special provisions for the powerful and wealthy who lived in their districts. For a powerful indictment of *both* parties' tax policies during this era, see Eisenstein 1961, 218–19.

32. Quoted in Witte 1985, 139–40.

33. This list included soil, dirt, turf, water, mosses, minerals from seawater, air, or similar inexhaustible resources. One can only surmise that those who mined these materials did not have a lobbyist in Washington—yet.

34. One should note the conflict between these complaints and reform objectives. On the one hand, reformers wanted the committees to be more responsive to party elites. On the other hand, individual members wanted the committee policy outputs to be responsive to individual members' constituency needs. The Ways and Means Committee under Mills was considered a sinner on both accounts. Mills neither bent to the wishes of the party leadership, nor was he willing to willy nilly pass out tax benefits for individual members' constituencies. The Finance Committee and the Senate generally were considered much more amenable to individual politicians' needs. Strahan 1986, 4.

35. *Congressional Quarterly Weekly Report,* 35, September 10, 1977, 1906, quoted in Reese 1980, 163.

36. "Remarks of the Honorable Al Ullman on the Tax Restructuring Act of 1979," *Congressional Record,* 96th Congress, 1st session, October 22, 1979, 29059. The proposal did, however, contain a series of tax expenditures designed to assuage the most obvious and powerful opposition to the plan: food, medical care, and residential housing were to be taxed at a reduced rate of 5 percent. There was to be no tax on charities, education, mass transit, nonretail sales by fishermen and farmers. U.S. Congress, House Committee on Ways and Means, *Hearing Announcement on the "Tax Restructuring Act of 1979" (HR 5665),* 96th Congress, 1st session, October 23, 1979, 6.

37. Butskell is a conflation of the names of two famous British chancellors, Hugh Gaitskell (Labour 1950–51) and R. A. Butler (Conservative 1951–55).

38. This exchange took place at the Brookings Conference entitled *A National Issues Forum on World Tax Reform: A Progress Report.* Washington, D.C.: November 12–13, 1987.

39. Parliamentary Debates, vol. 414, October 23, 1945. Some of Dalton's many reforms: he (1) lowered the standard and reduced rates; (2) increased various income tax allowances aimed at the poor; (3) increased the surtax to a maximum of 55 percent, which brought the combined income and surtax rates to levels very close to the wartime high, 86.5 percent; (4) removed the purchase tax on a variety of items, such as cooking and heating products; (5) introduced new, higher rates of purchase tax on luxury items; (6) significantly raised the tax on tobacco; (7) substantially increased the estate tax, increasing rates to a maximum of 75 percent—the world's highest; (8) introduced a new type of corporation tax called the split rate system, which taxed distributed and

undistributed profits at different rates; and finally, (9) to counterbalance the negative effect some of these measures might have on investment and employment, he reduced the wartime excess profits duty to 60 percent, and expanded some tax concessions for industrial investment.

40. Parliamentary Debates, vol. 414, October 24, 1945.

41. Dalton was forced to resign in 1948 because of a minor budget leak. For a comprehensive treatment of Dalton's ideas and accomplishments, see Morgan 1989.

42. The one-time capital levy (called a special contribution) placed an additional tax on investment incomes over £2,000 to be paid on top of the basic rate and surtaxes already in effect. The levy was to be paid on a graduated scale of 10 percent to 50 percent. This meant that a number of wealthy income tax payers suffered effective tax rates in excess of 100 percent of their income in this year.

43. Williams, Hansard, April 10, 1950.

44. The anger here was fanned by the fact that Gaitskell had also placed a cap on National Health Service spending. When the health service was nationalized in 1945 no one stopped to consider the revenue implications of this move. General tax revenue was simply assumed to be adequate. Klein 1984. By 1950 it was clear that this had been a major mistake.

45. The standard rate was brought down from 45 percent in 1951 to 39.5 percent in 1964. The maximum surtax rate was reduced from 53 percent to only 50 percent. The tax threshold was increased only from £190 in 1951 to £240 in 1964. Of course, these figures indicate only statutory nominal rates. Hence one would be widely off the mark to assume that these were "effective" tax rates. Interest payments and pension contributions were fully deductible for income tax purposes at this time, and capital gains were wholly untaxed.

46. Hansen (1969, 419–21) reported for the OECD that the British record of stabilization policy was the worst of the seven countries he studied. Policies were so badly timed and executed that they had the opposite of their intended effects and actually destabilized the economy.

47. Willis, interview with author, 1985.

48. Much effort was put into closing some of the major loopholes and thus making the tax less arbitrary. "Our first three budgets were thick with amendments aimed at increasing equity" (Diamond, interview, 1985). The Inland Revenue called the cancellation of the deductibility of nonmortgage interest a "radical change" in the taxation of personal income (IR Report, 1975).

49. SET was a tax on each worker (with different rates for workers according to age, sex, etc.) paid by the employer. A portion of SET revenues was rebated to specific industries. In these cases, generally manufacturing industries, which were heavily labor intensive and possessed strong, militant labor union movements, the rebate exceeded the contribution, and thus the tax was in fact an indirect subsidy.

50. The SET was expected to provide a covert subsidy to exports and thereby also help Britain's lagging balance of payments.

51. A very similar story can be told of the introduction of the first modern corporate

profits tax in Britain in 1966. See Steinmo 1986, chap. 7; Robinson and Sandford 1983, 28–31.

52. It must be noted that total revenue nearly doubled between 1963 and 1971. There was also a significant shift in the balance between customs and excise taxes and direct income taxes. Customs and excise receipts were reduced from 42.7 percent of total revenue to 33.4 percent in this period. Inflation was probably the biggest factor in this shift. See Karran 1985; and Morrissey and Steinmo 1987.

53. For example, the standard income tax rate was reduced from 41.25 percent to 38.75 percent; the "reduced rate" band of tax was abolished; and there were a number of increases in a whole range of personal, child and family allowances, provisions for separate taxation of husband and wife; repealed aggregation of child's investment income into parents' tax return; also, the income and surtax systems were unified into a comprehensive income tax base.

Chapter 6
Rethinking Modern Taxation

1. To list the critics of tax expenditure abuse could take volumes. For one of the most important early criticisms, see Surrey 1973.

2. There were also a number of studies (in the United States at least) that demonstrated that many huge and profitable corporations did not pay taxes. See, for example, any of the numerous publications of the citizens' watchdog/advocacy group Citizens for Tax Justice, Washington, D.C.

3. Pomper (1986, 2) reports, for example, that three out of four people surveyed in the United States believed that "the present tax system benefits the rich" and that four-fifths felt corporations pay too little in taxes. For a description of the degree of apathy and antipathy met by tax reform efforts in the United States, see Birnbaum and Murray 1987, 43.

4. Survey data from all three countries suggest that these feelings were indeed widespread. See, for example, Lewis 1982; Hadenius 1986; Laurin 1986.

5. Figures computed from *Fortune*, various years. See Steinmo 1991.

6. See Joint Committee on Internal Revenue Taxation, *General Explanations of the Economic Recovery Tax Act of 1981*, Washington D.C.: Government Printing Office, 1982.

7. Dole was able to muster support for closing loopholes worth $98 billion in the next three years. Angry over Dole's Tax Equity and Financial Reform Act (TEFRA) of 1982, the banking industry, which took a hit in this bill, mounted a huge campaign against one of TEFRA's main revenue features. In 1983 they won, and the offending provisions were repealed.

8. See, for example, Birnbaum and Murray 1987; Conlan et al. 1990; White and Wildavsky 1989.

9. The Tax Reform Act of 1986 was indeed a remarkable legislative achievement. Though the final bill was far from an ideal tax reform from an economic efficiency point of view, it did cut tax rates on virtually all income tax payers substantially, and it did

eliminate or reduce a sizable number of tax expenditures. For a more complete analysis of the 1986 reform see Joint Tax Committee, HR3838, 1986.

10. There were a huge number of highly particularistic measures retained for specific groups, industries, cities, regions of the country, and even individuals. A partial list of these includes reindeer hunters, chicken farmers, watchmakers, pen manufacturers, ministers, military personnel, timber growers, oil and gas investors, state and municipal bond investors, some commodity investors, building rehabilitators, steel manufacturers, tuxedo rental companies, firms with Puerto Rican operators, solid waste facilities, the estate of James H. W. Thompson, dependents of MIA's, foster parents, certain Indian tribes, the Miami Dolphins, Cleveland, Chicago, Memphis, and northern New Jersey. In addition, Senator Robert Packwood and Congressman Dan Rostenkowski retained $5 to $6 billion in revenues to use for "transition rules" in order to buy off particularly intransigent opponents to the tax bill in its final stages.

11. *Congressional Record,* vol. 132, no. 129, September 26, 1986. Given the complexity of the final bill and the multiple ways in which a reform of this size affects the economy, it is virtually impossible to tell whether the result of reform was revenue neutral (as promised) or whether the government lost or gained revenues.

12. Jeffrey Birnbaum, "Showdown at Gucci Gulch," speech to the Tax Institute, May 1987.

13. In her government's first budget, then, Thatcher lowered the maximum tax on earned income from 83 percent to 60 percent; increased tax thresholds and lowered the basic rate of tax from 33 percent to 30 percent; lowered the investment income tax surcharge from 15 percent to 10 percent (as well as increased the threshold of this tax from £1,701 to £5,000); and doubled most tax allowances. To pay for these cuts, she "reformed" the VAT from a two-rate (8 percent and 12.5 percent) system to a single 15 percent tax rate. Chancellor Sir Geoffrey Howe also announced that capital taxation and corporate taxation would go under review for future budgets.

14. In 1985, the land development tax was abolished, the VAT base was broadened, and some loopholes were closed. In 1986, some of the reforms included income tax rate cuts, the expansion of tax thresholds, halving the stamp tax, stricter taxation of pension funds, and the introduction of a Personal Equity Plan, which is somewhat like the American IRA.

15. There were also a large number of more detailed changes affecting capital and corporate taxation as well as the taxation of married couples. Finally, the basic rate was cut to 27 percent in 1987 and then to 25 percent in 1988. The top marginal rate was cut to 60 percent in 1987 and to 40 percent in 1988.

16. *Financial Times,* Wednbesday, March 16, 1988, 25.

17. The Labour government chancellor Denis Healey (1989, 393) admitted in his autobiography that measures he introduced left a company tax system in which "British companies are the most lightly taxed in the developed world; in fact no manufacturing company which re-invested its profits paid any tax at all thereafter."

18. It is of course possible that the chancellor was in fact lying and that he knew that this

reform would increase the burden borne by the corporate sector. Unfortunately, it is unlikely that we will ever know which explanation is correct.

19. Interview with author, 1985.

20. One could suggest that the increasing of the tax burden on the manufacturing sector, which received the biggest tax increase, was less than accidental. After all, the capital-intensive manufacturing sector, which had received the biggest tax breaks under Labour, was a stronghold for labor union power. We cannot know whether there is any truth to this proposition, however, because of the secrecy of budget deliberations.

21. Interview with author, June 8, 1988. Asked if he could think of any other specific examples in which the lack of consultation had recently led to poor policy choices from industry's point of view, Wilkins responded, "Of course. For example in the 1988 change in the definition of company residence there was absolutely no consultation. We believe that the government didn't even know that there were companies registered in Britain who have no operations in Britain at all. They weren't even aware that these companies existed. This rule change has had very negative consequences for these firms."

22. Interview with author, June 6, 1988.

23. *Paying for Local Government* Cmnd. 9714, London: Her Majesty's Stationery Office, January 1986. For a good introduction to the workings of the poll tax, see Ian Lomax, *A Guide to the Community Charge* (London: Fourmat Publishing, 1990).

24. I can neither detail here the many machinations that the reform underwent nor even adequately summarize the outcome. No sooner had the reform been introduced than it was changed. There was, moreover, so much public resistance and deliberate failure to comply with the poll tax that even after it had been implemented it was unclear what an average poll tax burden was across the country. The tax ranged, however, from approximately £100 per person in some areas to more than £400 per person in others ("Projected English Poll Tax Payments," *Times*, November 18, 1987).

25. The political impact of this new proposal was cushioned somewhat by the proposal to introduce the tax in Scotland, where the Tories were already political losers, and bring it into England only after 1987 (that is, after the next national election). This calculation appeared to work—at first. Though the Tories did indeed lose ten of the twenty-one Scottish constituencies they held before the election, the poll tax did not figure prominently among the general electorate, who understood the proposal poorly at best.

26. The *Times* of London reported that all but two members of the cabinet, Nicholas Riddley, whose Environment Department was responsible for working out the details of the reform, and Thatcher herself, were opposed to the new plan.

27. At the time of this writing, the poll tax is being repealed due to massive public protest and even violence in opposition to the regressive tax.

28. At one point, it appeared that the House of Lords would not yield its rubber stamp—but a few phone calls and a bit of arm twisting corrected this problem. The government solved this minicrisis by literally stacking the House of Lords with peers who

each stood to gain thousands of pounds in reduced taxes from this reform. See Paul Lashmar, "Lords are Cashing in on the Poll Tax," *Observer*, May 29, 1988.

29. Sweden moved from a multitiered income tax system with marginal tax rates rising to 80 percent to a much more simplified system in which the average taxpayer paid only the flat local income tax (approximately 30 percent, depending on the local commune) and those with high incomes paid an additional 20 percent national income tax. Under the new system the top rate was thus reduced to 50 percent, whereas in the old system middle-income workers paid at a 50 percent rate or higher.

30. For an interesting analysis of why the SAF changed strategies and what the likely effects of this strategy will be, see the "Debatt" article by the LO president Stig Malm, "De enögda ideologierna har tagit över SAF" *LO Tidningen* 12, March 23, 1990, 8.

31. Herein lies a major flaw in Mancur Olson's famous argument. It is not simply the *size* of Swedish unions that made them consider the national interest in their wage and political demands, but rather the political and institutional context that structures their interest differently from that of their British and American counterparts.

32. Interview with author, 1988.

33. Interview with author, 1988.

34. Once again the examples of this argument made even by Social Democrats is voluminous. See, for example, Villy Bergström and Jan Södersten 1987; Jonung 1982.

35. Domestic investment as a percentage of net domestic product fell from 16.3 percent in 1963–73 to 8.7 percent in 1974–82. See Bosworth and Lawrence 1987, table 2.2.

36. For the Moderate party's view of this reform, see "Århundradens skattereform och verkligheten," Moderate Party Press Release 12/21/83.

37. Kjell-Olof Feldt, "What Shall We Do with Capitalism?" in *Inside Sweden*, 1989.

38. Many would argue that under Wigforss, Sträng, and Feldt, the minister of finance was more powerful than the party leader in economic and especially tax affairs.

39. Ahlquist and Engquist 1984. This book was by no means exclusively focused on taxation matters. It instead attempted to activate a general debate on the nature of the Social Democratic model for Sweden. Taxation, however, was a central topic in this book and in the subsequent debate that it evoked.

40. Interest group publications included, for example, TCO Congress report, *White Collar Workers and Taxation* (Tjänstemännen och skatterna) (Stockholm: TCO, 1982); Gustaf Lindencrona, Nils Mattson, Ingemar Ståhl, and Jan Bröms, *Uniform Income Tax* (Enhetlig inkomst skatt) (Stockholm: SACO/SR, 1986). The latter book in itself demonstrates the extent to which some interest groups, the ministry, and academics supported tax reform. The publisher of this monograph was SACO/SR, a union consisting largely of academics; the first two authors listed are professors of tax law, the third worked as the chief secretary for the Royal Commission on Income Tax Reform, and the last is an economist for SACO/SR. See also Calmfors and Wadner 1980.

41. See *Skall Matmomsen Slopas?* (SOU, 1983), 54; *Reavinst Aktier Obligationer* (SOU, 1986), 37; *Förenklad Själv Deklaration* (SOU, 1984), 21; *Reformerade Mervardeskatte* (SOU, 1989), 35, vols. 1, and II, and *Reformerade Foretagsbeskattning* (SOU, 1989), 34, vols. 1, 2; *Reformerade Inkomstbeskattning* (SOU, 1989), 33, vols. 1–4. In the

case of the last two monumental studies, which are the foundation of the major tax overhaul introduced in December 1989, the chairman of both commissions was Erik Åsbrink, the undersecretary for tax policy from the Finance Ministry.

42. In the first few months after the Social Democrats returned to government in the fall of 1982 they were particularly active in trying to raise revenues. By February 1984 they had introduced forty-four separate tax measures that increased state revenues.

43. Instead of a tax return, taxpayers simply sign a document declaring that they received no outside income other than that reported to tax authorities by their employers.

44. As one might imagine, the Left of his party was less than enthusiastic about the proposals. Moreover, the LO, which had been explicitly excluded from participating on the commissions, was exceedingly restless. According to their calculations, the distributional effects of the commissions' proposals were distinctly regressive. Low-paid and part-time workers (mostly women) would lose an average of Skr 2,900 a year (approximately $450 U.S.), while people earning Skr 250,000 or more a year ($40,000 U.S.) would have their taxes lowered by an average of Skr 8,300 ($1,000 U.S.). See LO, press release, September 5, 1989, "Låginkomstaggare förlorar pa skatteomlagningen" (Low-paid lose in tax changes).

45. Each of the three bourgeois party commission members wrote their "reservations" against the final report, which in essence said, "In general we approve of the idea, but we don't like this and that." The specific this and that differed from party to party.

46. See series of articles in the LO weekly magazine, *LO Tidningen*, especially September 8, 1989, and September 29, 1989.

47. The Center party was included in the negotiations but in the end refused to sign off on the financing portion of the tax reform.

48. Indeed, on October 20 the government conceded to increasing the top marginal rate to 55 percent.

49. The most significant of these were: (a) the absolute highest tax bracket would be 50 percent; (b) tax brackets would be indexed to inflation, thus guaranteeing that government income tax revenue would not simply grow via inflation, and (c) the deductibility of consumer interest from tax liability was made more generous than Feldt and his economist-advisers preferred.

50. Number 45, November 10, 1989, 2.

51. Even before the Socialists left office, the Swedish economic resurgence of the mid-1980s had ground to a halt. For example, Sweden had the second lowest GDP growth in all the OECD in 1989. Growth in investment was expected to fall from 7 percent in 1989 to 0.5 percent in 1991. Unit labor costs were rising at a rate of 6.8 percent per year while the OECD average was only 2.4 percent. Wage increases averaged 10 percent in 1989 and were expected to continue rising. As a result, inflation was galloping at 8 to 9 percent a year in Sweden, twice the OECD average. Finally, Swedish labor relations were deteriorating beyond recognition; see, for example, *Financial Times*, "Strikes Threaten to Tear Apart Sweden's Consensus Society," February 7, 1990, 2.

52. See "Regeringens Krispacket i bitar" ("The government's crisis package in pieces"), *Riksdag & Departement* 7 (1990): 3, 4.

Chapter 7
Taxes, Democracy, and the Welfare State

1. The literature that can be cited to support this point is voluminous. See, for example, Hadenius 1986; Lewis 1982; Taylor-Gooby 1987; Ladd 1979; Citrin 1979; Hibbs and Madsen 1981.
2. It is clear, for example, that if the interviewer simply asks about taxes and does not mention benefits or programs, wide majorities will say that taxes are too high. If specific public programs are mentioned, the number of people who say that taxes are too high drops dramatically. When asked about specific programs first (e.g., health, education, etc.) and then if taxes are too high, only a minority believe their taxes should be cut if it means cutting public services.
3. The average European OECD nation collects 39.7 percent of GDP in taxes. Of course many economists would argue that because of "tax competition," the doubling of consumption taxes in the United States would drive out or reduce other revenue sources.
4. Data provided by Axel Hadenius, Uppsala, Sweden, from his study "A Crisis of the Welfare State?" (1986).
5. As we saw in chapter 6, Reagan later introduced a much more politically palatable tax proposal, which Congress then proceeded to "reform" so that it conflicted less with their reelection interests. Still, the desire to make good public policy played an important role in the passing of even this watered-down law.
6. Leif Muten noted, for example, "Rather few Swedes really like the tax burden imposed on them; a cost less tax reduction [as in the United States] would gain overwhelming support." Comments made at the 1986 Brookings Conference "World Tax Reform," Nov. 12–13, 1987, Washington, D.C.
7. A poll conducted in the United States in 1984 found that 70 percent of respondents agreed to the following statement: "The major reason I'm opposed to any new federal taxes is because you can't trust the government to spend the money wisely." Market Opinion Research, 1984, 102.
8. Remark made by an adviser to the prime minister. Quoted in Longley 1986.
9. The Labour party has, of course, promised to repeal the tax and, more generally, reintroduce progressivity into the British tax system. It was almost certainly the fear of another round of see-sawing that swung so many British voters against Labour in the last days of the 1992 election.

Bibliography

Aaron, Henry, and Harvey Galper. *Assessing Tax Reform*. Washington, D.C.: Brookings Institution, 1986.

Advisory Commission on Intergovernmental Relations (ACIR). "Changing Public Attitudes on Governments and Taxes." Washington, D.C.: ACIR, 1985.

Ahlquist, Berndt, and Lars Engquist. *Samtal Med Feldt*. Stockholm: Tiden, 1984.

Ahmad, Ehtisham, and Nicholas Stern. *The Theory and Practice of Tax Reform in Developing Countries*. Cambridge: Cambridge University Press, 1991.

Alt, James. "The Evolution of Tax Structures." *Public Choice* 41 (1984): 181–222.

Amenta, Edwin, and Theda Skocpol. "Redefining the New Deal: World War II and the Development of Social Provision in the United States." In *The Politics of Social Policy in the United States*, edited by Margaret Wier, Ann Shola Orloff, and Theda Skocpol, 81–122. Princeton: Princeton University Press, 1988.

Andersson, Krister. "Sweden." In *Comparative Tax Systems: Europe, Canada, and Japan*, edited by Joseph Pechman. Arlington, Va.: Tax Analysts, 1987.

Andersson, Staffan. "Lag Om Vinstdelningsskatt—Löntarfonder." *Svensk Skattefidning* 51.4–5 (1984): 181–93.

Anonymous. "Projected English Poll Tax Payments." *Times*, November 18, 1987.

———. "Britain's Budget Options: A Chance That Won't Come Again." *The Economist*, Feb. 20, 1987, 66–68.

———. "Strikes Threaten to Tear Apart Sweden's Consensus Society." *Financial Times*, February 7, 1990, 2.

Anton, Thomas. "Policy making and Political Culture in Sweden." *Scandinavian Political Studies* 4 (1969): 88–102.

Anton, Thomas, Claes Linde, and Anders Mellbourn. "Bureaucrats in Politics: A Profile of the Swedish Administrative Elite." *Canadian Public Administration* 16.4 (1973).

Arestis, Philip. "Post-Keynesian Economic Policies: The Case of Sweden." *Journal of Economic Issues* 20 (September 1986): 709–23.

Arnold, R. Douglas. "The Local Roots of Domestic Policy." In *The New Congress*, edited by Thomas Mann and Norman Ornstein, 250–87. Washington D.C.: American Enterprise Institute, 1981.

Aronson, J. Richard, and John Hilley. *Financing State and Local Government*. Washington, D.C.: Brookings Institution, 1986.

Åsard, Erik. *LO Och Lontagarfondsfragan*. Uppsala: Raben and Sjogren, 1978.

———. "Employee Participation in Sweden 1971–1979: The Issue of Economic Democracy." *Economic and Industrial Democracy* 1.2 (August 1980): 371–94.

———. "Industrial and Economic Democracy in Sweden: From Consensus to Confrontation." Paper presented to the 12th joint session of the European Consortium for Political Research (ECPR), 13–18 April 1984, Salzburg, Austria.

Åsbrink, Per. "Direct Och Indirect Beskattning." *Tiden*. 1950.

Ascher, William. "Risk, Politics and Tax Reform: Lessons from Some Latin American Experiences." In *Tax Reform in Developing Countries,* edited by Malcolm Gillis, 417–72. Durham and London: Duke University Press, 1989.

Ashford, Douglas E. "Structural Analysis and Institutional Change." *Polity* 19 (Fall 1986): 97–122.

Atkinson, Anthony B. *Taxation and Social Security Reform: Reflections on Advising a House of Commons Select Committee.* London: Economic and Social Science Research Council Program, 1984.

Atkinson, Anthony, and A. J. Harrison. *The Distribution of Personal Wealth.* Cambridge: Cambridge University Press, 1978.

Bagehot, Walter. *The English Constitution and Other Political Essays.* New York: Appleton, 1877.

Barnett, Joel. *Inside the Treasury.* London: André Deutsch, 1982.

Bates, Robert H. "A Political Scientist Looks at Tax Reform." In *Tax Reform in Developing Countries,* edited by Malcolm Gillis, 473–91. Durham and London: Duke University Press, 1989.

Beer, Francis A., et al. "War Cues and Foreign Policy Acts." *American Political Science Review* 81.3 (September 1987): 700–15.

Beer, Samuel. *British Politics in the Collectivist Age.* 2d ed. New York: Vintage Books, 1969.

————. *Britain against Itself.* London: Faber and Faber, 1982.

Bendix, Reinhard. *Nation-building and Citizenship.* Berkeley: University of California Press, 1964.

Berger, Suzanne. *Organizing Interests in Western Europe.* New York: Cambridge University Press, 1981.

Bergström, Hans. *Rivstart?* Stockholm: Tidens forlag, 1987.

Bergström, Villy. *Studies in Swedish Postwar Industrial Investments.* Uppsala: Almquist and Wicksell, 1982.

————. "Fordelnings Politiken Ökar Orattvisorna," *LO Tidningen,* December 15, 1989, 50–52.

Bergström, Villy, and Jan Södersten. "Do Tax Allowances Stimulate Investment?" *Working Paper Series* (Uppsala). University of Uppsala, Department of Economics, 1984.

————. "Kan Finance Politiken Styra Investeringar?" *Fackforeningsrörelsens Institute for Ekonomisk Forskning.* May 1987.

Bertmar, Lars. "Företags Beskattning—Behovs Den?" *Hur Klarar Vi 1990.* Stockholm: Riksbank Jubileums Fond, 1983.

Bird, Richard. *Tax Incentives for Investment: The State of the Art.* Toronto: Canadian Tax Foundation, 1980.

Birgesson, Bengt Ove, et al. *Sverige Efter 1900.* Stockholm: Bonnierfakta, 1981.

Birnbaum, Jeffrey, and Alan Murray. *Showdown at Gucci Gulch: Law Makers, Lobbyists and the Unlikely Triumph of Tax Reform.* New York: Random House, 1987.

Bittker, Boris. "Accounting for Federal 'Tax Subsidies'in the National Budget." *National Tax Journal* 22.2 (1969): 244–61.

Bjerlow, Torsten. *Riksdags Årsbok.* Stockholm: Norstens, 1938.

Blakey, Roy G., and Gladys C. Blakey. *The Federal Income Tax.* New York: Longmans, Green, 1940.

Blank, Stephen. "Britain: The Politics of Foreign Economic Policy, the Domestic Economy, and the Problem in Pluralistic Stagnation." In *Between Power and Plenty,* edited by Peter J. Katzenstein, 89–138. Madison: University of Wisconsin Press, 1978.

Blough, Roy. *The Federal Taxing Process.* New York: Prentice-Hall, 1952.

Board of Inland Revenue and Board of Customs and Excise. "Industry and the Weight of Taxation." *PRO T171/203.* January 1922.

Boskin, Michael J. "New Directions in Tax Policy." In *World Tax Reform,* edited by Michael J. Boskin and Charles E. McLure, Jr., 3–7. San Francisco: ICS Press, 1990.

Boskin, Michael J., and Charles E. McLure, Jr., eds. *World Tax Reform.* San Francisco: ICS Press, 1990.

Bossons, John. "The Impact of the 1986 Tax Reform Act on Tax Reform in Canada." *National Tax Journal* 40.3 (September 1987): 331–38.

————. "International Tax Competition: The Foreign Government Response in Canada and Other Countries." *National Tax Journal* 41.3 (September 1988): 347–55.

Bosworth, Barry, and Alice Rivlin, eds. *The Swedish Economy.* Washington, D.C.: Brookings Institution, 1987.

Bosworth, Barry, and Robert Lawrence. "Adjusting to Slower Economic Growth." In *The Swedish Economy,* edited by Barry Bosworth and Alice Rivlin, 22–54. Washington, D.C.: Brookings Institution, 1987.

Bovenberg, Lans A. "The Effects of Capital Income Taxation on International Competitiveness and Trade Flows." *American Economic Review* 79.5 (December 1989): 1045–64.

Brady, Richard. "The Puzzle of Participation in America." In *The New American Political System,* edited by A. King. Washington, D.C.: AEI, 1978.

Bratt, John, and Lars Fogelklou. *Skatt På Arv Och Skatt På Gava.* Stockholm: Norstedt and Sons, 1960.

Braun, Rudolf. "Taxation, Sociopolitical Structure, and State Building in Great Britain and Brandenburg, Prussia." *The Formation of Nation States in Western Europe.* Princeton: Princeton University Press, 1975.

Break, George. *Financing Government in a Federal System.* Washington, D.C.: Brookings Institution, 1980.

————. "The Tax Expenditure Budget—The Need for a Fuller Accounting." *National Tax Journal* 38.3 (September 1985): 261–65.

Break, George, and Joseph Pechman. *Federal Tax Reform: The Impossible Dream.* Washington, D.C.: Brookings Institution, 1975.

Brennen, G., and J. Buchanan. *The Power to Tax: Analytical Foundation of a Fiscal Constitution*. Cambridge: Cambridge University Press, 1980.

Brittain, Samuel. *Steering the Economy*. London: Secker and Warburg, 1969.

Brown, Chuck, and Cedric Sandford. "The Effects of Income Tax on Incentives: How the 1988 Income Tax Reductions Affected Accountants." *British Tax Reveiw*, nos. 11, 12 (1991): 414–20.

Brownlee, W. Elliot. "Taxation for a Strong and Virtuous Republic: A Bicentennial Retrospective." *Institute of Governmental Studies* (Berkeley) Working Paper no. 90–14 (1990).

Bruce-Gardyne, Jack, and Nigel Lawson. *The Power Game*. London: Macmillan, 1976.

Bruenker, John. *The Income Tax and the Progressive Era*. New York: Carland, 1985.

Buchanan, James M. *Public Finance in Democratic Process*. Chapel Hill: University of North Carolina Press, 1987.

Buchanan, James M., and Robert D. Tollison, eds. *The Theory of Public Choice—II*. Ann Arbor: University of Michigan Press, 1984.

Burnham, Walter Dean. *Critical Elections and the Mainstream of American Politics*. New York: W. W. Norton, 1970.

Butler, D., and R. Rose. *The British General Election of 1959*. London: Macmillan, 1960.

Butler, David, and Jennie Freeman. *British Political Facts*. London: St. Martin's Press, 1969.

Calmfors, Lars, and Göran Wadner, eds. *Sverige's Ekonomiska Kris*. Stockholm: Natur och Kultur, 1980.

Cameron, David. "The Expansion of the Public Economy: A Comparative Analysis." *American Journal of Political Science* 72 (1978): 1243–62.

————. "Social Democracy, Corporatism, and Labour Quiescence, and the Representation of Economic Interests in Advanced Capitalist Society." In *Order and Conflict in Contemporary Societies*, edited by John Goldthorpe, 143–78. Oxford: Oxford University Press, 1984.

————. "Distributional Coalitions and Other Sources of Economic Stagnation: On Olson's *Rise and Decline of Nations*." *International Organization* 42.4 (Autumn 1988): 561–601.

Cantril, Hadley. *Public Opinion*. Princeton: Princeton University Press, 1951.

Carlsson, Sten. "From Four Estates to Two Chambers: The Riksdag in a Period of Transition, 1809–1921." In *The Riksdag: A History of the Swedish Parliament*, edited by Michael Metcalf, 165–221. New York: St. Martin's Press, 1987.

Carstairs, Andrew McLaren. *A Short History of Electoral Systems in Western Europe*. London: George Allen and Unwin, 1980.

Casparsson, Ragnar. *Saltsjobads Avtalet I Historisk Belysning*. Stockholm: Tidens Forlag, 1966.

Castles, Francis. *The Social Democratic Image of Society*. London: Routledge and Kegan Paul, 1978.

————. "The Impact of Parties on Public Expenditure." In *The Impact of Parties: Politics of Parties: Politics and Policies in Democratic Capitalist States,* edited by Francis Castles, 21–96. Beverly Hills: Sage, 1982.

Caves, R., and L. Krause. "Introduction." *Britain's Economic Performance.* Washington, D.C.: Brookings Institution, 1980.

Central Statistical Office (CSO). *Income and Expenditure.* London: CSO, 1980.

————. *Annual Abstract of Statistics.* Vol. 94. London: Her Majesty's Stationery Office, 1957.

————. *Annual Abstract of Statistics.* Vol. 102. London: Her Majesty's Stationery Office, 1965.

————. *Statistical Abstract for the U.K., 1924–1938.* Vol. 83. Nendeln, Lichtenstein: Reprinted by Kraus Reprint Ltd., 1966.

————. *Statistical Abstract for the U.K., 1913, 1915–1928.* Vol. 73. Nendeln, Lichtenstein: Reprinted by Kraus Reprint Ltd., 1966.

————. *Statistical Abstract for the U.K., 1901–1915.* Vol. 63. Nendeln, Lichtenstein: Reprinted by Kraus Reprint Ltd., 1966.

————. *Annual Abstract of Statistics.* Vol. 104. London: Her Majesty's Stationery Office, 1967.

————. *Statistical Abstract of the U.K., 1938–1950.* Vol. 88. Nendeln, Lichtenstein: Reprint by Kraus Reprint Ltd., 1970.

————. *Annual Abstract of Statistics.* Vol. 116. London: Her Majesty's Stationery Office, 1980.

————. *Annual Abstract of Statistics.* Vol. 123. London: Her Majesty's Stationery Office, 1987.

Chalmers, Douglas. "Corporatism and Comparative Politics." In *New Trends in Comparative Politics,* edited by K. Wiarda, 56–79. Boulder: Westview Press, 1985.

Childs, Marquis. *Sweden: The Middle Way.* New Haven: Yale University Press, 1974.

Citrin, Jack. "Do People Want Something for Nothing: Public Opinion on Taxes and Government Spending." *National Tax Journal* 32.2 (supplement) (June 1979): 113–30.

Citrin, Jack, and Donald Green. "Public Opinion in California after Proposition 13." *National Tax Journal* 38.1 (1985): 15–36.

Clarke, Peter. *The Keynesian Revolution in the Making.* Oxford: Oxford University Press, 1988.

Coats, A. W. "Britain: The Rise of the Specialists." *History of Political Economy* 13.3 (1981): 1–15.

Coffield, James. *A Popular History of Taxation: From Ancient to Modern Times.* London: Longman, 1970.

Cohen, Richard E. "Democrats, GOP Wary of Long-term Fallout from Tax Reform." *National Journal* 23 (June 8, 1985): 1346–49.

Confederation of British Industries (CBI). *Annual Report.* London: CBI, 1975.

————. *Taxation in Western Europe.* London: CBI, 1965.

Congressional Budget Office (CBO). *The Economic and Budget Outlook: An Update.* Tables I-3, II-3, and II-8. November 1986.

————. *Tax Expenditures: Current Issues and Five-Year Budget Projections for Fiscal Years 1983–1987.* Table 3. November 1982.

————. *Tax Expenditures: Budget Control Options and Five-Year Budget Projections for Fiscal Years 1983–1987.* Washington, D.C.: Congressional Budget Office, 1983.

Conlan, Timothy J., Margaret T. Wrightson, and David R. Beam. *Taxing Choices: The Politics of Tax Reform.* Washington, D.C.: Congressional Quarterly, 1990.

Cook, Karen Schweers, and Margaret Levi, eds. *The Limits of Rationality.* Chicago: University of Chicago Press, 1990.

Cooper, George. *A Voluntary Tax? New Perspectives on Sophisticated Estate Tax Avoidance.* Washington, D.C.: Brookings Institution, 1979.

Coughlin, Richard. *Ideology, Public Opinion, Welfare Policy: Attitudes Towards Taxing and Spending in Industrial Societies.* Berkeley: Institute of International Studies, 1980.

————. "Payroll Taxes for Social Security in the U.S.: The Future of Fiscal and Social Policy Illusions." *Journal of Economic Psychology* 2 (1982): 165–85.

Creedy, John, and Richard Disney. "The New Pension Scheme in Britain." *Fiscal Studies* 9.2 (1988): 57–79.

Crenshaw, Albert B. "Has Our Tax System Outlived Its Usefulness?" *Washington Post National Weekly Edition,* April 24–30, 1989, 20.

Crocker, Royce. "Federal Government Spending and Public Opinion." *Public Budgeting and Finance* (Autumn 1981).

Crosland, Anthony. *Socialism Now: And Other Essays.* London: Jonathan Cape, 1974.

Crossman, Richard. *Diaries of a Cabinet Minister.* New York: Holt, Rinehart and Winston, 1975.

Daley, Charles. *Tax Cuts and Tax Reform: The Quest for Equity.* Washington, D.C.: AEI, 1978.

Dalton, Hugh. *Memoirs, 1945–60, High Tide and After.* London: Federich, 1962.

Darman, Richard G. "Beyond Tax Populism." *Society* 24.6 (September-October 1987): 35–38.

De Geer, Hans. *SAF I Forhandlingar.* Arlov: SAFs forlag, 1986.

————. *Rationaliseringsrörelsen I Sveriga. Effektivitetsideer Och Socialt Ansvar Under Mellankrigstiden.* Uddevalla: Studiefobundet Naringsliv och Samhalle, 1978.

Denton, Geoffrey. "Financial Assistance to British Industry." In *Public Assistance to Industry,* 120–64. London: Macmillan 1976.

Department of Environment. *Paying for Local Government.* London: Her Majesty's Stationery Office, CMND 9714, 1986.

Department of the Committee on National Debt and Taxation. CMND 2800. 1927.

Derthick, Martha. *Making Policy for Social Security.* Washington, D.C.: Brookings Institution, 1979.

Devereux, M. P., and C. P. Mayer. *Corporation Tax: The Impact of the 1984 Budget.* London: Institute of Fiscal Studies, 1984.

Dickie, Robert B., and Thomas A. Layman. *Foreign Investment and Government Policy in the Third World.* New York: St. Martin's Press, 1988.

Dilnot, A., and J. Kay. "The U.K. Tax System, Structure and Progressivity, 1948–1982." *Scandinavian Journal of Economics* 86.2 (1985): 150–65.

——— . "Tax Reform in the United Kingdom: The Recent Experience." In *World Tax Reform,* edited by Michael J. Boskin and Charles E. McLure, Jr., 149–76. San Francisco: ICS Press, 1990.

Dilnot, A., and G. Stark. "The Distributional Consequences of Mrs. Thatcher." *Fiscal Studies* 7.2 (1986): 48–53.

Dilnot, A. W., and C. N. Morris. "The Tax System and Distribution 1978–1983." *Fiscal Studies* (London) 4.2 (May 1983): 54–64.

——— . "Progressivity and Graduation in Income Tax." *Fiscal Studies* 5.4 (1984): 23–29.

Dilnot, A. W., J. A. Kay, and C. N. Morris. "The U.K. Tax System, Structure and Progressivity, 1948–82." *Scandinavian Journal of Economics* 86.2 (1984): 150–65.

Dilnot, Andrew, Ian Walker, Steven Webb, and Graham Stark. "The 1987 Budget in Perspective." *Fiscal Studies* 8.2 (May 1987): 49–57.

Dilnot, Andrew, Steven Webb, and Michael Kell. "The 1988 Budget and the Structure of Personal Taxation." *Fiscal Studies* 9.2 (1988).

Dilnot, Andrew, and Steven Webb. "Reforming National Insurance Contributions." *Fiscal Studies* 9.4 (1988): 1–9.

——— . "The 1988 Social Security Reforms." *Fiscal Studies* 9.3 (1988): 26–53.

DiMaggio, Paul J., and Walter W. Powell. "Introduction." In *The New Institutionalism in Organizational Analysis,* edited by Walter W. Powell and Paul J. DiMaggio, 1–38. Chicago: University of Chicago Press, 1991.

Dodd, Lawrence. "Congress and the Quest for Power." In *Congress Reconsidered,* 1st ed., edited by Lawrence Dodd and Bruce Oppenheimer. New York: Praeger, 1977.

Dodd, Lawrence C., and Richard L. Schott. *Congress and the Administrative State.* New York: John Wiley and Sons, 1979.

Doernberg, Richard. "The Market for Tax Reform: Public Pain for Private Gain." *Tax Notes* (November 28, 1988): 965–69.

Dooley, Michael P. "Capital Flight: A Response to Differences in Financial Risks." *IMF Staff Papers* 35.3 (September 1988): 422–36.

Downs, Anthony. *An Economic Theory of Democracy.* New York: Harper and Row, 1957.

——— . "Why the Government's Budget is Too Small in a Democracy." *World Politics* 12 (1960): 541–63.

Drucker, Peter F. "The Changed World Economy." *Foreign Affairs* 64.4 (Spring 1986): 768–91.

Duverger, M. *Political Parties.* New York: John Wiley and Sons, 1954.

Eberstein, Gosta. *Om Skatt Til Stat Och Kommun.* Stockholm: Norstedt and Sons, 1937.

Edvardson, Leif. *Utskiffningsskatt Vid Fusion . . .* Stockholm: Odenbyra AB, 1984.

Eisenstein, Louis. *The Ideologies of Taxation*. New York: Roland Press, 1961.

Eismeier, Theodore J. "Public Preferences about Government Spending: Partisan, Social and Attitudinal Sources of Policy Differences." *Political Behavior* 4.2 (1982): 133–45.

Eklund, Klas. "Den Bistra Sanningen." *Tidens Debatt*. Kristianstad: Leif Zetterling Production, 1982.

———. "Den Tredje Vägen—Och Alternativet." *Tiden* 3 (1985): 143–49.

———. "Vad Göra Med Skatterna?" *Affärsvärlden* 29.2 (1984): 7–17.

Ekstein, Harry. *Pressure Group Politics: The Case of the Medical Association*. Stanford: Stanford University Press, 1960.

Eliasson, Gunnar. *Investment Funds in Operation*. National Institute of Stockholm: Economic Research, 1965.

Ellis, Elmer. "Public Opinion and the Income Tax, 1860–1900." *Mississippi Valley Historical Review* 27 (June 1940): 225–42.

Elvander, Nils. *Svensk Skattepolitik 1945–1970*. Stockholm: Raben and Sjogren, 1972.

———. *Den Svenska Modellen*. Stockholm: Liber Forlag, 1988.

Englund, Goran. *Beskattning Av Arv Och Gava*. Stockholm: Norstedts, 1982.

Epstein, Leon. "What Happened to the British Party Model?" *American Journal of Political Science* 74.1 (1980): 9–23.

———. *Votes and Taxes*. Madison: Institute of Governmental Affairs, University of Wisconsin, 1964.

Esping-Anderson, Gösta. *Politics against Markets: The Social Democratic Road to Power*. Princeton: Princeton University Press, 1985.

———. *Power, Equality and Efficiency: The Perennial Dilemmas of Swedish Social Democracy*. Florence: European University Institute, 1988.

Esping-Anderson, Gösta, and Walter Korpi. "Social Policy as Class Politics in Postwar Capitalism: Scandinavia, Austria and Germany." In *Order and Conflict in Contemporary Capitalism*, edited by John Goldthorpe, 179–208. Oxford: Claredon Press, 1984.

Evans, Peter, Dietrich Rueschemeyer, and Theda Skocpol. "On the Road to a More Adequate Understanding of the State." In *Bringing the State Back In*, edited by Peter Evans, Dietrich Rueschemeyer, and Theda Skocpol, 347–66.

Federation of British Industries. *Taxation in the Proposed European Free Trade Area*. London: Federation of British Industries, 1957.

Feinstein, C. H. *National Income, Expenditure and Output of the United Kingdom 1855–1965*. Cambridge: Cambridge University Press, 1972.

Feldt, Kjell-Olof. "Löntagara Och Demokrati." *Tiden* 7 (1980).

———. "S—Politiken Offensiv Mot Nyliberalismen." *Tiden* 3 (1985): 137–42.

———. *Alla Dessa Dagar: I Regeringen 1982–1990*, Stockholm: Norstedts, 1991.

Fenno, Richard F. *The Power of the Purse: Appropriations Politics in Congress*. Boston: Little, Brown, 1966.

Fiegehen, G. C., and W. B. Reddaway. *Company Tax Incentives and Senior Managers*. Oxford: Oxford University Press, 1981.

Finansdepartementet. *Finansplanen Prop. 84:100*. Stockholm: Norstedts Trykeri, 1983.

Finansutskottet (FIU). 1981/82.

————. 1982/83.

————. 1983/84.

Finer, Sam. "Adversary Politics and Electoral Reform." In *Adversary Politics and Electoral Reform*, edited by Sam Finer, 3–34. London: Anthony Wigram, 1975.

Fiorina, Morris. *Congress: Keystone of the Washington Establishment*. New Haven: Yale University Press, 1977.

Fisher, Peter. "Investment Tax Credits, Capital Gains Taxation and the Re-industrialization of the American Economy." *Journal of Economic Issues* 15.3 (1981): 769–73.

Forsman, Anders. *En Teori Om Staten Och de Offentliga Utgifterna* (A theory of the state and state expenditures). Uppsala: Gleerup, 1980.

Fraser, Derek. *The Evolution of the British Welfare State*. London: Macmillan, 1973.

Frazen, Thomas. "Skatternas Effect På Arbetsviljan." In Staten Offentliga Utredningar (SOU), *Oversyn av skatte systemet* (Stockholm: SOU) 91 (1977): 357–96.

Free, Lloyd, and Hadley Cantril. *The Political Beliefs of Americans*. New Brunswick: Rutgers University Press, 1967.

Freeman, Gary. "National Styles and Policy Sectors: Explaining Structured Variation." *Journal of Public Policy* 5.4 (1985): 467–96.

Friedland, Roger, and Robert R. Alford. "Bringing Society Back In: Symbols, Practices, and Institutional Contradictions." In *The New Institutionalism in Organizational Analysis*, edited by Walter W. Powell and Paul J. DiMaggio, 232–63. Chicago: University of Chicago Press, 1991.

Frontline. *Taxes Behind Closed Doors*. Boston: WGBH Transcripts, 1986.

Gable, A. M., and S. A. Walkland. *The British Party System and Economic Policy, 1945–1983*. Oxford: Clarendon Press, 1984.

Gammie, Malcome. "Has Nigel Lawson Really Reformed Business Taxation?" *Fiscal Studies* 2 (1984): 82–93.

————. *The Enactment of Tax Legislation: An Analysis of the Consultative Process and the Finance Acts of 1979–1987*. London: Law and Society of England and Wales, 1988.

Garestad, Peter. "Industrialisering Och Beskattning I Sveriga 1861–1914." Ph.D. diss., Uppsala University, 1985.

Genberg, Torsten. "Skatteutvecklingen Sedan Sekelskiftet." *Meddelanden Från Skattebetalarnas Forening* 76 (1942).

Gershenkron, Alexander. *Economic Backwardness in Historical Perspective*. Cambridge: Harvard University Press, 1962.

Gilbert, Bentley. *David Lloyd George: A Political Life*. Columbus: Ohio State University Press, 1987.

Gillis, Malcolm. "Comprehensive Tax Reform: The Indonesian Experience, 1981–1988." In *Tax Reform in Developing Countries*, edited by Malcolm Gillis, 79–114. Durham and London: Duke University Press, 1989.

Giovannini, Alberto. "International Capital Mobility and Capital-income Taxation." *European Economic Review* 34.2–3 (May 1990): 480–88.

Gourevitch, Peter. *Politics in Hard Times: Comparative Responses to International Economic Crises.* Ithaca: Cornell University Press, 1986.

———. "Keynesian Politics: The Political Sources of Economic Policy Choices." *The Political Power of Economic Ideas: Keynesianism across Nations,* edited by Peter A. Hall, 87–106. Princeton: Princeton University Press, 1989.

Grant, R. M. "Appraising Selective Financial Assistance to Industry: A Review of Institutions and Methodologies in the United Kingdom, Sweden and W. Germany." *Journal of Public Policy* 3.4 (1983): 369–96.

Grant, Wyn. "Large Firms and Public Policy in Britain." *Journal of Public Policy* 4 (February 1984): 1–18.

Greenstone, David. *Labor in American Politics.* New York: Knopf, 1969.

Greider, William. "The Education of David Stockman." *Atlantic Monthly* December 1981, 5.

Gretton, John, and Anthony Harrison, eds. "Attitudes to Public Spending." *Public Money* 4.1 (June 1984).

Grosskopf, Göran. "Forenklad Företagsbeskattning." *Hur Klarer Vi 1990?* Riksbank Jubileums Fond., 1983.

Gulati, Sunil. "Capital Flight: Causes, Consequences and Cures." *Journal of International Affairs* 42.1 (Fall 1988): 165–85.

Gustavsson, Bo. *The Causes of the Expansion of the Public Sector in Sweden in the 20th Century.* Uppsala: Kung. Humanistiska Vetenskapliga-Samfundet i Uppsala, 1982.

Haag, Martin. "Election Year 1985: The Swedish Economy in the Right Direction?" *Current Sweden* 333 (May 1985).

Haas, Lawrence J. "Slippery Slope." *National Journal* 21.10 (March 11, 1989): 583–86.

Hadenius, Axel. *Facklig Organizationsutveckling: En Studie Av Lansorganisationen I Sverige.* Lund: Gleerup, 1966.

———. *Spelet Om Skatten.* Lund: Norstedts, 1981.

———. "Citizens Strike a Balance: Discontent with Taxes, Content with Spending." *Journal of Public Policy* 5.3 (August 1985): 349–63.

———. *A Crisis of the Welfare State? Opinions about Taxes and Public Expenditure in Sweden.* Stockholm: MiniMedia AB, 1986.

Hall, Peter. *Governing the Economy.* New York: Oxford University Press, 1986.

———. "The Movement from Keynesianism to Monetarism: Institutional Analysis and British Economic Policy in the 1970s." In *Structuring Politics: Historical Institutionalism in Comparative Analysis.* edited by Sven Steinmo, Kathleen Thelen, and Frank Longstreth, 90–113. New York: Cambridge University Press, 1992.

———. "Introduction." *The Political Power of Economic Ideas: Keynesianism across Nations,* edited by Peter A. Hall, 3–26. Princeton: Princeton University Press, 1989.

Ham, Adrian. *Treasury Rules: Recurrent Themes in British Economic Policy.* London: Quartet Books, 1981.

Hamilton, Alexander, James Madison, and John Jay. *The Federalist Papers*. New York: New American Library, 1961.

Hancock, Donald. *Sweden: The Politics of Postindustrial Change*. Hinsdale, Ill.: Dryden Press, 1972.

Hansard Society. *Politics and Industry—The Great Mismatch*. London: Hansard Society, 1979.

Hansen, Bent. *Fiscal Policies in Seven Countries*. Paris: OECD, 1969.

Hansen, Susan B. *The Politics of Taxation: Revenue without Representation*. Westpoint, Conn.: Praeger, 1983.

Hansson, Ingemar, and Charles Stuart. "Sweden: Tax Reform in a High-tax Environment." In *World Tax Reform*, edited by Michael J. Boskin and Charles E. McLure, Jr., 127–48. San Francisco: ICS Press, 1990.

Harberger, Arnold C. "Lessons of Tax Reform from the Experiences of Uruguay, Indonesia, and Chile." In *Tax Reform in Developing Countries*, edited by Malcolm Gillis, 27–43. Durham and London: Duke University Press, 1989.

Harriss, C. Lowell. "Taxation, Incentives and Disincentives, and Human Motivation." *American Journal of Economics and Sociology* 44 (April 1985): 129–36.

Håstad, Elis. *Gallup—Den Svenska Valjararen*. Uppsala: Almquist and Wicksell, 1950.

Hatfield, Michael. *The House the Left Built*. London: Victor Gollanez, 1978.

Hawley, Ellis. *The New Deal and the Problem of Monopoly*. Princeton: Princeton University Press, 1966.

Hays, Samuel P. *The Response to Industrialism 1885–1914*. Chicago: University of Chicago Press, 1957.

Head, John, and Richard Bird. "Tax Policy Options for the 1980s." In *Comparative Tax Studies*, 3–29. Amsterdam: North Holland, 1983.

Heald, David. *Public Expenditure*. Oxford: Martin Robertson, 1983.

Healy, Denis. *The Time of My Life*. London: Penguin Books, 1989.

Hecksher, Gunnar. "Sweden's Anti election: A Lot to Vote Against." *Wall Street Journal*, September 8, 1982, 33.

———. *Staten Och Organisationerna*. Stockholm: Kooperativa forbundet, 1946.

Heclo, Hugh. *Modern Social Politics in Britain and Sweden*. New Haven: Yale University Press, 1974.

Heclo, Hugh, and Aaron Wildavsky. *The Private Government of Public Money*. London: Macmillan, 1981.

Heclo, Hugh, and Henrik Madsen. *Policy and Politics in Sweden*. Philadelphia: Temple University Press, 1987.

Hedborg, Anna, and Rudolf Meidner. *Folkhemsmodellen*. Stockholm: Raben and Sjögren, 1984.

Heidenheimer, Arnold, Hugh Heclo, and Carolyn Adams. *Comparative Public Policy: The Politics of Social Choice in Europe and America*. New York: St. Martin's Press, 1975.

Hennessy, Peter. *Whitehall*. New York: Free Press, 1989.

Henning, Roger. *Företagen I Politiken*. Stockholm: Studieforbundet Naringslivet och Samhalle, 1977.

Hermanson, C. H. *Formogenheter, Inkomster, Profiter Och Löner*. Stockholm: STK Arbetskulture, 1944.

Hettich, Walter, and Stanley Winer. "A Positive Model of Tax Structure." *Journal of Public Economics* 24 (1984): 67–87.

Hibbs, Douglas A., Jr., and Henrik Jess Madsen. "Public Reactions to the Growth of Taxation and Government Expenditure." *World Politics* 33.3 (April 1981): 413–35.

————. "Political Parties and Macroeconomic Policy." *American Political Science Review* 71 (1977): 1467–87.

————. "On the Political Economy of Long Run Strike Activity." *British Journal of Political Science* 7 (1978): 153–77.

Hills, John. "Look Out, Its High-Tax Nigel." *New Statesman*, March 13, 1987, 13.

————. *Changing Tax: How the Tax System Works and How to Change It*. London: CPAG, 1988.

Hines, James. "Taxation and U.S. Multinational Investment." In *Tax Policy and the Economy*, edited by Lawrence Summers. Cambridge: MIT Press, 1988.

Hobsbawm, E. J. *Industry and Empire*. London: Penquin Books, 1969.

Hochstein, Madelyn. "Tax Ethics: Social Values and Noncompliance." *Public Opinion*, February/March 1985, 11–14.

Hockley, G. C. *Monetary Policy and Public Finance*. New York: Augustus M. Kelley, 1970.

Hoerner, J. Andrew. "Tax Reform around the World." *Tax Notes*, April 30, 1990.

Hofstadter, Richard, ed. *The Progressive Movement, 1900–1915*. Englewood Cliffs: Prentice-Hall, 1963.

Holmberg, Sören. *Riksdagen Representar Svenske Folket: Empiriska Studier I Representative Demokrati*. Lund: Studentlitteratur, 1974.

————. *Svenska Väljarne*. Stockholm: Liber forlag, 1981.

————. *Väljare I Forändring*. Stockholm: Liber forlag, 1984.

Holmberg, Sören, and Mikael Gilljam. "Valjase Och Val I Sverige." Stockholm: Bonnier Fakta Bokforlag AB, 1987.

Hoskyns, Sir John. "Whitehall and Westminster: An Outsider's View." *Fiscal Studies* 3.3 (1982): 162–72.

Howell, Thomas R., et al. *The Microelectronics Race: The Impact of Government Policy on International Competition*. Boulder: Westview Press, 1988.

Huntington, Samuel. "American Ideals versus American Institutions." *Political Science Quarterly* (Spring 1982): 1–37.

Ikenberry, John. "Conclusion: An Institutional Approach to American Foreign Economic Policy." *International Organization* 42 (Winter 1988): 219–26.

Ikenberry, John, David Lake, and Michael Mastanduno. "Introduction: Approaches to Explaining American Foreign Economic Policy." *International Organization* 42 (Winter 1988): 1–15.

Ikenberry, John, ed. *The State and American Foreign Economic Policy*. Ithaca: Cornell University Press, 1988.

Ilersic, I. R. *Government Finance and Fiscal Policy in Postwar Britain.* London: Staples Press, 1955.

Immergut, Ellen. "The Rules of the Game: The Logic of Health Policy-making in France, Switzerland, and Sweden." In *Structuring Politics: Historical Institutionalism in Comparative Analysis,* edited by Sven Steinmo, Kathleen Thelen, and Frank Longstreth, 57–89. New York: Cambridge University Press, 1992.

Industri Departementet. *Industri Och Industripolitik.* Stockholm: Industri Departementet, 1982.

Industries Utredning Institutet. *Economic Growth in a Nordic Perspective.* Stockholm: I.U.I., 1984.

Ingham, Geoffrey. *Strikes and Industrial Conflict.* London: Macmillan, 1974.

Institute of Economic Affairs. *The State of Taxation.* London: IEA, 1977.

International Fiscal Association. *Determination of Taxable Profit of Corporations.* LXIIb. Jerusalem: Cashiers de Droit Fiscal International, 1977.

International Monetary Fund (IMF). *International Financial Statistics* 4(5). Washington, D.C., May 1951, 86–87.

———. *Supplement on Government Finance.* 11. Washington, D.C., 1986.

———. *International Capital Markets: Developments and Prospects.* Washington, D.C.: IMF, 1990.

Internal Revenue Service, IRS Pub 1304. "Individual Income Tax Returns 1987, Table 1.1: Selected Income & Tax Items, by Size of Adjusted Gross Income." *100% tax on income over 100k* (rev 8–90) 1990, 20.

Isaksson, Anders. "Ett Parti Utan Inre Kompass." *Tiden* 3 (1983).

Isberg, Magnus. "The First Decade of the Unicameral Ridsdag: The Role of the Swedish Parliament in the 1970s." *Forsknings Rapporter* (University of Stockholm) 1 (1982). Statsvetenskapliga Institution.

Israel, Joachim. "Swedish Socialism and Big Business." *Acta Sociologica* 21.4 (1978): 341–53.

Jackman, Robert. "Political Institutions and Voter Turnout in the Industrial Democracies." *American Political Science Review* 81.2 (June 1987): 405–23.

Jakobsson, Ulf, and Göran Normann. *Inkomstbeskattning I Den Ekonomiska Politiken.* Stockholm: Almquist and Wicksell, 1974.

James, S., and C. Nobes. *The Economics of Taxation.* London: Phillip Allen, 1981.

Jenkins, Glenn P. "Tax Changes before Tax Policies: Sri Lanka, 1977–88." In *Tax Reform in Developing Countries,* edited by Malcolm Gillis, 233–51. Durham and London: Duke University Press, 1989.

Joint Committee on Taxation. *Estimates of Federal Tax Expenditures for Fiscal Years 1983–1988.* Washington, D.C.: Government Printing Office, 1983.

———. "Summary of Conference Agreement on H.R. 3838 (Tax Reform Act of 1986)." Washington, D.C.: Government Printing Office, 29 August (1986).

Jones, Carolyn. "Taxes to Beat the Axis: A Comparison of American and British Income Tax Publicity during World War II." Paper presented to the Tenth International Economic Congress, Leuven, Belgium, June 12, 1990.

Jonung, Lars. *Skatter.* Malmö, Sweden: Libertrykk, 1982.

Josefsson, Martha. "Listed Companies—A Comparison with Previous Years." *Skandinavisha Enskilda Banken Quarterly Review* 4 (1987): 84–95.

Jowell, Roger, and Colin Airey, eds. *British Social Attitudes: The 1984 Report*. London: Social and Community Planning Research, 1984.

Judge, Ken, Jillian Smith, and Peter Taylor-Gooby. "Public Opinion and the Privatization of Welfare: Some Theoretical Implications." *Journal of Social Policy* 12 (October 1983): 469–89.

Kahneman, David, Paul Slovic, and Amos Tversky, eds. *Judgement under Uncertainty: Heuristics and Biases*. New York: Cambridge University Press, 1982.

Kaldor, Nicholas. *Reports on Taxation I*. New York: Anchor Press, 1980.

Karran, T. *The Determinants of Taxation in Britain: An Empirical Test*. Glasgow, Scotland: Center for the Study of Public Policy, University of Strathclyde, 1985.

Katz, Claudio, Vincent Mahler, and Michael Franz. "The Impact of Taxes on Growth and Distribution in Capitalist Countries: A Cross-National Study." *American Political Science Review* 77.4 (December 1983): 871–86.

Katzenstein, Peter. *Small States in World Markets: Industrial Policy in Europe*. Ithaca: Cornell University Press, 1984.

Kay, J. A. "Tax Policy: A Survey." *The Economic Journal* 100.399 (1 March 1990): 18–75.

———. "Tax Reform in Context: A Strategy for the 1990s." *Fiscal Studies* 7.4 (1988): 1–17.

Kay, J. A., and M. King. *The British Tax System*. London: Oxford University Press, 1983.

Keith, Gordon. "The Excess Profits Tax Act of 1950." *National Tax Journal* 5 (1951).

Kenneth O. Morgan. *Labour in Power: 1945–1951*. Oxford: Oxford University Press, 1986.

Key, V. O. *The Responsible Electorate*. Cambridge: Harvard University Press, 1966.

Keynes, John Maynard. "National Self-sufficiency." *The Yale Review* 22 (Summer 1933).

———. *The General Theory of Employment, Interest and Money*. London: Macmillan, 1936.

Kies, Ken. "The Current Political, Budgetary, and Tax Policy Environment Suggests the Possibility of Major Federal Tax Legislation in the 100th Congress." *Tax Notes* 35.2 (April 13, 1987): 179–89.

King, Anthony. "Ideas, Institutions and Policies of Governments: A Comparative Analysis, Part I." *British Journal of Political Science* 3.4 (1974): 291–313.

King, Desmond S. "The Establishment of Work-welfare Programmes in the United States and Britain: Politics, Ideas, and Institutions." In *Structuring Politics: Historical Institutionalism in Comparative Analysis,* edited by Sven Steinmo, Kathleen Thelen, and Frank Longstreth, 217–50. New York: Cambridge University Press, 1992.

King, Mervin. "Comment by Mervin King." In *Britain's Economic Performance,* edited by R. E. Caves and L. B. Krause, 254–60. Washington, D.C.: Brookings Institution, 1980.

————. *Public Policy and the Corporation*. London: Chapman Hall, 1977.

King, Ronald. "From Redistributive to Hegemonic Logic: The Transformation of American Tax Politics." *Politics and Society* 12.1 (1983): 1–52.

————. "Tax Expenditures and Systematic Public Policy: An Essay on the Political Economy of the Federal Reserve Code." *Public Budgeting and Finance* (Spring 1984): 14–31.

Kjellander, Claes-Göran. "The New Tax Structure Splits the Bloc Structure of Swedish Politics." *Current Sweden* 287 (May 1982): 2–9.

Klein, Rudolf. *The Politics of the National Health Service*. London: Longman, 1984.

Korpi, Walter. *The Working Class in Welfare Capitalism*. London: Routledge and Kegan Paul, 1978.

————. *The Democratic Class Struggle*. London: Routledge and Kegan Paul, 1983.

Korpi, Walter, and Michael Shalev. "Strikes, Industrial Relations and Class Conflict in Capitalist Societies." *British Journal of Sociology* 30.2 (June 1979): 164–87.

Krasner, Stephen. "Approaches to the State: Alternative Conceptions and Historical Dynamics." *Comparative Politics* (January 1984): 223–46.

Krieger, Joel. *Reagan, Thatcher and the Politics of Decline*. Oxford: Polity Press, 1986.

Kristol, Irving. *Two Cheers for Capitalism*. New York: Basic Books, 1978.

Labour Party. *Looking to the Future*. London: Labour Party, 1990.

Ladd, Everett Carll, Jr., et al. "The Polls: Taxing and Spending." *Public Opinion Quarterly* 43.1 (Spring 1979): 126–35.

————. "Tax Attitudes." *Public Opinion*, February/March 1985, 8–10.

Lange, Peter, and Geoffrey Garret. "Organization and the Political Determination of Economic Performance." *Journal of Politics*, 1985.

Lanke, Jan, and Bo Bjurulf. "En Granskning Av Den Svenska Vallagen." *Stats Vetenskaplig Tidskrift* 89.2 (1986): 123–29.

Larsson, Torbjörn. *Rejeringen Och Dess Kansli*. Lund: Studentlitteratur, 1986.

Lash, S. "The End of Neocorporatism?: The Breakdown of Centralized Bargaining in Sweden." *British Journal of Industrial Relations* 23 (July 1985): 215–39.

Lashmar, Paul. "Lords Are Cashing in on the Poll Tax." *Observer*, May 29, 1988.

Laurin, Urban. *På Heder Och Samvete*. Stockholm: Norstedts, 1986.

Lee, Dwight R., and Richard B. McKenzie. "The International Political Economy of Declining Tax Rates." *National Tax Journal* 42.1 (March 1989): 79–83.

Leijonhufud, Sigfrid. "New Departures from the Middle Road." *Current Sweden* 295 (October 1982).

Lembruch, Gerhard. "Introduction: Neocorporatism in Comparative Perspective." In *Patterns of Corporatist Policy-making*, edited by Philippe Schmitter and Gerhard Lembruch, 1–29. London and Beverly Hills: Sage Publication, 1982.

Leuchtenburg, William. *Franklin Roosevelt and the New Deal*. New York: Harper Torchbooks, 1963.

Lever, Harold. "The Barbara Castles Diaries." *The Listener*, November 22, 1984.

Levi, Margaret. *Of Rule and Revenue*. Berkeley: University of California Press, 1988.

Lewin, Leif. *Planhushållningsdebatten*. Stockholm: Almquist and Wicksell, 1970.

————. *Ideologi and Strategi*. Stockholm: Norstedts, 1985.

Lewin, Leif, Bo Jansson, and Bo Sorbom. *The Swedish Electorate*. Stockholm: Almquist and Wicksell, 1972.

Lewis, Alan. "Perceptions of Tax Rates." *Tax Review* 6 (1978): 358–65.

———. *The Psychology of Taxation*. Oxford: Martin Robertson, 1982.

Leys, Colin. "Thatcherism and British Manufacturing: A Question of Hegemony." *New Left Review* (May/June 1985): 2–25.

Light, Paul. *The Artful Work*. New York: Random House, 1985.

Lindbeck, Assar. *Svensk Ekonomisk Politik*. Stockholm: Aldus/Bonniers, 1975.

———. "The Political Economy of Redistribution and the Expansion of the Public Sector." Stockholm, 14 June 1983.

Lindblom, Charles. "Decision-making in Taxation and Expenditures." National Bureau for Economic Research Report, *Public Finance: Needs, Sources and Utilization*, 295–329. Princeton: Princeton University Press, 1961.

———. *Politics and Markets*. New York: Basic Books, 1973.

Lindencrona, Gustav. "Skatteformågaprincip Och Individuel Beskattning." *Festskrift Til Jan Heller*. Stockholm: Norstedt and Sons, 1984.

———. "President Reagan's Tax Proposal." *Scandinaviska Enskilda Banken* 4 (1985): 104–09.

Lindquist, L. L. *The Hare and the Tortoise: Clean Air Policies in the United States and Sweden*. Ann Arbor: University of Michigan Press, 1980.

Lippman, Walter. *Public Opinion*. New York: Harcourt, Brace, 1922.

Lipset, Seymour Martin. "Why No Socialism in the United States?" In *Sources of Contemporary Radicalism*, edited by Seweryn Bialer, 31–149. Boulder: Westview Press, 1977.

Livesey, D. A. "The Uncertain Foundations of Fiscal Policy." In *Public Policy and the Tax System*, edited by G. A. Hughes and G. M. Heal, 194–224. London: George Allen and Unwin, 1980.

Lloyd, Susan. "A Maturing Market." *Accountancy* 102.1134 (February 1988): 73–74.

LO. *Samordnad Närinspolitik*. Stockholm: LO, 1963.

Lockhart, Charles. "Explaining Social Policy Differences among Advanced Industrial Societies." *Comparative Politics* 16.3 (April 1984): 335–50.

Lodin, Sven-Olof. *Skatter I Kris*. Lund: Norstedt and Sons, 1982.

Lodin, Sven-Olof, et al. *Beskattning Ay Inkomst Och Förmögenhet, del 1 Och del 2*. Lund: Studentlitteratur, 1978.

Lohr, Steve. "Sweden: Home of Tax Reform, Arms Scandals and a Strong Defense." *New York Times*, September 6, 1987.

Lomax, Ian. *A Guide to the Community Charge*. London: Fourmat, 1990.

Longley, Lawrence. *Changing the System: Electoral Reform Politics in Great Britain and the United States*. Appleton, Wis.: Lawrence University Press, 1986.

Low Pay Unit. *An Abundance of Poverty*. London: Child Poverty Action Group (CPAG), 1988.

Lowi, Theodore. "Why Is There No Socialism in the United States? A Federal Analysis." In *The Costs of Federalism*, edited by R. Golembrewski and Aaron Wildavsky, 37–54. New Brunswick: Transaction Books, 1984.

Lownertz, Susanne. "De Svenska Skatternas Historia." *Riksskatteverkets Utbilding och Information*, April 1983.

Lubick, Donald, and Gerald Brannon. "Stanley Surrey and the Quality of Tax Policy Argument." *National Tax Journal* 38.3 (September 1985).

Lundberg, Erik. "The Rise and Fall of the Swedish Model." *Journal of Economic Literature* 23 (March 1985): 1–36.

———. "Mangefåld Och Förvirring—Den Ekonomiska Politikens Målutvekling." *Skandinaviska Enskilda Banken Kvartalstidskrift* 7 (1976).

MacInnes, John. *Thatcherism at Work*. Philadelphia: Open University Press, 1987.

Mackie, Thomas, and Richard Rose. *The International Almanac of Electoral History*. New York: Facts on File, 1983.

Mackuen, Michael, and Courtney Brown. "Political Context and Attitude Change." *American Political Science Review* 81.2 (June 1987): 471–90.

Maier, Charles. "Preconditions for Corporatism." *Order and Conflict in Contemporary Capitalism*, edited by J. H. Goldthorpe, 39–59. London: Clarendon Press, 1984.

Malmström, Åke. "Regeringen Kan Tvingas Avgå Efter Krav Från Majoriteten." *Skanska Dagbladet*, December 3, 1970.

Manley, John. *The Politics of Finance*. Boston: Little, Brown, 1970.

Mansfield, Charles Y. "Tax Administration in Developing Countries: An Economic Perspective." *IMF Staff Papers* 35.1 (March 1988): 181–97.

March, James. "Bounded Rationality, Ambiguity, and the Engineering of Choice." *Bell Journal of Economics* (1978): 587–608.

Mardsen, Keith. "Taxes and Growth." *Finance and Development* 20 (September 1983): 40–43.

Market Opinion Research. *The Federal Deficit and Tax Policy*. Washington, D.C.: Market Opinion Research, 1984.

Martin, Andrew. "The Dynamics of Change in a Keynesian Political Economy: The Swedish Case and Its Implications." In *State and Economy in Contemporary Capitalism*, edited by Colin Crouch, 88–121. New York: St. Martin's Press, 1979.

Martin, Cathie Jo. "Business Influence and State Power: The Case of U.S. Corporate Tax Policy." *Politics and Society* 17.2 (1989): 189–223.

Matthiessen, Lars. *A Study in Fiscal Theory and Policy*. Stockholm: Economic Research Institute, 1973.

Mattson, Nils. "Some Current Questions of Tax Policy." *Faculty of Law at Uppsala University*. Uppsala University, 1976.

Mattson, Nils, et al. "Tax Law." In *An Introduction to Swedish Law*. Stockholm: Norstedts, 1983.

Mayhew, David. *Congress: The Electoral Connection*. New Haven: Yale University Press, 1974.

McClosky, Herbert, and John Zaller. *The American Ethos*. Cambridge: Harvard University Press, 1984.

McConnell, Grant. *Private Power and American Democracy*. New York: Knopf, 1966.

McDaniel, Paul, and Stanley Surrey. *International Aspects of Tax Expenditures: A Comparative Study*. Deventer, The Netherlands: Kluwer, 1985.

McKenzie, Richard. *Competing Visions: The Political Conflict over America's Economic Future*. Washington, D.C.: Cato Institute, 1985.

————. "Capital Flight: The Hidden Power of Technology to Shrink Big Government." *Reason* 20.10 (March 1, 1989): 22–26.

McLure, Charles E., Jr. "Lessons for LDCs of U.S. Income Tax Reform." In *Tax Reform in Developing Countries,* edited by Malcolm Gillis, 347–90. Durham and London: Duke University Press, 1989.

Meade Committee. *The Structure and Reform of Direct Taxation*. London: IFS/George Allen and Unwin, 1978.

Meidner, Rudolf. "Our Concept of the Third Way: Some Remarks on the Sociopolitical Tenets of the Swedish Labor Movement." *Economic and Industrial Democracy* 1.3 (August 1980): 343–70.

Meijer, Hans. "Bureaucracy and Policy Formation." *Scandinavian Political Studies* 4 (1969): 103–16.

Mellon, Andrew. *Taxation: The People's Business*. New York: Macmillan, 1924.

Messerer, Ken. "Tax Levels, Structures, and Systems: Some Intertemporal and International Comparisons." In *Secular Trends of the Public Sector,* edited by Hoist Claus Recktenwald. Paris: Editions Cujas, 1976.

————. "Trends in OECD Tax Revenue." In *Comparative Tax Studies,* 31–57. Amsterdam: North Holland, 1983.

Metcalf, Michael, ed. *The Riksdag: A History of the Swedish Parliament*. New York: St. Martin's Press, 1987.

Micheletti, Michele. "From Saltsjobaden to Harpsund, Haga and the Fourth of October." Manuscript. Dept. of Political Science, University of Stockholm, 1984.

Middlemas, Keith. *Politics in Industrial Society*. Thetford, Norfolk, U.K.: André Deutsch, 1979.

Middleton, Roger. *Towards a Managed Economy*. London: Methuen, 1985.

Milner, Henry. *Sweden: Social Democracy in Practice*. Oxford: Oxford University Press, 1989.

Minarik, Joseph J. *Making America's Budget Policy: From the 1980s to the 1990s*. Armonk, N.Y.: M. E. Sharpe, 1990.

Montgomery, Edward. "Income Security and Economic Growth." *Journal of Contemporary Studies* 7 (Fall 1984): 79–102.

Morgan, Kenneth O. *Labour in Power: 1945–1951*. Oxford: Oxford University Press, 1989.

Morris, C. N. "The Structure of Personal Income Taxation and Support." *Fiscal Studies* 3.3 (November 1982): 210–18.

Morrissey, Oliver, and Sven Steinmo. "The Influence of Party Competition on Postwar UK Tax Rates." *Policy and Politics* 15.4 (1987): 195–206.

Morrissey, Oliver, John Cullis, and Peter Jones. "Poll Tax Paradoxes and the Analysis of Tax Reform." Dept. of Economics Discussion Paper, no. 90/5. Nottingham, U.K.: Nottingham University, Dept. of Economics, April 1990.

Mosely, Paul. *The Making of Economic Policy: Theory and Evidence from Britain and the U.S. since 1945*. London: Wheatsheaf Books, 1984.

Mowat, Charles Loch. *Britain between the Wars, 1918–1940*. Chicago: University of Chicago Press, 1955.

Muellbauer, John. "The Community Charge, Rates and Tax Reform." *Lloyds Bank Review,* October 1987, 7–19.

Murray, Alan, and Jeffery Birnbaum. "Tax Reform: The Bill Nobody Wanted." *Public Opinion* 9.6 (March/April 1986): 41–60.

Musgrave, R. A., and P. B. Musgrave. *Public Finance in Theory and Practice.* New York: McGraw Hill, 1980.

Muten, Leif, and Karl Faxen. "Sweden." In Brookings Institution, *Foreign Tax Policies and Economic Growth*, 337–89. New York: Columbia University Press, 1966.

———. "Tax Reform—An International Perspective." *Vårt Ekonomiska Läge.* Stockholm, 1988.

Myrdal, Gunnar. "Dags for Ett Båttre Skattesystem." *Skatter.* Malmö: Liberforlag, 1982.

Nachmias, David, and Ann L. Green. "Governance Dilemmas in an Age of Ambiguous Authority." *Policy Sciences* 14 (1981/82).

Nelson, Michael. "An Empirical Analysis of State and Local Tax Structure in the Context of the Leviathan Model of Government." *Public Choice* 49 (1986): 283–94.

Nettle, J. P. "The State as a Conceptual Variable." *World Politics* 20 (1968): 559–92.

Neustadt, Richard. *Presidential Power.* New York: Wiley, 1980.

Newton, K., and L. Sharpe. *Does Politics Matter?* Oxford: Clarendon Press, 1984.

Nordlinger, Eric. *On the Autonomy of the Democratic State.* Cambridge: Harvard University Press, 1981.

Normann, Göran. "Sweden." *The Value Added Tax: Lessons from Europe.* Washington, D.C.: Brookings Institution, 1981.

Normann, Göran, and Jan Södersten. *Skattepolitik Resursstyrning Och Inkomstutjämnning.* Stockholm: I.U.I., 1978.

Norr, Martin, Frank Duffy, and Harry Steiner. *Taxation in Sweden.* Boston: Little, Brown, 1959.

North, Douglas. *Structure and Change in Economic History.* New York: Norton, 1981.

———. *Institutions, Institutional Change and Economic Performance.* Cambridge: Cambridge University Press, 1990.

Olson, Mancur. *The Rise and Decline of Nations.* New Haven: Yale University Press, 1982.

———. "The Political Economy of Comparative Growth Rates." In *The Political Economy of Growth*, edited by Dennis Mueller, 7–52. New Haven: Yale University Press, 1983.

———. "A Theory of Incentives Facing Political Organizations." *International Journal of Political Research* 7.2 (1986): 165–89.

Office of Technology Assessment (OTA). *U.S. Industrial Competitiveness: A Comparison of Steel, Electronics, and Automobiles.* Washington, D.C.: OTA, 1981.

Organization for Economic Cooperation and Development (OECD). *Company Tax Systems in OECD Members Countries.* Paris: OECD, 1973.

————. *The Treatment of Family Units in OECD Member Countries under Tax and Transfer Systems*. Paris: OECD, 1977.

————. *Income Tax Schedules: Distribution of Taxpayers and Revenues*. Paris: OECD, 1981a.

————. *Long-Term Trends in Tax Revenues of OECD Member Countries: 1955–1980*. Paris: OECD, 1981b.

————. *The Impact of Consumption Taxes on Different Levels of Income*. Paris: OECD, 1981c.

————. *Tax/Benefit Position of Selected Income Groups: In OECD Member Countries 1974–1978*. Paris: OECD, 1982.

————. *Tax Expenditures: A Review of the Issues and Country Practices*. Paris: OECD, 1984.

————. *Personal Income Tax Systems under Changing Economic Conditions*. Paris: OECD, 1986.

————. *Structural Adjustment and Economic Performance*. Paris: OECD, 1987.

————. *Taxing Consumption*. Paris: OECD, 1988a.

————. *Why Economic Policies Change Course*. Paris: OECD, 1988b.

————. *International Direct Investment and the New Economic Environment*. Paris: OECD, 1989a.

————. *Economies in Transition: Structural Adjustments in OECD Countries*. Paris: OECD, 1989b.

————. *The Personal Income Tax Base: A Comparative Survey*. Paris: OECD, 1990a.

————. *Taxpayers' Rights and Obligations: A Survey of the Legal Situation in OECD Countries*. Paris: OECD, 1990b.

————. *Revenue Statistics: Statistiques Des Recettes Publiques 1965–1990*. Paris: OECD, 1990c.

————. *Strategic Industries in a Global Economy: Policy Issues for the 1990s*. Paris: OECD, 1991.

Panitch, Leo. "The Development of Corporatism in Western Democracies." In *Trends towards Corporatist Intermediation,* edited by Philippe Schmitter and Gerhard Lembruch, 119–49. Beverly Hills: Sage, 1979.

Patterson, James. *Congressional Conservatism and the New Deal*. Lexington: University of Kentucky Press, 1967.

Paul, Randolph E. *Taxation in the United States*. Boston: Little, Brown, 1954.

Peacock, Alan, and Jack Wiseman. *The Growth of Public Expenditure in the United Kingdom*. Princeton: Princeton University Press, 1961.

Pechman, Joseph, and Benjamin Okner. *Who Bears the Tax Burden?* Washington, D.C.: Brookings Institution, 1974.

Pechman, Joseph, ed. *What Should Be Taxed: Income or Expenditure?* Washington, D.C.: Brookings Institution, 1980.

————. *Federal Tax Policy*. Washington, D.C.: Brookings Institution, 1983a.

————. "Anatomy of the U.S. Individual Income Tax." *Comparative Tax Studies*. Amsterdam: North Holland, 1983b.

———. "The Rich, the Poor and the Taxes They Pay." *The Public Interest* 77 (1984): 28–36.

———. *Who Paid the Taxes 1965–1985*. Washington, D.C.: Brookings Institution, 1985.

———. "Introduction: Recent Developments." *Comparative Tax Systems: Europe, 1987*. 1–32.

———. "The Future of Income Tax." *The American Economic Review* 80.1 (March 1990): 1–20.

———, ed. *World Tax Reform: A Progress Report*. Washington, D.C.: Brookings Institution, 1988.

Peet, Richard. "Class Struggle, the Relocation of Employment, and Economic Crisis." *Science and Society* 48 (Spring 1984): 38–51.

Pimlott, Ben. *Hugh Dalton*. London: Jonathan Cape, 1985.

Pirages, Dennis. *Global Technopolitics*. Pacific Grove, Cal.: Brooks and Cole, 1989.

Platt, C. J. *Tax Systems in Western Europe*. London: Gower, 1985.

Pollard, Sidney. *The Wasting of the British Economy*. London: Croom Helm, 1982.

———. *The Development of the British Economy*. Baltimore: Edward Arnold, 1983.

Polsby, Nelson. "The Institutionalization of the House of Representatives." *American Political Science Review* 62.1 (1968): 144–68.

———. *The Consequences of Party Reform*. Oxford: Oxford University Press, 1983.

Polsby, Nelson, and Aaron Wildavsky. *Presidential Elections*. New York: Charles Scribner, 1980.

Polsby, Nelson, et al. "The Growth of the Seniority System in the House of Representatives." *American Political Science Review* 63 (1969): 787–807.

Pomper, Gerald. "The Politics of Tax Reform." *News for Teachers of Political Science* 50 (1986).

Pontusson, Jonas. "Labor Reformism and the Politics of Capital Formation in Sweden." Ph.D. diss., University of California, 1986.

———. "Radicalization and Retreat in Swedish Social Democracy." *New Left Review* 165 (September/October 1987): 5–33.

———. "Labor, Corporatism, and Industrial Policy: The Swedish Case in Comparative Perspective." *Comparative Politics* 23, no. 2 (1991): 163–74.

———. *The Limits of Social Democracy: Investment Politics in Sweden*. Ithaca: Cornell University Press, 1992.

Porter, Michael E. *The Competitive Advantage of Nations*. New York: Free Press, 1990.

Powell, G. Bingham. *Contemporary Democracies: Participation, Stability, Violence*. Cambridge: Harvard University Press, 1982.

Premforss, Rune. "Governmental Commissions in Sweden." *American Behavioral Scientist* 26 (May/June 1983): 623–42.

Prezworski, Adam, and Henry Teune. *The Logic of Comparative Social Inquiry*. New York: John Wiley and Sons, 1970.

Prowse, Michael. "An End to Old-Fashioned Egalitarianism." *Financial Times*, March 16, 1988.

Public Opinion. "Ethnicity in America: Opinion Roundup." *Public Opinion* 7 (October/November 1984): 17–51.

————. "Five Years of Public Opinion: Stability in Attitudes." *Public Opinion* 6 (April/May 1983): 21–33.

————. "Tax Philosophy: An Interview with Barber Conable and Joseph Pechman." *Public Opinion* (February/March 1985): 207.

————. "Tax Americana: Opinion Roundup." *Public Opinion* 8 (February/March 1985): 19–29.

Rabushka, Alvin. "The Tax Reform Act of 1986: Concentrated Costs, Diffuse Benefits, An Inversion of Public Choice." *Contempory Policy Issues* 6.4 (1988): 50–64.

Ratner, Sidney. *Taxation and Democracy*. New York: John Wiley, 1942.

Rauch, Jonathan. "Interest Groups Preparing for Worst as They Lobby against Budget Cuts." *National Journal* 16 (December 15, 1984): 2380–85.

Reese, Thomas. *The Politics of Taxation*. Westport, Conn.: Quorum Books, 1980.

Rehn, Gösta. "Ekonomisk Politik Vid Full Sysselsättning." *Tiden*. 1948.

Richardson, Jeremy, ed. *Policy Styles in Western Europe*. London: George Allen and Unwin, 1982.

Ridge, Michael, and Stephen Smith. "The First Months of the Community Charge." *Fiscal Studies* 11.3 (August 1990): 39–54.

Riksrevisionsverket (RRV). *Statistika Meddelanden*. 1983. Vol. 7.1. Stockholm: Statistika Centralbyran, 1983.

Robinson, A., and C. Sandford. *Tax Policy Making in the United Kingdom*. London: Heinemann, 1983.

Rodriguez, Enrique. *Offentlig Inkomstexpansion: En analys av drivkrafterna bakom de offentliga inkomsternas utveckling i Sverige under 1900-talet*. Uppsala: Gleerup, 1980.

————. *Den Svenska Skatt Historien*. Lund: Liber Laromedel, 1981.

Rodriguez, Enrique, and Sven Steinmo. "The Development of the American and the Swedish Tax Systems: A Comparison." *Intertax* 3 (1986): 68–79.

Roper Organization. *The American Public and the Federal Income Tax System*. Study commissioned by H & R Block, Kansas City, 1986.

Rose, Richard. *Maximizing Revenue and Minimizing Political Costs: Taxation by Inertia*. Glasgow: Center for the Study of Public Policy, n.d.

————. *Do Parties Make a Difference?* 2d ed. New York: Macmillan, 1980.

————. "Electoral Systems: A Question of Degree or of Principle?" *Choosing an Electoral System*, edited by Arendt Lijphart and Bernard Gorfman. New York: Praeger, 1984.

————. *Understanding Big Government: The Programme Approach*. London: Sage Publications, 1984b.

Rose, Richard, and Guy Peters. *Can Governments Go Bankrupt?* New York: Basic Books, 1982.

Rose, Richard, and Terrance Karran. "Inertia or Incrementalism? A Long-Term View of the Growth of Government." *Comparative Resource Allocation.* London and Beverly Hills: Sage Publications, 1983.

————. *Taxation by Political Inertia.* London: Macmillan, 1986.

Rothgeb, John M. *Myths and Realities of Foreign Investment in Poor Countries: The Modern Leviathan in the Third World.* New York: Praeger, 1989.

Rothstein, Bo. "State and Capital in Sweden: The Importance of Corporatist Arrangements." *Scandinavian Political Studies* 11.3 (1988): 235–60.

————. "En Hysterisk Rymt." *Dagens Nyheter,* December 28, 1990.

————. "Den Svenska Byråkatins Uppgang Och Fall." *Häften for Kritiska Studier* 15.5 (1982a): 26–46.

————. *Den Social-demokratiska Staten.* Lund, Sweden: Arkiv Avhandinesserie, 1986.

————. "Labor Market Institutions and Working-Class Strength." *Structuring Politics: Historical Institutionalism in Comparative Analysis,* edited by Sven Steinmo, Kathleen Thelen, and Frank Longstreth, 3–56. New York: Cambridge University Press, 1992.

————. "Swedish Interest Organizations: From Solution to Problem." *Svensk Democrati I Forändring,* edited by Johan P. Olsen. Uppsala: Carlssons, 1990.

Rudder, Catherine. "Committee Reform and the Revenue Process." In *Congress Reconsidered,* edited by Lawrence Dodd and Bruce Oppenheimer. New York: Praeger Books, 1977.

————. "Fiscal Responsibility and the Revenue Committees." In *Congress Reconsidered,* 3d ed., edited by Lawrence Dodd and Bruce Oppenheimer, 211–22. Washington: Congressional Quarterly, 1984.

Ruin, Olof. "Patterns of Government Composition in Multiparty Systems: The Case of Sweden." *Scandinavian Political Studies* 4 (1969): 71–87.

————. "Sweden in the 1970s: Police-making (*sic*) Becomes More Difficult." In *Policy Styles in Western Europe,* edited by Jeremy Richardson, 141–67. London: George Allen and Unwin, 1981.

Russakoff, Dale. "Bill Bradley Becomes a Player—Again." *Washington Post Magazine,* February 1, 1987, 10–37.

Rustow, Dankwart. *The Politics of Compromise.* Princeton: Princeton University Press, 1955.

————. "Sweden's Transition to Democracy: Some Notes Towards Genetic Theory." *Scandinavian Political Studies* 6 (1971): 9–26.

Rytohonka, Risto. "Beskattning I Norden—en Jämforelse." *Svensk Skattetidning* 52.1–2 (1985): 475–81.

Sabine, B. E. V. *A History of Income Tax.* London: George Allen and Unwin, 1966.

————. *British Budgets in Peace and War 1932–1945.* London: George Allen and Unwin, 1970.

————. *A Short History of Taxation.* London: Butterworths, 1980.

Sverigas Arbeiter Förening (SAF). *Fakta Om Sveriges Skatter.* Stockholm: SAF, 1983.

Sainsbury, Diane. *Swedish Social Democratic Ideology and Electoral Politics 1944–1948*. Stockholm: Almquist and Wicksell, 1980.

———. "Theoretical Perspectives in Analyzing Ideological Change and Persistence: The Case of Swedish Social Democratic Party Ideology." *Scandinavian Political Studies* 4 (1981): 273–94.

Salant, Walter S. "The Spread of Keynesian Doctrines and Practices in the United States." In *The Political Power of Economic Ideas: Keynesianism across Nations*, edited by Peter A. Hall, 27–52. Princeton: Princeton University Press, 1989.

Sandford, Cedric. *Taxing Personal Wealth*. London: George Allen and Unwin, 1971a.

———. *Realistic Tax Reform*. London: Chatto and Windus, 1971b.

———. "Open Government and the Use of Green Papers." *The British Tax Review*. 1980a.

———. "The Diamond Commission and the Redistribution of Wealth." *British Journal of Law and Society* 7 (1980b).

———. "Capital Taxes—Past, Present and Future." *Lloyds Bank Review*, October 1983.

———. *The Economics of Public Finance*. Oxford: Pergamon Press, 1984.

Sansonetti, Patrick. "International Venture Capital: Reaching New Markets." *Small Business Reports* 14.1 (January 1989): 40–42.

Särlvik, Bo. "Party Politics and Electoral Opinion Formation." *Scandinavian Political Studies* 2 (1967): 167–202.

Saunders, Laura, ed. "Who Got Reformed?" *Forbes* 143.1 (January 9, 1989): 297–98.

Savage, James D. *Balanced Budgets and American Politics*. Ithaca: Cornell University Press, 1988.

Scase, Richard. *Social Democracy in Capitalist Society*. London: Croom Helm, 1977.

Schattschneider, E. E. *Party Government*. New York: Holt, Rinehart and Winston, 1942.

———. *The Semi-Sovereign People*. New York: Holt Rinehart, 1960.

Scherwin, Don. "Historic Compromise and Pluralist Decline? Profits and Capital in the Nordic Countries." In *Order and Conflict in Contemporary Societies*, edited by John Goldthorpe, 231–56. Oxford: Oxford University Press, 1984.

———. "Does Corporatism Matter? Economic Crisis, Politics and Rates of Unemployment in Capitalist Democracies in the 1970s." In *Patterns of Corporatist Policy Making*, edited by Philippe Schmitter and Gerhard Lembruch, 237–58. London: Sage, 1982.

———. "The Welfare State and the Economy in Periods of Economic Crisis: A Comparative Study of Twenty-three OECD Nations." *European Journal of Political Research* 11 (1983): 1–26.

Schmitter, Philippe. "Reflections on Where the Theory of Neo-corporatism Has Gone and Where the Praxis of Neo-corporatism May Be Going." In *Patterns of Corporatist Policy Making*, edited by Philippe Schmitter and Gerhard Lembruch, 259–80. London: Sage Publications, 1982.

———. "Still a Century of Corporatism." *Review of Politics* 36 (1974).

Schwartz, John E. "Exploring a New Role in Policy Making: The British House of

Commons in the 1970s." *American Political Science Review* 74.1 (1980): 23–37.

Sears, David, and Jack Citrin. *Tax Revolt: Something for Nothing in California.* Cambridge: Harvard University Press, 1985.

Shalev, Michael, and Korpi Walter. "Working Class Mobilization and American Exceptionalism." *Economic and Industrial Democracy* 1 (1980).

Shehab, F. *Progressive Taxation: A Study in the Development of the Progressive Principle in the British Income Tax.* Oxford: Oxford University Press, 1953.

Shepsle, Kenneth A. "Institutional Equilibrium and Equilibrium Institutions." In *Political Science: The Science of Politics,* edited by Herbert Weisberg, 51–81. New York: Agathon Press, 1986.

Shirras, G. Findlay, and L. Rostas. *The Burden of British Taxation.* Cambridge: Cambridge University Press, 1943.

Shonfield, Andrew. *Modern Capitalism: The Changing Balance between Public and Private Power.* Oxford: Oxford University Press, 1965.

Silverman, Dan. *Reconstructing Europe after the Great War.* Cambridge: Harvard University Press, 1982.

Simon, Herbert. "Human Nature and Politics: The Dialogue of Psychology with Political Science." *American Political Science Review* 79 (1985): 293–304.

Sinn, Hans-Werner. "U.S. Tax Reform 1981 and 1986: Impact on International Capital Markets and Capital Flows." *National Tax Journal* 41.3 (September 1988): 327–40.

———. "The 1986 U.S. Tax Reform and the World Capital Market." *European Economic Review* 32 (1988): 325–33.

Skidelsky, R. *Politicians and the Slump.* London: Macmillan, 1967.

Skocpol, Theda. "Bringing the State Back In: Strategies of Analysis in Current Research." In *Bringing the State Back In,* edited by Peter Evans, Dietrich Rueschmeyer, and Theda Skocpol, 3–43. Cambridge: Cambridge University Press, 1985.

———. "Political Response to Capitalist Crisis: Neo-Marxist Theories of the State and the Case of the New Deal." *Politics and Society* 10.2 (1980): 155–201.

Skocpol, Theda, and Edwin Amenta. "States and Social Policies." *Annual Review of Sociology* 12 (1986): 131–57.

Skocpol, Theda, and John Ikenberry. "The Political Formation of the American Welfare State: In Historical and Comparative Perspective." *Comparative Social Research* 6 (1983): 87–148.

Skowronek, Stephen. *Building a New American State: The Expansion of National Administrative Capacities 1877–1920.* Cambridge: Cambridge University Press, 1982.

Slemrod, Joel. "Effect of Taxation with International Capital Mobility." In *Uneasy Compromise,* 115–47. Washington, D.C.: Brookings Institution, 1988.

———. "Tax Principles in an International Economy." In *World Tax Reform,* edited by Michael J. Boskin and Charles E. McLure, Jr., 11–24. San Francisco: ICS Press, 1990.

Smail, Robin, and Chris Pond, eds. "The 1988 Budget and the Poor." *Low Pay Review* 33 (Spring 1988).

Smith, Geoffrey, and Nelson Polsby. *British Government and Its Discontents*. New York: Basic Books, 1981.

Smith, Rogers M. "Political Jurisprudence, the 'New Institutionalism,' and the Future of Public Law." *American Political Science Review* 82.1 (March 1988): 89–108.

Smith, S. R., and D. L. Squire. "The Local Government Green Paper." *Fiscal Papers* 9.1 (1986): 18–28.

Snowden, Philip. *An Autobiography*. London: Nicholson and Watson, 1934.

Söderpalm, Sven Anders. *Arbetgivarna Och Saltsjöbadspolitik*. Stockholm: SAF, 1980.

Södersten, Bo, and Cecilia Gunne, Anders Kristoffersson, Ingemar Hansson Carl-Gustav Fernlund. *Den Stora Reformen*. Stockholm: SNS Forlag, 1990.

Södersten, Jan. *Skatt På Bolagskapital*. Stockholm: Thomas Lindberg, 1983.

Söderstrom, Lars, and Bo Larsson. *Svensk Skatteforskning*. Stockholm: Riksbank Jubileumsfond, 1981.

Sola, Eduardo Fayos. "The Individual Income Tax and the Distribution of Its Burden: The Swedish Case." Stockholm: University of Stockholm International Graduate School, 1975.

Spaulding, Harrison. *The Income Tax in Great Britain and the United States*. London: P. S. King and Sons, 1927.

Ståhl, Ingemar. "Skattebaser Och Beskattning-tekniker 1990." In *Hur Karar Vi 1990?* edited by Alf Lindquist and Kerstin Stigmark, 7–26. Stockholm: Riksbankens Jubileumsfond, 1983.

Statens Offentilga Utredningar (SOU). *1921 Ars Kommunalskatte Kommitte's Betänkande Angående Den Kommunal Beskattning*. Volume 53. Stockholm: SOU, 1924.

―――. *1923 Års Taxeringssakkunnigas Betänkande Angående Omsorganisation Av Taxeringsväsendet*. Volume 27. Stockholm: SOU, 1925.

―――. *Utredning Angående Den Kommunala Skatteutjämning en Av Karl W. U. Kylenstierna*. Volume 35. Stockholm: SOU, 1925.

―――. *Promemorior Rörande Vissa Beskattnings Frågor Av 1927 Års Skatte Beredning*. Volume 33. Stockholm: SOU, 1927.

―――. *Det Samlade Skattetrycket*. Volume 18. Stockholm: SOU, 1936.

―――. *1936 Utredningar Rörande Det Samlade Skattetryket: Sverige Och Utlandet. Av Inom Finansdepartementet Tillkällade Sakkuniga*. Volume 18. Stockholm: SOU, 1936.

―――. *1936 Års Skattekommittee Betänkande*. Volume 42. Stockholm: SOU, 1937.

―――. *1945 Års Skatteberedning. Betänkande Med Förslag Till Omläggning Av Den Direkta Statsbeskattningen Samt Angående Kvarlåtenskapsskatt M.m.* Volume 79. Stockholm: SOU, 1946.

―――. *Förslag Till Ändrad Företag Beskattning*. Volume 19. Stockholm: SOU, 1954.

―――. *Den Statliga Indirekta Beskattningen Betänkande. Avgivet Av 1952 Års Kommittee for Indirekta Skatter*. Volume 13. Stockholm: SOU, 1957.

―――. *Beskattning Av Företag*. Volume 86. Stockholm: SOU, 1977.

———. *Löntagarfond Och Kapital*. Volume 9. Stockholm: SOU, 1979.

———. *Löntagarfond Och Kapital Tilväxt*. Volume 105. Stockholm: SOU, 1981.

———. *Statistika Meddelanden*. Volume 7.1. Stockholm: SOU, 1983.

———. *Skall Matmomsen Slopas?* Volume 54. Stockholm: SOU, 1983.

———. *Utredning Om Taxeringsförfarandet Och Skatteprocessen*. Volume 24. Stockholm: SOU, 1982.

———. *Utredning Om Reformerad Inkomst Beskattning*. Volume 29. Stockholm: SOU, 1987.

———. *Reavinst Aktier Obligationer*. Volume 37. Stockholm: SOU, 1986.

———. *Förenklad Själv Deklaration*. Volume 21. Stockholm: SOU, 1984.

———. *Reformerade Mervärdeskatte*. I, II, III. Volume 35. Stockholm: SOU, 1989.

———. *Reformerade Företagsbeskattning*. I, II. Volume 34. Stockholm: SOU, 1989.

———. *Reformerade Inkomstbeskattning*. I, II, III, IV. Volume 33. Stockholm: SOU, 1989.

Stein, Herbert. *The Fiscal Revolution in America*. Chicago: University of Chicago Press, 1969.

Steinmo, Sven. "Taxes, Institutions and the Mobilization of Bias," Ph.D. diss., University of California, Berkeley, 1986a.

———. "So What's Wrong with Tax Expenditures: A Re-evaluation Based on Swedish Experience." *Journal of Public Budgeting and Finance* (Summer 1986b).

———. "Social Democracy vs. Socialism: Goal Adaptation in Social Democratic Sweden." *Politics and Society* 16.4 (1988): 403–46.

———. "Political Institutions and Tax Policy in the United States, Sweden and Britain." *World Politics* 41.4 (1989): 500–35.

———. "The End of Redistribution?" Manuscript, 1991.

———. "Rethinking American Exceptionalism: Culture or Institutions?" In *Dynamics of American Politics: Approaches and Interpretations*, edited by Lawrence Dodd and Calvin Jillson. Boulder: Westview Press, 1993.

Stephens, J. D. *The Transition from Capitalism to Socialism*. London: Macmillan 1979.

Stern, Philip. *The Rape of the Taxpayer*. New York: Random House, 1973.

Steuerle, Eugene. "The New Tax Law." *Deficits, Taxes and Economic Adjustments*, edited by Phillip Lagar, 275–303. Washington, D.C.: American Enterprise Institute, 1987.

Steuerle, Eugene, and Michael Hartzman. "Individual Income Taxation 1947–1979." *National Tax Journal* 34.2 (June 1981): 145–66.

Stevenson, John, and Chris Cook. *The Slump: Society and Politics during the Depression*. London: Quartet Books, 1979.

Stewart, Michael. *The Jekyll and Hyde Years: Politics and Economic Policy since 1964*. London: J. M. Dent and Sons, 1977.

Stiglitz, Joseph. "Some Aspects of the Taxation of Capital Gains." *Journal of Public Economics* 21.2 (July 1983): 257–94.

Stjernquist, Nils. "From Bicameralism to Unicameralism: The Democratic Riksdag, 1921–1986." In *The Riksdag: A History of the Swedish Parliament*, edited by Michael Metcalf, 223–304. New York: St. Martin's Press, 1987.

Stockholm Economic Studies (SES). "Wages in Sweden 1900–1913, Part 1, Table 26." *Socialstyrelsen lönestatistik* 2 (1914).

Stockman, David. "The Triumph of Politics." *Newsweek,* April 21, 1986.

Strachey, John. *The Coming Struggle for Power.* New York: Covici-Friede, 1933.

Strahan, Randall. "Agenda Change and Committee Politics in the Post-Reform House." *Legislative Studies Quarterly* 13.2 (May 1988): 177–97.

Sträng, Gunnar. "Stabiliseringspolitikens Medel." *Tiden* 6 (1956a).

——. *Fast Economisk Politik Och Rättvis Beskattning.* Stockholm: Social Demokratiska Arbetarparti och Tiden Forlag, 1956b.

——. *Facta Om Skatten.* Stockholm: Prisma, 1970.

Strom, Kaare. "Party Goals and Government Performance in Parliamentary Democracies." *American Political Science Review* 79.3 (September 1985): 738–54.

Sundquist, James L. *Dynamics of the Party System.* Washington, D.C.: Brookings Institution, 1973.

Surrey, Stanley. *Pathways to Tax Reform.* Cambridge: Harvard University Press, 1973.

——. "Our Troubled Tax Policy." *Tax Notes,* February 2, 1981.

Surrey, Stanley, and William Hellmuth. "The Tax Expenditure Budget—Response to Professor Bittker." *National Tax Journal* 22.4 (1969): 528–37.

Swenson, Peter. *Fair Shares: Unions, Pay, and Politics in Sweden and West Germany.* Ithaca: Cornell University Press, 1989.

——. "Labor and the Limits of the Welfare State." *Comparative Politics* 23.4 (July 1991): 379–99.

Tanzi, Vito. *The Individual Income Tax and Economic Growth: An International Comparison.* Baltimore: Johns Hopkins University Press, 1969.

——. "The Impact of Macroeconomic Policies on the Level of Taxation and the Fiscal Balance in Developing Countries." *IMF Staff Papers* 36.3 (September 1989): 633–56.

Taverne, Dick. "Looking Back." *Fiscal Studies* 4.3 (1983): 1–7.

Taylor, John. "The Swedish Investment Funds System as a Stabilization Rule." *Brookings Papers on Economic Activity* 1 (1982): 57–100.

Taylor-Gooby, Peter. "Citizenship and Welfare." In *British Social Attitudes: The 1987 Report,* edited by Roger Jowell, Sharon Witherspoon, and Lindsay Brook, 1–29. Gower Publishers, Social and Community Planning Research, 1987.

Teuber, Jack. "With Estimates in the Spotlight, Their Methods Come Under Scrutiny." *Tax Notes* 33.9 (December 1, 1986): 788–91.

——. "Revenue Estimates Play a New Role as Numbers Dictate Policy." *Tax Notes* 33.8 (November 24, 1986): 698–701.

Thelen, Kathleen, and Sven Steinmo. "Historical Institutionalism in Comparative Politics." In *Structuring Politics: Historical Institutionalism in Comparative Analysis,* edited by Sven Steinmo, Kathleen Thelen, and Frank Longstreth, 1–32. New York: Cambridge University Press, 1992.

Thorell, Per. *Skattelag Och Åffarsed.* Lund: Nordenstens and Söner, 1984.

Thurow, Lester C. "The Other Deficit." *Resources,* Spring 1985, 5–9.

Tilton, Timothy. "A Swedish Road to Socialism: Ernst Wigforss and the Ideological Foundations of Swedish Social Democracy." *American Political Science Review* 73.2 (1979): 505–20.

Tingsten, Herbert. *Den Svenska Socialdemokratins Ide Utvekling.* Stockholm: Tiden, 1941.

————. *The Swedish Social Democrats: Their Ideological Development.* Totowa, N.J.: Bedminster Press, 1973.

Tjänstemannens Centralorganisation (TCO). *Ekonemernas Höst Rapport.* Stockholm: TCO, 1980.

————. "Tjänstemänen Och Skatterna." *Kongresstryk* 9 (1982).

Todd, Paul. "The Diamond Commission and the Redistribution of Wealth." *British Journal of Law and Society* 7 (1980): 286–96.

Tomasson, Richard. "Government Old-Age Pensions under Affluence and Austerity." *Research in Social Problems and Public Policy* 3 (1984): 217–72.

Touche Ross & Co. *Investment and Taxation in Sweden.* Stockholm: Touche Ross International, 1979.

Truman, David. *The Governmental Process.* New York: Knopf, 1951.

Tsbelis, George. *Nested Games: Rational Choice in Comparative Politics.* Berkeley: University of California Press, 1990.

U.S. News and World Report. "Is America Better Off These Days?" April 2, 1984, 26–27.

Uhr, Carl G. "The Emergence of the 'New Economics' in Sweden: A Review of a Study by Otto Steiger." *Journal of History of Political Economy* 7, no. 1 (1977): 89–121.

United Kingdom. *Report on National Debt and Taxation.* London: HMSO cmnd. 2800, 1927.

Vallinder, T. *I Kamp for Demokratin.* Stockholm: Natur och Kulture, 1962.

Verney, Douglas. *Parliamentary Reform in Sweden, 1866–1921.* Oxford: Oxford University Press, 1957.

Vickery, Graham. "Tax Reform: What Impact on Industry?" *OECD Observer* 155 (December 1, 1988): 35–38.

Vogel, Joquim. *Aspirationer, Möjligheter Och Skattemoral.* Volume 25. Stockholm: SOU, 1970.

Von Beyme, K. "Do Parties Matter?" *Government and Opposition* 19.1 (1984): 5–30.

Von Sydow, Björn. *Vagen Til Enkammar Riksdagen.* Stockholm: Tiden 1989.

————. *Vägen Till Enkammar Riksdagen: Demokratisk Författningspolitik I Sverige 1944–1968.* Stockholm: Tidens forlag, 1989.

Vylder, Stefan de. "Funderingar Kring Krisen." *Zenit* 73.5 (1981).

Walkland, S. A. *The Legislative Process in Great Britain.* London: Allen and Unwin, 1968.

Wallace, Cynthia Day. "Foreign Direct Investment in the Third World: U.S. Corporations and Government Policy." In *Foreign Direct Investment in the 1990s: A New Climate in the Third World,* edited by Cynthia Day Wallace. Doerdech, The Netherlands: Nijhoff, 1990.

Walters, Peter. " 'Distributing Decline': Swedish Social Democrats and the Crisis of the Welfare State." *Government and Opposition* 20, no. 3 (1985): 356–69.

Walters, Sir Allen. "Comment." *Taxation in International Perspective*. Vancouver: Frazer Institute, 1984.

Waltman, Jerold. *Political Origins of the U.S. Income Tax*. Jackson: University of Mississippi Press, 1985.

Walton, Victor. *Income Tax, Super-tax and Sur-tax*. London: Sir Isaac Pitman and Sons, 1928.

Weatherford, M. Stephan. "Evaluating Economic Policy: A Contextual Model of the Opinion Formation Process." *Journal of Politics* 45 (November 1983): 866–88.

Weber, Carolyn, and Aaron Wildavsky. *A History of Taxation and Expenditure in the Western World*. New York: Simon and Schuster, 1986.

Weaver, Kent R. "Political Foundations of Swedish Economic Policy." In *The Swedish Economy*, edited by Barry P. Bosworth and Alice M. Rivlin, 289–324. Washington, D.C.: Brookings Institution, 1987.

Weir, Margaret. "The Federal Government and Unemployment: The Frustration of Policy Innovation from the New Deal to the Great Society." In *The Politics of Social Policy in the United States*, edited by Margaret Weir, Ann Shola Orloff, and Theda Skocpol, 149–97. Princeton: Princeton University Press, 1988.

———. "Ideas and the Politics of Bounded Innovation." In *Structuring Politics: Historical Institutionalism in Comparative Analysis*, edited by Sven Steinmo, Kathleen Thelen, and Frank Longstreth, 188–216. New York: Cambridge University Press, 1992.

———. "Ideas and Politics: The Acceptance of Keynesianism in Britain and the United States." In *The Political Power of Economic Ideas: Keynesianism across Nations*, edited by Peter A. Hall, 53–86. Princeton: Princeton University Press, 1989.

Weir, Margaret, and Theda Skocpol. "State Structures and Possibilities for 'Keynesian' Responses to the Great Depression in Sweden, Britain and the United States." In *Bringing the State Back In*, edited by Peter Evans, Dietrich Rueschmeyer, and Theda Skocpol, 107–68. Cambridge: Cambridge University Press, 1985.

Wiseman, Jack. *Comparative Aspects of Taxation of Business in Germany and the United Kingdom*. London: David Green, 1980.

White, Joseph, and Aaron Wildavsky. *The Deficit and the Public Interest: The Search for Responsible Budgeting in the 1980s*. Berkeley: University of California Press, 1989.

Whittington, Geoffrey. *Company Taxation and Dividends*. London: IFS, 1974.

Wicksell, Knut. *Vara Skatter, Hvilka Betala Och Hvilka Börde Betala*. Stockholm, 1894.

Wigforss, Ernst. *Government Proposition, N158, Bihang Till Riksdagens Protokoll 1938*. Stockholm: Norstedts Trykeri, 1938.

———. *Socialism I vor Tid*. Stockholm: Tidens, 1952.

————. *Are You a Socialist?* Framtiden, 1962.

————. *Skrifter and Urval, Vol. III, Financeministern.* Stockholm: Tiden, 1980.

Wildavsky, Aaron. "Keeping Kosher: The Epistemology of Tax Expenditures." *Journal of Public Policy* 5.3 (August 1985): 413–31.

Wilensky, Harold. *The Welfare State and Equality.* Berkeley: University of California Press, 1975.

————. *The New Corporatism: Centralization and the Welfare State.* London: Sage Publications, 1976.

————. "The Political Economy of Income Distribution: Issues in the Analysis of Government Approaches to the Reduction of Inequality." In *Major Social Issues: A Multidisciplinary View,* edited by Milton Yinger and Stephen J. Cutler, 87–108. New York: Free Press, 1978.

————. "Taxing, Spending and Backlash: An American Peculiarity?" *Taxing and Spending,* July 1979, 6–11.

————. "Leftism, Catholicism, and Democratic Corporatism: The Role of Political Parties in Recent Welfare Development." *The Development of Welfare States in Europe and America,* edited by Peter Flora and Arnold Heidenheimer, 345–82. New Brunswick: Transaction Books, 1982.

————. "Nothing Fails Like Success: The Evaluation-research Industry and Labor Market Policy." *Industrial Relations* 24.1 (Winter 1985).

————. "Political Legitimacy and Consensus: Missing Variables in the Assessment of Social Policy." In *Evaluating the Welfare State: Social and Political Perspectives,* edited by S. E. Spirow and E. Yuchtman-Yaar, 51–74. New York: Academic Press, 1983.

Wilensky, Harold, et al. *Comparative Social Policy.* Berkeley: Institute of International Studies, 1985.

Wilkinson, Margaret. "Tax Expenditure and Public Expenditure in the U.K." *Journal of Social Policy* 15 (January 1986): 23–49.

Willis, J. R. M., and P. J. W. Hardwick. *Tax Expenditures in the United Kingdom.* London: Heinemann Educational Books, 1984.

Wilson, Frank. "Interest Groups and Politics in Western Europe: The Neo-corporatist Approach." *Comparative Politics* 16.1 (1983): 105–23.

Wilson, John Douglas. "Trade, Capital Mobility, and Tax Competition." *Journal of Political Economy* (Chicago) 95.4 (August 1987): 835–56.

Wilson, T. "The Economic Costs of the Adversary System." In *Adversary Politics and Electoral Reform,* edited by Samuel Finer, 99–116. London: Anthony Wigram, 1975.

Wilson, Woodrow. *Congressional Government.* Boston: Houghton Mifflin, 1885.

Witte, John. "The Distribution of Federal Tax Expenditures." *Policy Studies Journal* 12 (September 1983): 131–46.

————. *The Politics and Development of the Federal Income Tax.* Madison: University of Wisconsin Press, 1985.

Wolman, Clive. "Dramatic Gains for the Rich." *Financial Times,* March 16, 1988.

Yointek, Thom. "Government and Popularity in Great Britain under Conditions of Economic Decline." *Political Studies* 33 (September 1985): 467–83.

Zaller, John. "The Effects of Political Awareness on Public Attitudes and Voting Behavior." *X-rox* (Los Angeles), July 23, 1987, University of California.

Zysman, John. *Governments, Markets and Growth.* Ithaca: Cornell University Press, 1983.

Index